D0463504

CROSSING CULTURES

CROSSING CULTURES

Essays in the Displacement of Western Civilization

Daniel Segal, editor

THE UNIVERSITY OF ARIZONA PRESS

Tucson & London

The University of Arizona Press
Copyright © 1992
The Arizona Board of Regents
All Rights Reserved
♾ This book is printed on acid-free,
archival-quality paper.
Manufactured in the United States of America.

97 96 95 94 93 92   6 5 4 3 2 1

Library of Congress Cataloging-in-Publication Data

Crossing cultures : essays in the displacement of western civilization
  / Daniel Segal, editor.
      p.   cm.
   Includes bibliographical references and index.
   ISBN 0-8165-1277-9 (cloth)
      1. Civilization, Western—History.   2. Culture diffusion—History.
   3. Europe—Colonies—History.   I. Segal, Daniel Alan, 1958–   .
   CB245.C695   1992
   970—dc20   91-35113
                                                          CIP

British Library Cataloguing-in-Publication data are available.
A catalogue record for this book is available from the British Library.

CONTENTS

List of Illustrations

Acknowledgments

Earlier versions of these essays were commissioned for a conference held at the Claremont Colleges in 1989 and funded by the Mellon Foundation. I am indebted to both Harry Liebersohn, who organized the conference with me, and Al Bloom, then Dean of Pitzer College, who provided much institutional support for the conference. Susie Spitzer, David Glass and Sandy Hamilton ensured that the conference ran smoothly. The conference benefited greatly from the enthusiastic participation of many Claremont colleagues, including Agnes Jackson, Pieter Judson, Stuart McConnell, and Sam Yamashita. In addition to the essays printed here, the conference included a paper by Brackette Williams; I regret that other commitments prevented the inclusion of her essay here, for it was integral to the theme of both the conference and this volume.

While preparing these papers for publication, it was my great good fortune to be able to call upon the counsel of three exemplary scholar-editors: Don Brenneis, Kris Fossum, and George Stocking. Sandy Corbett provided valuable assistance with notes, references, and much else in the final preparation of the manuscript.

The publication of this volume provides me an opportunity to redress an omission in my previously published book with the University of Arizona Press. For that publication and this, it has been my good fortune to have worked with such an attentive, meticulous, and helpful press; I am particularly indebted to Greg McNamee and Marie Webner.

Portions of David Prochaska's essay previously appeared in different form in the *Journal of Historical Sociology*, vol. 3, no. 4; Peter Linebaugh and Marcus Rediker's essay previously appeared in *Journal of Historical Sociology*, vol. 3, no. 3. Derek Sayer's essay previously appeared in *Past and Present: A Journal of Historical Studies*, no. 131, published by the Past and Present Society, 175 Banbury Road, Oxford, England. We gratefully acknowledge permission to reprint these essays here.

INTRODUCTION

Harry Liebersohn and Daniel Segal

The papers in *Crossing Cultures* examine post-Columbian cultural encounters. In so doing, they struggle to represent both the exercise of power and the presence of difference. Issues of power and difference have, in recent years, become an important focus for anthropology, history, and literary studies—the disciplines represented in this volume. This convergence of interest occurs in the midst of a broader debate about the place of 'Western Civilization' in the undergraduate curriculum.[1] Our goal here is twofold: to introduce the papers in this volume, and to place them collectively in the context of that broader debate.

'The West' became a privileged topic of study in the age of European expansion, as part of an intellectual affirmation of European superiority. In the late nineteenth century, for example, world histories imaged 'Europe' as the pinnacle of a universal historical evolution toward 'civilization' (Harbsmeier and Larsen 1989). This sociocultural evolutionary paradigm (Stocking 1987) did much to shape the subsequent history of the human sciences, and in particular, to preempt a study of the historical contingency and instability of the distinction between European and non-European identities and persons. On the unilinear timeline-yardstick of this paradigm, observed social formations were imaged as distinct cases—that is, as historically isolated societies. If the contrary were true—if social orders were related through either a shared history or diffusion—then evidence of diachronic convergence would not prove the social evolutionary thesis that human societies progressed along a single, historical path. In short, the logical warrant of social evolutionary theory is that social orders are distinct cases, or isolates, and not parties to intercultural exchange—or even, to invoke a more recent concern, dialectical differentiation vis-à-vis those deemed 'other.'

Although today we confidently disavow sociocultural evolutionary theory, its supposition of distinct cases has nonetheless been bequeathed to us in the less obvious form of the opposition between 'simple' and 'complex' societies.[2] The *comparatively perceived* complexity of the West has given rise to an array of disciplines (sociology, psychology, economics, political science, history, literary studies . . .) which study separately what is joined together in the anthropology of the rest. In our disciplinary lives, this formal asymmetry continues to assert the incomparability, and hence distinctness, of two species of societies: the West and the rest, between whom mixing is supposed to have occurred only of late and only as a shaping of the rest by a stable West. Moreover, this asymmetry confronts us in public life with panels of experts—economists, sociologists, political scientists, etc.—who profess scientific laws of human behavior and welfare derived from a highly constrained sampling of what Ruth Benedict once called "the great arc" of human possibilities ([1934] 1959: 24). The prevailing social scientific discourse of human nature and welfare ignores both the greater portion of this "arc" ('the rest') and the dynamics of cultural crossings.

Yet, if important features of sociocultural evolutionary theory inhabit the present, there is nonetheless a long history of this paradigm's disintegration. Self-doubts within European liberalism, the outbreak of barbarism within the heartlands of "civilization," and the decline of the European states to the status of second-rate powers, all rendered out-of-date Victorian versions of historical teleology and racial anthropology. More recently, the economic decline of England, East Asia's high-tech prosperity, and the puncturing of boundaries between Europe East and West have further reshaped the familiar outline of (Western) 'civilization.' As we approach the quincentenary of Columbus's collision with Asia/America, the conventions of 'Western civilization' *circa* 1900 have the quaint and odd look of a British Empire map of the world.

As we have already suggested, however, scholarly conventions are not discarded as easily as old maps. In embarking on self-critique, we may unintentionally reproduce the analytic habits we wish to contest. Such habits often persist in the very act of declaring opposition, and there is no convenience store with an instant product for unlearning them. Some of the most notable recent attempts at telling a different story of the West attest to this.

Counterhistories, which attempt to displace the 'rise of the West' by narrating the history of the West's domination of the rest, contain the danger of fighting the dominant discourse with its own means and sounding like it in the end. For example, Eric Wolf (1982) assembles post-Columbian colonial encounters into a narration that is lucidly chronological in form and admirably global in coverage. And certainly, Wolf's text succeeds in presenting the historical emergence of industrial capitalism as a world phenomenon, rather than as a European phenomenon which eventually spread outward. Yet the book's rock-steady, univocal narrative voice elides the strangeness and polyphony of colonial encounters, and presents them as leading inexorably to a monolithic late-capitalism. In Wolf's text, cultures do not cross, they fall in line. Wolf's book thus enacts in narration its author's historical perception of the destruction of cultural difference (cf. Clifford 1988: 14).

Other authors, more reflexive than Wolf, have promoted experimentation with narrative conventions with the aim of introducing greater polyphony into accounts of cultural difference (Clifford 1988; Marcus and Fisher 1986; Handler and Segal 1990). To note a recent example, having criticized various stylistic claims to ethnographic authority, James Clifford now urges a shift toward representing ethnographic research as travel encounters rather than as stays in homes-away-from-home (forthcoming). Such a shift, argues Clifford, will move us away from objectifying 'cultures' as boundaried social wholes with fixed, emblematic traits, and will increase the visibility of "constructed and disputed *historicities*, sites of displacement, interference and interaction" (12). Yet, as James Boon's essay in this volume reminds us, narratives which transgress the boundary between travel tales and ethnography are an aspect of, rather than something outside, the history of 'Western' writing about exotic others (see also, Boon 1990). So too, Mary Campbell's essay tells us, are moral doubts about colonial conquest itself. That such transgressions of genre and pangs of conscience are older than many postmodernist texts claim does not mean these transgressions and pangs are without value. It does remind us that neither provides a once-and-for-all 'solution' to the problem of relating Europe to the non-European world.

Neither, of course, do the essays in this volume. What we claim on their behalf is more modest—that they participate vigorously in a longstanding and not-soon-to-be-ended struggle with Eurocentrism in the writing of histories and ethnographies. The essays participate in this struggle *via* detailed case studies of cultural crossings, hazily perceived and fragmentarily documented. We use the term "crossing" to refer to the mutual conditioning which takes place in cultural encounters, altering both sides. For the most part the essays do not attempt to document the diffusion of cultural goods: proving the 'influence' of, say, African masks in Picasso paintings is not their point. Rather, these essays show how cultural differences shaped historical events, and how, in turn, new differences emerged from encounters—how, that is, the identities and groupings that have emerged as European and non-European were forged and reforged in colonial encounters, and indeed, are being reforged in postcolonial encounters now.

The authors of these essays approach cultural crossings from a wide range of theoretical perspectives. Arguing for the determinacy of relations to the mode of production, Peter Linebaugh and Marcus Rediker show how the experiences of European and African workers in eighteenth-century Atlantic ports shaped a common identity—a class consciousness. Writing in a markedly different vein—with the persona of a roving ethnographer-tourist—James Boon examines the instability of the demarcation of natives and ethnographers in post-colonial Bali and New York. For all the differences between an essay operating primarily with the category of class, and one distilling (and ironizing) personal memory, these two essays nonetheless share this volume's perception of cultural encounters as sites of the displacement of identities. Neither geography nor genetics nor cultural objectification (nor anything else) creates unambiguous selves or others; the crossings (between African and European workers, between ethnographers and informants) suggest how permeable demarcations have been and remain.

One specific type of crossing characterizes the colonial encounters studied in all the essays in this volume: the reciprocity of moral regimes. The threat and use of force was a prevalent feature of colonial encounters. But as Weber observed long ago, sheer force never rules for very long. Routinized power relationships are inseparable from representations of power, and together these form what we term a moral regime. In such moral regimes, the more and less powerful are defined and shaped vis-à-vis each other. In contrast to collective representations of an "organic," Durkheimian sort, such moral regimes emerge not from an experience of belonging, but from dialectical and reciprocal demarcations of identities and groupings.[3] This means, as Pauline Strong tells us in her study of captivity on the British Amerindian Frontier, that "oppositions between White and Red"—or any other self/Other pair—"also involve a subtle identification between [them]" (see page 41 below).

To identify moral regimes as characteristic of colonial encounters is not to suggest that colonized persons acquiesced to their subordination or conquest.[4] Rather, it is to argue that in colonial encounters, there emerged meaningful patterns of relations between demarcated social groupings. Moral regimes defined both normative models of order serving the interest of dominant classes, and various forms of resistance to domination—although, historically, they did more to enable the former than the latter.

All of the papers in this volume probe the reciprocity of moral regimes. Mary Campbell's essay examines Fracastoro's poetic grappling with the etiology of syphilis. Lacking a later Europe's sense of being inevitably, absolutely, and simply 'a victor,' Fracastoro, according to Campbell, inadvertently testifies to the mutual and morbid objectification of self and other, conqueror and conquered, master and slave, which European colonialism set in motion. Pauline Strong examines how the complex experiences of European captives were resolved into the moral certainties of Puritan allegories, in part by the captors themselves and more fully in retellings by Puritan authorities, notably Cotton Mather. Peter Linebaugh and Marcus Rediker's paper shows us that geographically dispersed experiences of class subordination could unify (and not just divide) workers whom historians today delineate by race. Linebaugh and Rediker thus bring into view a subsequently obscured resistance to both class exploitation and racial fragmentation. All three of these papers re-member the reciprocity of moral regimes which now seem more simply one-sided.

The papers by David Prochaska and Derek Sayer explore moral regimes within early twentieth-century colonial societies in which state institutions were highly developed and seemingly entrenched. Prochaska reveals how the opposed nationalisms of European settlers and colonized Algerians emerged from shifting, triangular relations among settlers, Algerians, and metropolitan France. Sayer reconstructs British moral responses to the Amritsar massacre, finding that liberals who condemned the killings contributed, in turn, to a belief in a British moral superiority which transcended the occasional shortcomings of imperial rule.

In the volume's concluding essay, James Boon reexamines his own ethnographic encounters with long-crisscrossed, formerly colonized, and now touristic Bali: here the ethnographer finds informants intent upon and adept at 'mastering' his language and culture. Boon brings to our attention, as well, the venerability of the 'Western' tradition of reclaiming magical-coincidence from the exoticized, reciprocally defined periphery of the West's disenchanted self.

Crossing Cultures goes to press at a moment when American colleges and universities are debating the place in the undergraduate curriculum of something widely known as 'Western Civilization.' Defenders of 'Western Civ' courses represent themselves as keeping morality and order firmly in place. Against liberalizing demands for a multicultural curriculum and practical calls for studies of the Pacific rim, they invoke the stability of a metaphorized geography ('the West'). The essays gathered here question whether there has ever been, at least since Fracastoro (and Columbus), a 'West' defined independent of reciprocal relations with those deemed 'Other,' including many within the supposed 'West.' Thus these essays suggest a need to go beyond the reformist impulse to add other 'cultures' to the curriculum—as if each and every 'culture' could be represented alike by a dish at a large, but finite, smorgasbord (cf. Handler 1988: 195). Rather, these essays suggest the importance of telling students of the long history of cultural-crossings that has produced the institutions and customs conventionally attributed to essentialized, cultural isolates.[5] The papers collected here are forays in the displacement of Western civilization; they seek to undermine its established boundaries by demonstrating their permeability and shifting locations. Together, these essays testify to the view that the multicultural, creolizing world of the present is a consequence of a multicultural, creolizing past.

NOTES

Richard Handler, Pieter Judson and Laurie Shrage read drafts of this introduction; their comments helped us greatly to clarify our thinking about these issues.

1. We use single quotation marks to indicate a term or phrase we have set off for analysis. We reserve double quotation marks for quoted material from a specific source.

2. It is worth noting that after Boas's robust attacks on social evolutionary theory, the evolutionary opposition between 'complex' and 'simple' societies was retained by Boasian anthropology. For an important example, see Benedict ([1934] 1959: 17–18, 52–56). As many have noted, the rendering of social orders as isolates is even more obviously a characteristic of British structural-functionalism. Our goal is to call attention to some of the less obvious instances of this objectifying practice.

3. For this use of reciprocity, see Simmel ([1890] 1966; [1900] 1978).

4. Here our notion of moral regimes departs significantly from Weber's notion of legitimacy. In Weber, whereas the upper class (comprised notably of male intellectuals) is innovative and creative, subaltern classes and women are merely reactive (Weber 1978: 399–634).

5. For us, one of the most important and stimulating examples of such a historical narrative is C.L.R. James's ([1938] 1963) account of the mutual shaping of the classes and revolutions of Haiti and France. Segal (1988, 1990) attempts to build upon James's study of the colonial context of the French Revolution.

REFERENCES

Benedict, Ruth. [1934] 1959. *Patterns of Culture*. Boston: Houghton Mifflin.

Boon, James. 1990. "Travel Writing and Circumcision, from the Sixteenth Century and Since." Paper presented at the annual meeting of the American Historical Association, New York.

Clifford, James. 1988. *The Predicament of Culture: Twentieth-Century Ethnography, Literature, and Art*. Cambridge, Mass.: Harvard University Press.

————. Forthcoming. "Traveling Cultures." In *Cultural Studies*, eds. Larry Grossberg, Cary Nelson, and Paula Treichler. New York: Ron Hedge.

Handler, Richard. 1988. *Nationalism and the Politics of Culture in Quebec*. Madison: University of Wisconsin Press.

Handler, Richard, and Daniel Segal. 1990. *Jane Austen and the Fiction of Culture: An Essay on the Narration of Social Realities*. Tucson: University of Arizona Press.

Harbsmeier, Michael, and Mogens Trolle Larsen. 1989. *The Writing of World Histories*. Vol. 5, *Culture and History*. Copenhagen: Akademisk Forlag.

James, C.L.R. [1938] 1963. *The Black Jacobins*. New York: Vintage Books.

Marcus, George, and Michael Fisher. 1986. *Anthropology as Cultural Critique*. Chicago: University of Chicago Press.

Segal, Daniel. 1988. "Nationalism, Comparatively Speaking," *Journal of Historical Sociology* 1:300–321.

————. 1990. "Some Colonial Meanings of 'European.'" Paper presented at the annual meeting of the American Anthropological Association, New Orleans.

Simmel, Georg. [1890] 1966. *Uber Soziale Differenzierung*. Amsterdam: Liberas.

————. [1900] 1978. *Philosophy of Money*. Trans. Tom Bottomore and David Frisby. London: Routledge & Kegan Paul.

Stocking, George. 1987. *Victorian Anthropology*. New York: The Free Press.

Weber, Max. 1978. *Economy and Society*, eds. Guenther Roth and Claus Wittich. Vol. 1. Berkeley and Los Angeles: University of California Press.

Wolf, Eric. 1982. *Europe and the People Without History*. Berkeley and Los Angeles: University of California Press.

CROSSING CULTURES

1

Carnal Knowledge:

Fracastoro's *De Syphilis* and the Discovery of the New World

Mary B. Campbell

> O my America! My new-found land,
> My kingdom, safeliest when with one man manned,
> My mine of precious stones, my empery,
> How blest I am in this discovering thee!
> To enter in these bonds is to be free;
> Then where my hand is set, my seal shall be.
>
> —John Donne, "Elegy XIX. To His Mistress Going To Bed"

Among the first and for a long time most important imports from America were syphilis and its popular cure, the bark of the guaiacum tree. In fact, the geographical origin of syphilis remains controversial to this day. Although in 1986 some declared it settled by the discovery in the Caribbean of pre-Columbian bones bearing syphilitic lesions, it will be remembered that in 1986 Western science had only recently given up identifying the Caribbean island of Haiti as the original home of AIDS. The reassignment of AIDS to Africa may be medically warranted and it may not. Certainly in the sixteenth century the etiology of venereal diseases was a matter beyond the reach of medical science; the European search for origins was contaminated a priori by symbolic and political conceptions of both venereal disease and the places from which it may have been contracted. To analyze a fragment of sixteenth-century speculation on the origin and treatment of syphilis is inevitably to confront the intermingled issues of sexuality, xenophobia, conquest, and guilt in a period before any European community had reached a consensus as to the nature or future of its contact with the New World.

We will examine here a Renaissance poem in which an Italian physician committed to a medical theory that discounted the American origin is nevertheless led to reimagine the discovery of the New World as tragically pathogenic. Girolamo Fracastoro's 1530 poem, *De Syphilis, sive morbum gallicum*, offers a total of four independent etiologies for syphilis, only two of which identify the disease as American. The resulting incoherence of the work signals, to me at least, a case of serious cognitive distress, and permits me to read the poem as inadvertent testimony to the inherent morbidity of the colonial relation.[1] That testimony is important to our understanding of the prehistory of modern European colonialism, but for good reasons, it cannot be derived from the poem's explicit argument. *De Syphilis* reveals the distress of its author and its culture through the arrangement and derangement of literary materials and techniques; it speaks all the more clearly for its historical moment through such structural and conventional features as its genres, its allusions, its reliance on preexisting mythic cliché. To unravel Fracastoro's literary nightmare we will accordingly need to look at the contemporary and conventional significance of these materials as well as at their particular combinations in this poem.

In the currently rather lively place where literary and cultural studies meet, a monolithic image of European power politics is emerging which I think needs some modifications. Fracastoro's poem reveals a Europe more nearly conscious of moral failure in the exercise of its colonial expansion than the critiques of the New Historicism suggest. The terms were in place by 1530 for a European self-criticism, or at any rate a perception of conquest as ambiguous. There is a greater appreciation of loss in Fracastoro's poem than in many of our contemporary narratives of New World exploration and exploitation, for all their moral anguish over a domination we have come to see as both successful and complete.

Stephen Greenblatt offers one such New World narrative in *Renaissance Self-Fashioning* (1980), a classic of the New Historicism. From an account of Guyon's destruction of the Bower of Bliss and the chaining of its resident nymph in the *Faerie Queene*, Greenblatt is moved to consider the analogous and contemporary destruction of the Indies: "A whole civilization was caught in a net, and, like Acrasia, bound in chains of adamant; their gods were melted down, their palaces and temples razed, their groves felled. 'And of the fairest late, now made the foulest place' " (183). Greenblatt comes to the vision of "sexual colonialism" from an immersion in English romance, and speaks of it in a discussion of the literary and social construct "gentleman"—i.e., in the central chapter of *Renaissance Self-Fashioning*, "The Fashioning of a Gentleman." By contrast, I come to the vision of "sexual colonialism" from the opposite horizon, finding later in romance what I had found first in travel accounts of the period, and in the process of constructing, if not a lady, at any rate a female—what John Donne called "my America, my new found land," in the elegy to his mistress quoted at the beginning of this essay. The center in which we meet is not quite a place of agreement, although we do agree on a central principle of the New Historicism. In Greenblatt's words, "it is not adequate for a cultural poetics to describe the destruction of the Bower of Bliss or any literary text as a *reflection* of its circumambient culture; Spenser's poem is one manifestation of a symbolic language that is inscribed by history on the bodies of living beings" (179).

Although that last clause is intended metaphorically, Tzvetan Todorov invites us to imagine it literally when he dedicates his recent *Conquest of America* (1984) "to the memory of a Mayan woman devoured by dogs." Todorov joins current discussion of the Conquest from the perspective of a cultural historian, reading the events of history as though history were *in fact* romance, and the hero's Other won, like Juliet or Dante's Francesca, with language. Interestingly, neither Greenblatt nor Todorov pays much attention to the literary figure of America as a woman, or to the actual American women inscribed *in* history. It is hard to see why not. For Todorov's thesis, that the Conquest was a linguistic victory on a heavily eroticized field of play, the figure of Malinche—Cortes's mistress, native interpreter, intermediary and namesake—should have been an irresistible topic. And for Greenblatt's thesis, that the conquest was a "sexual" one, the inescapable presence of directly feminizing and erotic tropes in the discovery literature ought to have provided textual support.

So it is in the peculiar footsteps of their inattention that I will set out to find what, after all, could not have been the goal of either man's

quest; they are concerned with the success of the Conquest and I with
its failure. The failure of the Conquest is not a congenial topic for the
New Historicism; the reasons are directly related to the assumptions
behind my essay and should perhaps be aired before we turn to Fracastoro's poem. Most of the essays in this volume treat episodes in the
history of imperial hegemony occurring after the point at which empire and colonialism had become indubitable facts. But in the history
of colonialism, the Renaissance is almost prehistorical. In 1530 we can
barely see Europe contemplating, or even repressing consciousness
of, colonialism. It is not clear what the future holds. Pizarro has not
yet conquered Cuzco; the mineral wealth of South America is still an
educated guess. Of course, *we* know what the future holds—it holds
us. Greenblatt eloquently declares this as a ground of inquiry for the
New Historicism, in the chapter of *Self-Fashioning* from which I have
already quoted:

> We sense . . . that we are situated at the close of the cultural
> movement initiated in the Renaissance and that the places in which
> our social and psychological world seems to be cracking apart are
> those structural joints visible when it was first constructed. In the
> midst of the anxieties and contradictions attendant upon the threat-
> ened collapse of this phase of our civilization, we respond with
> passionate curiosity and poignancy to the anxieties and contradic-
> tions attendant upon its rise. To experience Renaissance culture is to
> feel what it was like to form our own identity . . . (174–175).

This intuition of our nostalgic personal fellowship with Renaissance culture is confessed in deference to another principle of New
Historicism—the recognition, as Louis Montrose puts it, "That this
project of historical resituation is necessarily the textual construction
of critics who are themselves historical subjects" (1986: 304). It therefore behooves the critic to situate his own practice and expose the
nature of his stake in the matters he examines. Both Greenblatt and
Montrose are admirably responsive to their duty; Montrose admits
that he is impelled not only by Greenblatt's "poignancy" of identification but "by a questioning of our very capacity for action—by a

nagging sense of professional, institutional and political impotence" (352). The Foucauldian message of most New Historicist analysis is not immediately designed to relieve any such nagging sense of impotence—it seems, rather, a projection of it.

But I have used the masculine pronoun intentionally in the previous paragraph. Both the concern with impotence and the perception of sourceless and totalizing systems of power, arising in the Renaissance and still triumphant (as that "history" to which we are ourselves "subject"), seem to me to betray a primarily masculine dynamic of identification.[2] The same critics oppressed by the inescapability of that power so admirably figured in the conquests and colonizations of the early modern period seem to derive at least some comfort from identification with it, and from an intellectual "mastery" of it.[3] The decision to see in the Renaissance the origins of a cultural hegemony which, threatened or not, persists in our time (and not to the entire inconvenience of white male American professors) is to have some stake in its inevitability and totality.

My assumptions might be better described as proclivities. I will be examining the epidemiology of conquest, as far as possible, from the point of view of Fracastoro, who did not "know" it would lead to world domination and had not yet chosen a mythology of Manifest Destiny in which to view it. That the discovery and conquests of America were the forerunners of colonial empires in the New World is obviously the case. But the unambiguous success recorded by Todorov, the one-sided power of destruction so lamented by Greenblatt—these are not the whole story. The picture at short range, as seen by a poetizing doctor steeped in the ambivalence of Virgil, is a corrective. Greenblatt's description of America's destruction at Europe's hands ("their goods . . . melted down, palaces and temples razed, their groves felled") finds an eerie echo in Fracastoro's picture of contemporary Europe: "we have seen an unusual disease, . . . we have seen harsh disastrous wars, and household gods drenched in their owners' blood and towns and cities burned and kingdoms overthrown and temples and altars violated, robbed of their sacred objects; . . . woods uprooted in mid-flood" (II, 16–21). "Parthenope [Naples], . . .

tell of the deaths of kings and spoils and plunder and the necks of your citizens bound captive" (I, 426–427).[4] It is a moment of European impotence we will be observing here, and the contribution of that impotence to what became, but was not yet and was never only, a domination.

De Syphilis: Materials

It is neither an insignificant nor a merely wonderful coincidence that a contemporary historical romance exists which narrates the initial encounter of imperial Spain with its first colony. In Fracastoro's *De Syphilis*, the historical allegory of Spenser and the allegorical history implied in Todorov's "reading" of the Conquest meet in a single text: a text which is historical artifact, poetical history, and genetic romance all at once. *De Syphilis* is a brief conflation of epic and georgic materials in Latin hexameters, which combines an account of Columbus's discovery with an account of the origins and treatment of the disease which took its name from this poem. The poet and his poem are famous among historians of medicine for providing a diplomatic solution to the nationalistic war of names then raging in Europe, where neighbor nations pointed accusing fingers at each other with such labels as "the French disease," "the Spanish disease," "the Naples disease," "the German disease" and "the Polish disease." His poem located the enemy at a more distant remove—in that same Haiti, in fact, which we first blamed for AIDS.

We need to look at *De Syphilis* from two angles, in the context of European perception of the colonial relation and also in its own more immediate literary context. In the case of a geographical discovery like Columbus's, postulated almost entirely on literary rather than scientific evidence, these contexts overlap to an unusual degree. But the poem remains a poem: it is a response to, as well as a part of, the history it imagines. And because it is a poem, it provides simultaneous access to a great density and variety of significations, revealing as perhaps no prose discourse could the interconnectedness of the medical, erotic, and colonial aspects of what historians so suggestively term "the contact period."

To judge from two of the most pervasive image clusters in sixteenth-century literature on the New World, that America was a woman is not open to doubt, nor that she was "golden." Columbus's Caribbean was "a woman's nipple"; Waldseemüller feminized Amerigo Vespucci's name to title the continent; "Ammerices" is the name of the tutelary nymph in Fracastoro's myth. In de Bry's illustration for the *Great Voyages* (1590–1634, vol. 9A, plate lxi), she is depicted as Eve offering fruit to the Spaniards. Las Casas wants to marry her to the Spanish crown, Ralegh to rape her, George Chapman to set foot on her "broad breast" (Columbus 1930–33: 2, 30; Waldseemüller 1507; de Bry 1590–1634; Las Casas 1583: F4r; Ralegh 1595: 115; and Chapman 1596). All the early explorers are drawn to the nakedness and comeliness of the Carib and Arawak women, who quickly become welcoming parties of nymphs for writers as disparate as the historian Peter Martyr and the poet Fracastoro. Eventually, America is Donne's pet name for his mistress and Acrasia, as Greenblatt so amply demonstrates, Spenser's pet name for America.

If we bear in mind the traditional Western notion of nature itself as female, the female image absorbs as well the insistent identification of the American landscape as purely (if fantastically) natural (Merchant 1980, ch. 1). Few and far between lie European depictions of American agriculture, or even of any masculine restraint in the natural landscape, which is as wanton and profuse as the tendrils of Milton's Eve (or the luxurious foliage of his Eden—as clearly a female body as the body of Donne's mistress is an American colony).

If the female, and in particular the female body, is the matrix of American metaphor, the metonym is gold. Long before it was found it was sought hysterically and attested to repeatedly: America's sands were gold dust, its rivers gold-bearing, its mountainsides gleamed with gold, its women were decked with it, its womb teemed with it. The obvious connection between the female body and buried treasure is old among the topoi of European literature. Carolyn Merchant quotes from Pliny's explanation of earthquakes as the trembling of ravished nature: "We penetrate her entrails, and seek for treasure . . ." (30). Ovid complains in a similar figure: "Not only did men demand of the bounteous fields the crops and sustenance they owed, but they delved as well into the very bowels of the earth; and the wealth which the creator had hidden away and buried deep amidst the very Stygian shades, was brought to light, wealth that pricks men on to crime" (1984: I, 137–40).

Robert Baker is leaning on an old tradition when he pens in prison, in 1563, an irate verse letter about his frustrating voyages for gold to the Guinea Coast:

> And Orpheus past I wot
>> the passage quietly
> Among the souls in Charon's boat
>> and yet to say truly
> I never read that he
>> paid for his passage there
> Who past and repast for to see
>> if that his wife there were,
> Nor yet that he paid ought
>> or any bribe there gave
> To any office, while he sought
>> his wife again to have.
> Whereby I surely guesse
>> these men with whom that we
> Have had to do, are fiends more fierce
>> than those in hell that be.
>
> (In Hakluyt 1582: 130)

Baker's lines reintroduce, in an African context, the figure of Hades we saw in Ovid's "Stygian shadow" and which some have seen, oddly disguised, in Spenser's Bower of Bliss. That figure will reappear in full force in Conrad's *Heart of Darkness*, but it is mostly absent from sixteenth-century writing about America. For the men of this period, the "new-found land" was not a hell but a paradise: a paradise lost or destroyed or blemished by savagery, but a figure of desire, not of horror.

Browsing through the literature for images, one ends up in a dismaying hall of mirrors. To separate figure from ground when the figure of the woman is so easily translated into the figure of the ground from which the gold will come—and then to find gold as Baker's figure for Eurydice, herself the figure of the supreme object of desire and even, in her elusiveness, of desire itself—this is unsettling. And when America becomes the poet's figure for the woman, as in Donne, we have come around the circle on a ferris wheel, and I, at least, am dizzy.

The fifteenth and sixteenth centuries saw the great flowering of European romance, both as genre and as literary "mode." In verse and prose, narrative and drama, Boiardo, Ariosto, Tasso, Camoens, Malory, Sidney, Spenser, Shakespeare: we are used to these romancers' names as the major literary names of the later Renaissance. But their favored literary mode was not restricted to works of imaginative literature, and it flowered from roots in precisely the literatures Columbus (and later explorer-writers) found so fertile: travel literature, the allegorically suggestive pastoral of antiquity, the Greek "Alexander romances" that fed Pliny and through him the subsequent Western tradition of exotic travel writing.

This mode and the topoi that accompany it dominate most early accounts of the New World, even the most naïve. Landscapes are almost always reducible to the conventionalized features of the *locus amoenus*, and their human inhabitants are as inhumanly innocent and eager to satisfy the European visitor as any bevy of nymphs or maidens in Arcadia. There is no winter, no drought, no alien culture to baffle or distract the reader; people and places alike function as fantastic and ornamental background to the *aventur* of the exploring knight.[5] A quick glance at the main historical features of European response to the discovery shows us that romance was a mode of understanding and acting as well as of writing—that the New World was the "Other World" to explorers and kings and popes and historians and mapmakers and scientists and even to such great commercial outfits as the Fuggers, who organized more than one ill-fated expedition to El Dorado.

The primitive literary original both of romance and of European perception of the New World lies in Genesis: de Bry's frontispiece to Volume I of the *Great Voyages* portrays Adam and Eve and the Serpent standing (and coiling) around the Tree of Knowledge (see figure 1-1). This is already, in 1590, an ironic commentary on the paradisal image complex underlying European reception of America over the course of the century. (It was perhaps in honor of this same Serpent that the Spanish physician Ruy Diáz de Isla had called venereal syphilis "Morbo Serpentino" in his treatise of 1539.) The romance of Genesis ends on a sour note—indeed, *history* begins, and history, as historians of the Discovery noted early on, is sour stuff.

From the original depictions of the Caribbean as another garden of Eden—according to Columbus perhaps even the same one—accounts degenerated with grim rapidity into the detailing of another Fall, a Fall to which Las Casas was the most eloquent and influential witness:

> Upon these lambes so meeke, so qualified and endewed of their maker and creator, as hath been said, entred the Spanish incontinent as they knewe them, as wolves, as lions, and as tigres most cruel of long time famished: and have not done in those quarters these 40 yeres be past, neither yet doe at this present, ought els save teare them in peeces, kill them, martyre them, afflict them, torment them, and destroy them by straunge sorts of cruelties never neither seene, nor reade, nor hearde of the like . . . so farre foorth that of above three Millions of soules that were in the Ile of Hispaniola, and that we have seene, there are not nowe two hundreth natives of the countrey. . . . (1583: A1v–A2r)

But the Fall is not simply an image of the inevitable corrupting influence of man's greed, for which God sentences him to death. It is also an account of woman's guilt, and authorizes her subjection: "Because thou hast done this . . . in sorrow shalt thou bring forth children; and thy desire shall be to thy husband, and he shall rule over thee" (Genesis 2:16). This subjection is so natural to the male European imagination of the sixteenth century that even Las Casas, the most guiltily sensitive of its historians, quotes approvingly at the end of his denunciation of Spanish colonial practice a letter from a Mexican bishop who speaks of it as a redemptive possibility:

Figure 1-1. *Adam and Eve* from Part ("America") of Theodor de Bry's *Great Voyages*, Frankfurt, 1590. Courtesy of the John Carter Brown Library at Brown University.

> I say, sacred Majestie, that the way to redresse this countreye, is
> that his Majestie deliver her out of the power of Stepfathers, and
> give unto her an husbande whiche may increase her as is reason, and
> according as thee discerneth. (1583: F4r)

That the New World should be married to her imperial Spanish colo-
nizer is not seen as a tragic consequence in the figure of the Second
Fall, but as an *undoing* of Spain's guilt and America's trauma. This
marriage will set things right again for the Spanish Argonauts and the
American nymphs.

But in this erotic figure, essential to the romance equally of Genesis and the *Faerie Queene*, lies the rub. For it was from the literally
erotic relations of the early Argonauts and the Caribbean nymphs that
the pestilential penance of Europe sprang. Fracastoro's romance re-
capitulates the bitterness of Genesis while, with inadvertent precision,
it displaces the fact of that sexual contact into an image of unmoti-
vated and fatal aggression. When Fracastoro's heroic mariners reach
America, they call down divine wrath on themselves, not for the more
historically probable rape of the nymphs, but by aimlessly shooting
and killing a flock of talking birds.

Books I and II: Alternative Etiologies

Fracastoro's poem has not received much attention from literary critics recently, although in his own time Scaliger and Sannazoro thought
highly of it—Scaliger called it "divine."[6] The problem may be partly
that, to modern tastes, disease is no subject for epic hexameters, or for
any serious poetic treatment. Sixteenth-century readers and writers
did not share our distaste, and Fracastoro's is not the only poetic
treatment of the disease, nor was Fracastoro the only physician-poet.[7]
The two professions merged more easily then, in the days of a more
philosophical and poetic language of medicine. It was not lost on any
humanist that Apollo was the god of both poetry and healing, and
indeed, poetry itself had been a medieval therapeutic (Olson 1982).

The hook is the body, of course—the most fertile source of metaphor we know, and as such a particular object of interest to the
analogy-mad intelligentsia of the Renaissance, which saw the body

as a microcosm of the entire universe, and whose period is still em-
blematized for us, on textbook covers and calls for scholarly papers,
in Da Vinci's proportional diagram of the (male) human figure.

The body is Fracastoro's high theme; the diseased body his tragic
subject. It is everywhere his ruling figure, or the figure behind his
figures, and it is always gendered. And so, in his animated landscape,
is everything else: the earth, the sea, the sky, the sun, the moon,
the Caribbean, the woods and streams, the mines, the ships, the victims of syphilis, and more abstractly, the source of the disease and of
its curatives. The actions that provoke or manifest the pestilence are
imagined as forms of sexual abuse and violation, and the *mise-en-scène*
of the poem is quite literally sex-soaked: in Book I Fracastoro imagines the pestilence as a seminal rain infecting the air of the entire globe.

The poem is also soaked in Virgil; the language carries frequent
echoes from the *Aeneid*, and the plot events of Book III allude directly
to the events of Aeneas's exploration of his Italian New World. But
the poem is not an epic. It follows the *Georgics*, rather than the *Aeneid*,
in devoting ninety lines of Book I to a close description of the course
and symptoms of syphilis and well over half of Book II to treatments and medical recipes. The average reader—doctor, patient, or
potential sufferer—must have felt a painfully immediate engagement
unavailable to the *Aeneid*'s original audience.

De Syphilis provides a mythos not only for the scourge of syphilis
but for the wars and the catastrophic floods that immediately preceded
its outbreak (in Italy) in 1495, for the Spanish and Portuguese explorations, and for the projected Crusade of Pope Leo X. Fracastoro knew
he was occupying an historical moment worthy of epic treatment.
But he leaves the narrative of the wars and explorations explicitly to
other poets: when he says at the beginning of Book II that he "will
expound the wonderful discoveries of men" (II, 4), he means remedies
for syphilis.[8] "For me it is enough to recall the powers of a single tree
and its use" (III, 26–27). When he gives Europe its first poem of the
New World in Book III, it is an account of the discovery of guaiacum,
which at the time of Book III's composition was the most popular
source of pharmaceutical remedies.[9]

In fact Book III was an afterthought, and the thought was not even Fracastoro's own. In 1525 he gave a copy to his friend and neighbor, the poet (as well as humanist, botanist, alchemist, and bishop) Pietro Bembo, to whom the work was dedicated. At that point it was composed of only two books, culminating in the myth of the discovery of the mercury cure, but Bembo urged him to update it. Ulrich von Hutten's enormously popular work on the "French disease" and the guaiacum cure had come out in 1519, and the drug itself had just reached Italy.

John Alden's chronological bibliography, *European Americana* (1980), includes all European works referring to America up to 1776 and also includes, as far as the year 1600, all works with references to syphilis. This criterion goes a long way towards increasing the size of the bibliography's first volume; the predominance of works included for the syphilis connection indicates that Fracastoro's epidemiological perspective on the New World was something more than an accident of his professional orientation. In 1530, for instance, the year of *De Syphilis*'s publication, ten of the twenty-eight works listed by Alden are included for the syphilis connection. On the other hand, it is also the case that as the author-to-be of two important medical treatises, *De Contagionibus* and *Sympathia et Antipathia*, Fracastoro was probably the perfect man for the task at hand. Sympathy, antipathy, and contagion are certainly appropriate conceptual anchors in the business of assessing the contact of two such mutually fascinating and alien populations as were those of Europe and the Caribbean in the early sixteenth century. Add to this the romance consciousness of the period, and the subliminal connections between the ideas of the female body and terra incognita, and it comes to seem almost inevitable that the most material repercussions of the "contact period" were in fact venereal syphilis and smallpox.

Given this armature of facts, figures, and genres, the natural concern of a physician with disease and of a Renaissance poet with the body, one might imagine *De Syphilis* practically writing itself. What is interesting, then, is to observe its self-contradictions, its displacements, its uncomfortable evasion of what could have been the tidy moral fable of a second descent, in a second Eden, into carnal knowledge and morality.

Although our main concern is with Book III, the account of the discovery of America, the structures and motifs of the poem's two earlier etiological narratives provide important internal evidence of the dishevelment we find in Book III. The scenario of Book I is simply contradicted by the later etiologies, while that of Book II sets up a symbolic structure that is elaborated and criminalized in Book III's ' many-layered romance narrative of the discovery.

In Book I (as later in the prose treatise, *De Contagionibus*), Fracastoro proves that syphilis could *not* have come from America: the disease seems to have broken out in too many places at once, and as he says more clearly in the treatise, it was predicted by "astronomos" some years before its appearance. Thus, its origin is more profound ("rerumque latenior ordo," I, 78) than mere contagion. The origin he provides is a properly Virgilian decree of the gods, themselves submitting to the urgency of Fate. At a council personifying a recent conjunction of the planets Mars and Saturn in the sign of Cancer (the same abhorrent conjunction that had presaged the Black Death), Jupiter winces, and then the "strange rains" fall. There is no transgression and no guilt, though transgression and guilt will structure all the subsequent etiologies in the poem. The blame is laid squarely, and neutrally, at the door of Air, "the father of all things and the author of their origin. This same [element] often brings serious illness to mortals" (I, 126–27). Mother Earth (*tellus parens*) is rudely inseminated, but the specific victim is "the one [species] that is great through its mind, the human race" (I, 301–2). Fracastoro's illustration, a blameless, Marcellian "youth of Verona," is simply stricken and simply (albeit horribly) dies.

This etiology, though personified, relays Fracastoro's mature scientific understanding. As a physician of his age he could imagine such an allegory without stepping far outside the bounds of his professional jargon: *semina* was as much the word for germ as for sperm, and planetary conjunctions an acknowledged cause of epidemics. And yet something will lead him to a far more resonant and compelling etiology in Book III, despite his scientific opinion; its implied redistributions of source and agency are probably behind the lyric protest attached to Nahum Tate's English translation of 1686:

Blame not the stars; 'tis plain it neither fell
From the distempered Heav'ns; nor rose from Hell,
Nor need we to the distant Indies rome;
The curst Originals are nearer home.
Whence should that fould infection's torment flow
But from the banefull source of all our wo?
That wheedling, charming sex, that draws us in
To ev'ry punishment and ev'ry sin.

(n.p.)

Although Fracastoro revised Books I and II after adding the third, he leaves intact the contradiction between the two theories of origin—one sign among many of his discomposure at the implications of the American origin.

After a detailed *regimen sanitatem*, Book II concentrates on a description of the gold-bearing womb of the earth, where nymphs are nurses and midwives for the minerals that supply the forges of the Cyclopes.[10] Its exemplary victim, Ilcaeus, has accidentally slain a stag of Hecate's, and at Hecate's request Apollo has smitten him with syphilis. The nymph to whom Ilcaeus had innocently offered up the stag hears his lament and advises supplication to Ops, Night, and the nymphs of the unknown powers (*numina ignota*), followed by a trip to the penetralia of the "blind earth"—the underworld not of Pluto but of Proserpine. Once there, he is succored by another nymph, who bathes him in a "living stream" of quicksilver: "Thrice she bathed him in the silver fount of salvation, thrice with her virgin hands she scooped the river water over his limbs, thrice cleansed the body of the youth in its entirety" (II, 410–14).[11] His final rite is a prayer to "chaste Diana."

This is an almost entirely female world, except for its central agents and victims: the sacred stag, the hunter/victim, the god who administers the penalty of disease. All places, local powers, and substances are feminine: groves, streams, earth, metals, nymphs, goddesses. Feminine also are the agencies of cure and purification, the subject of insult, and the immediate object of supplication. This is the world of romance—a world of diffuse femininity traversed and penetrated by the direct and concentrated plotlines of male action and suffering. Fracastoro's underworld is nothing new, of course. Even to the pagan writers of antiquity, whose underworld was ostensibly ruled by Pluto, it is Proserpine/Persephone who haunts the place, and female spirits who guide the hero there and back.

Nor does this poetic stereotype clash with Fracastoro's more strictly medical view of the therapeutic scene. Before he arrives at the harsh (*acerbis*) remedy of mercury, his most emphatic recommendations have been to "avoid the soft pleasures of love-making" ("Parce tamen Veneri, mollequi ante omnia vita/Concubitus," II, 113–14) and to seek out the citron, fruit of the tree of Venus. The whole *regimen sanitatem* in fact mirrors the female power and danger animating the mercury narrative: the sufferer (conceived entirely as male, although women and babies suffered too, as the good doctor well knew) is to be active and strenuous, to hunt, wrestle, climb mountains, plough his fields. He is to avoid repose and dalliance, humid or soft airs; his diet is of wild vegetables and "those [fish] which the rocks and the conflicting currents of rivers and sea tire" (II, 123). He must eschew milk and aphrodisiacs, wine and truffles. The reversal of emphasis in the final stage is interesting: as the body approaches normalcy again, milk and wine become therapeutic, and the final treatment is a luxuriously purifying bath in fragrant herbs. The herb that closes the *regimen* and Book II is the androgynous (and oxymoronic) "sweet-scented herb of Hercules."[12]

As we enter Book III, then, we are prepared for female numina and phenomena, male activity, and the transgression of taboo as generating circumstance. But with all the Virgilian emphasis on destiny and sacred decree so far, we are perhaps not so ready for the suddenly Judeo-Christian moral frame, and a close reader will be surprised by the displacements of the previously more overt sexuality of the scenario. The fact is, Fracastoro's high theme and tragic subject, and the traditional romance into which he has refracted them, have come face to face with themselves in history. We have met the metaphor, and it is fact.

Book III: Venereal America

In Book III, the poet-doctor who refuted the theory of an American origin for syphilis, and passed up the task of rendering the European discovery of America, is up against it at last, and his imagination goes wild. The book is practically bursting with its intertextual evasions, contradictions, admissions and denials of the "tidy moral fable" I mentioned earlier. What transformations and confusions it performs with materials from Virgil, Ovid, Columbus, and the Bible are too complex to present in full detail. The first conclusion one can draw from tracking them all down is that Fracastoro is skittish in the face (or at the rear) of his own conclusions about this land "fertile with gold, but made far richer by one tree . . . Guaiacum" (III, 34–35).

In fact, the Fuggers stood to gain a better profit from guaiacum than anyone yet had from hopes of gold, and no one would have needed it if it hadn't been for the discovery of the place from which it came.[13] And a worse fact for the patriotic European poet—the disease was unquestionably venereal. How do you represent its characteristic transmission inside a literary mode that operates by idealizing and diffusing the crucial mechanism? Especially when that mode had already absorbed into itself the discourse of colonialism, and your own poem has set up an ineluctably gendered terminology? Like Jupiter in Book I, Fracastoro winces. Like Jesus in that other Garden, he asks to be let off: another poet "might sing . . . of how all which the Ocean's great waters embrace was travelled and measured by one keel [carina] . . . . But for me it is enough to recall the powers of a single tree and its use" (III, 23–27). But the tree is at the center of the garden, and the garden, according to the poet's protagonist, is Eden: "these lands," Columbus had said after his third voyage, are those "in which I am assured in my heart that the earthly paradise is" (1930–33: 1, 47).

Fracastoro's first plunge into this abysmal paradise brings us the explorers' landfall on Ophir (Haiti), a landfall to which they have been guided by nymphs, after praying to Phoebe, out of an ocean linked to the power not of Neptune but of his consort Amphitrite. Sent to seek out "Nereus' concealed waters, where the sun sets and has his couch" (III, 93–94), they are "invited" by "groves and sweet waters from the river" ("invitant nemora, et dulces e flumine lymphae") to an island "undulating with shady woods and echoing with a running river, which . . . brought sands shining with gold down to the sea" (III, 138–42). After praying in gratitude to the local nymphs and laying out a banquet, the first action of their sudden leisure is to snatch up their guns and shoot down a flock of birds "flying among the lofty trees" (III, 155). The description of the shooting is itself peculiarly elaborate and phallic; afterwards the fallen birds lie lifeless, the air quivers, the earth moans, and a surviving bird utters a long, postcoital prophecy of punishment. The prophecy covers most of the current events already referred to in Book I, and it ends: "a day lies in wait for you, close at hand, when, your bodies filthy with an unknown disease, you will in your wretchedness demand help of this forest until you repent of your crimes" (III, 189–92).[14] Although the scene echoes Aeneas's landing on the Strophades and the invasion of his picnic by the furious Harpies, here it is the protagonists who are the violators. Fracastoro has violated his own pattern, too, by rendering as criminal and brutal the ignorant and piously innocent transgression motif of Book II's mercury narrative.

Perhaps he had read the *Letter* of Columbus, which so oddly combines a breathless wonder at the beauty of the islands (in particular, the colors and songs of its birds) with coldblooded references to kidnapping and to the ease with which the Noble Savages might be conquered and enslaved. Perhaps he knew the story of La Navidad—a garrison erected on Haiti during the first voyage and demolished before Columbus's return by islanders outraged at the rapes and thefts of the Spanish left to man it. At any rate, the narrative is a guilty one.

Fracastoro follows it almost immediately with another guilty narrative, in which the Ophirian king explains the origins of a yearly purification rite the mariners have arrived in time to see performed— another echoing of the *Aeneid* in which, again, the poet shifts the attribution of blame in his original. In the *Aeneid* the indigenous Italian king Evander explains to Aeneas the origin in gratitude of his people's yearly devotions to Hercules, who had once freed them from the depredations of a cannibal giant. Here, the shift provides us with *guilty* indigenes (rather than innocent victims), explaining the ultimate origin of syphilis as the punishment for an act of blasphemy and idolatry: the shepherd Siphilis, sick of the tropical heat, had defied the sun god and erected altars to his more tangible kind, Alcithous. The disease is Apollo's revenge, but as in the mercury narrative, expiation is performed to female deities, and assistance provided by nymphs. If properly appeased, advises the nymph Ammerices, "Juno will give you seeds of happiness (*foelicia semina*) from on high; the Earth will train up a green wood from the happy seed: whence your salvation" (III, 349–51). Thus the parthenogenesis of the guaiacum tree—and a far cry from the pestilential *semina* of Book I's male sky god, the floods and diseases brought forth on Earth from those seeds of *bad* omen.

Fracastoro has taken his names from Ovid's *Metamorphoses*: the Ovidian models for the characters of Siphilus and Alcithous are both women, one of whom (Alcithoe) whiles away her time, while refusing to participate in the annual rites of Bacchus ("nay, so bold is she that she denies Bacchus to be Jove's son" (IV, 2–3), telling the story of the transformation of Hermaphroditus while he is being raped by a nymph in a spring.[15] It would be fun to map out the multiple and delightful ironies of this intertextual tour de force, but it would take many pages. Suffice it to say that the most secret of the stories hidden in Fracastoro's puzzle is the story of Hermaphroditus and the rapacious nymph, who are fused into a single being during the rape. That being seems to retain the self of Hermaphroditus, who prays to his parents—Mercury and Venus, the opposed forces of Fracastoro's mercury treatment—to curse the spring: "whoever comes into this pool as man, may he go forth half a man, and may he [suddenly] weaken at touch of the water" (IV, 385–86).

This tale of a man feminized and diseased by intercourse with an aggressive nymph in a landscape of pastoral innocence has an obviously generative power for Fracastoro's etiological myth of an enervating venereal disease. I am interested here in the psychology of literary allusion, that is, in the author's own psychological process in simultaneously alluding to and erasing a narrative apparently so much closer to his purpose than the narrative of blasphemy we are given in Book III. The gender arithmetic of this tale brings Fracastoro's poem into contact with two similar stories: it reverses and parodies Aristophanes's comic myth of desire in the *Symposium*, which story postulates an original and affectless hermaphrodite cut into gendered and desiring halves by an angry Jupiter, and the first event in the Genesis story of the Fall. In Genesis, as in the *Symposium*, God makes two crucially fertile beings of different gender out of one sterile and genderless *h'adam*[16]; in the *Metamorphoses*, Ovid makes a sterile one out of two. Fracastoro plays a different game with numbers and genders, turning Ovid's female protagonists into male characters and replacing male deities with female. What all these stories have in common is the connection of risky metamorphosis with gender in the context of a fall into carnal knowledge and desire. And that is what they have in common, too, with the dynamic of colonialism, the sadomasochistic perversion of international love, the corrupt and corrupting embrace that ends in syphilis though it begins in Eden.

In her article "Master and Slave" (1983), the psychoanalyst Jessica Benjamin gives a lucid account of sadomasochism which depends on Hegel's account of the master–slave relationship but does not quite approach the topic of colonialism. What is most interesting for our purposes is her emphasis on the inherent *failure* of this relation. I want to quote from her description before returning to Fracastoro's play with gender and the problem of romance as history. Benjamin has based her analysis on the infant's paradoxical problem of differentiating itself from the mother it wholly desires. It wants to be recognized, and cannot bear its dependence on her for that recognition. The price of success is isolation, the price of failure, self-annihilating dependence. Sadomasochism crudely mimics this costly struggle.

> The sadist . . . is caught in the dialectic of objectification where
> the subject becomes increasingly like the objectified other he con-
> sumes. . . . Controlling the other person out of existence is the
> inevitable end. The relation of domination is built simultaneously
> on the effort to push the other outside the self and the denial of the
> other's separate reality. Eventually the other's unreality becomes
> more powerful than the sadist's effort to separate himself. The frus-
> tration of feeling there is no person there, no one to recognize me, is
> repeated. (1983: 292)

Fracastoro has begged off the job of narrating the colonial adventure: some other poet will sing "of new wars and military standards advanced throughout a whole new world, the imposing of laws and our names" (III, 21–22). He'll stick to the body and venereal disease. But all this narrowing of focus does is bring him closer to the heart of the matter, for the matter is literally a female matter, a gold-bearing female body personified by nymphs, a terra incognita, a *penetralium*, an Other World, an Other, a woman. Or as Nahum Tate's lyrical friend put it, "the curst Original."[17]

Odd signs of the poet's ambivalent semiconsciousness of these implications are everywhere in the language of the poem. Book III contains a number of verbs and participles that refer to the idea of mingling, but they are always followed and compensated for by references to separation and differentiation, as if the one idea led, by the route of panic, inevitably to the other. He buries the guilt of his Europeans in a parallel tale of Ophirian guilt, and ends that second narrative with the lines, "with these and other stories . . . *the peoples who had mingled together from opposite parts of the world* whiled away the time" ("talibus, atque aliis tempus per multa trahebant/ Diversis populi commixti e partibus orbis," III, 380–81, emphasis mine). He hopes the seed of the Ophirian guaiacum will multiply in Italian soil, then distinguishes the Italians from the Ophirians as the "race of gods" (*gentem deorum*)— a strange identification in light of the guilt he has just attributed to the Orphirians, of deifying their human kind. To escape European guilt he attributes similar guilt to Caribbeans, and in escaping the consequent similarity becomes guilty of their very crime.

" 'I am not you,' " says Benjamin's sadist. "He is using her to establish his objective reality by imposing it on her. . . . Violence, in the service of reason, has the . . . intention of asserting the self-boundary of control" (288).[18]

But the violence Fracastoro's Europeans perpetrate calls down on them the very curse from which the Caribbeans suffer, and soon "your bodies filthy with an unknown disease, you will in your wretchedness demand help for this forest" (III, 190–91). "They must never become dependent," says Benjamin. "Otherwise they would suffer the fate of Hegel's master, who in becoming dependent on his slave, gradually loses subjectivity to him. A further danger for the master is that the subject always becomes the object he consumes. ('You are what you eat')." (288) My favorite of Fracastoro's games with words for "mingle" appears in his description of the first human contact: a feast. The Ophirians arrive bearing gifts of gold, corn, and honey (all "golden" fruits of their femininely fertile land), and the Europeans give them clothes, the sign of civilization that differentiates human and "natural" life. ("Unto Adam and to his wife did the Lord God make coats of skins, and clothed them" [Genesis 3:21].) From "you are what you eat" we might deduce the inverse, that you are also what you wear. In this primal gift exchange the Europeans have made their hosts fully human, by covering their "natural" nakedness have made them, paradoxically, into objects of possible and lawful desire.[19] Then, "welcomed (separated out) with the unmixed [wine] they mingled (brewed) new delights" ("exceptique mero nova gaudia miscent," III, 212). Is this the scene where the embraces are hiding in Fracastoro's syphilitic romance?

No matter. What matters is that the embraces in this account, like the rape of Hermaphroditus, *are* hidden. They are too real. "Go, go," says T. S. Eliot's little bird, "humankind cannot bear very much reality."

It is perhaps clearer now why all the objects of Fracastoro's *regimen sanitatem* are male, and why they must avoid love and wine and truffles until they are better, why they must be strong and active and keep to themselves. Paradise is as contagious as she is beautiful, and "any man who enters [her] . . . will suddenly grow weak and effeminate." For all the *populi commixti* of Book III, there is no scene to parallel the lovely orgy that ends the narrative of De Gama's voyage in Camoëns's *Lusiads*, though his orgy begins with a volley of shots very like that of Fracastoro's mariners: "And now [Cupid's] quiver was empty, nor was there left in all the ocean a nymph alive" (Camoëns 1952: 208).

Even that orgy ends in a prophecy Camoëns calls "matter for the tragic, not the comic muse"—the long tale, told by a nymph of Venus, of "how such pagan rulers as refused to bow the neck to their yoke would feel the weight of their anger and of the strong right arm until finally they surrendered, if not to it, to death" (219–20). "The sadist," says Benjamin, "is seeking not to injure the other but to combat the other's will." But "the mastery he achieves over the other is unsatisfactory, because when the other is drained of resistance she can only be vanquished by death" (292).[20]

All that ends in a romance is supposed, generically, to end well.

It is the genre of fantasy fulfilled. But no romance ends satisfactorily, because the fantasy on which it is built—the fantasy of control, of a dominated landscape, of a world *absorbed* by its protagonists—is one that, by its own logic, ends in failure. A realistic (though perhaps even less satisfactory) romance would end, as Malory's does, in ambivalence or death. Spenser's, which Greenblatt sees as achieving the costly reinstatement of control, does not, in fact, end at all. Nor does Fracastoro's narrative, which comes to a close in the subjunctive mood, praying that Europe might absorb the guaiacum tree into its own soil, thus absolving itself from dependence on its colonial mistress.

Of course his prayer was not answered, and the rule of violence in the Spanish colonies contributed mightily to the decimation of the native American population—down to ten million by 1600, from an estimated eighty million at the time of the first discovery.[21] The combined efforts of Las Casas, Pope Alexander, and the Spanish crown itself could not end it: as Benjamin suggests, there is no closure but death to such a narrative.

Most of the American deaths can be attributed to epidemiological virginity. The Spanish brought devastating epidemics of smallpox and influenza in their wake. These were particularly demoralizing to the Americans because, as William McNeill and others have pointed out before, the Spanish were more or less immune to these diseases. Here seemed a "race of gods" indeed, and the Spanish did not often try to correct this impression. It suited them: in Benjamin's phrase, it drained the Americans of their resistance. According to the Cakchiquel Mayas,

> the mortality was terrible. Your grandfathers died, and with them
> died the son of the king and his brothers and kinsmen. So it was
> that we became orphans, oh, my sons! So we became when we
> were young. All of us were thus. We were born to die (*Annals of the
> Cakchiquels*, quoted in Crosby [1972: 58]).

Epidemiology works both ways, of course, and there was European disease and mortality, too. Syphilis was slow to appear and slow to kill, and the Indians did not see these deaths. But Fracastoro did, and when he looked at them in the context of America he saw them as the wages of sin. In the century of romance and the first century of modern colonialism, in the world which still believed that Nature and Earth were mothers, the poet of venereal disease tried hard to be unconscious, and probably succeeded. But if a poet *could* restrict his song to "a single tree," it would only be a song about a tree. Images are contagious, too, and a tree in such a garden becomes a tree of carnal knowledge. Beneath it stand our sexy, naked parents—Adam, who will die from its fruit, and Eve, who will be ruled.

NOTES

1. The term "colonial" is used loosely; we cannot help but see in the conquests and exploitative trading practices of early sixteenth-century Europe an adumbration of colonialism. But of course there were no permanent European settlements in America by the time of *De Syphilis*, only the military garrisons of the conquests that preceded colonization. Explorers, conquistadors, imperial administrators, and missionaries are not necessarily colonists; not all empires are colonial.

2. For a detailed analysis of the tense relations between feminism and the New Historicism, see Boose (1987), especially pp. 719–42. Other feminist critiques, at least partly sympathetic to New Historicism and cultural materialism ("the new Marxism"), include Waller (1987), Neely (1988) and Pollak (1988). Skura (1988) provides a corrective example of historicized analysis that escapes the "flattening effect" of much New Historicist practice, offering a "sense of how discourse is related to the individual who was creating, even as he was participating in, that discourse."

3. Montrose writes: "Every representation of power is also an appropriation of power" (331).

4. All quotations from Fracastoro's *De Syphilis* are from the 1984 bilingual edition prepared by Geoffrey Eatough. I have relied on his translation, but literalized some of what is quoted in this essay.

5. For the last word, at least from a Marxist point of view, on the relation of *aventur* to the rise of commercial exploration and venture capitalism in this period, see Nerlich (1987: vol. 1).

6. A brief account of critical reaction as far as Hallam is attached to the 1935 Wynne-Finch edition of *De Syphilis*. Scaliger's comment is included in a bibliographical description of an early edition in *A Bibliography of the Poem Syphilis*, 45.

7. Alden (1980) lists eight poetic treatments of syphilis in the sixteenth century, four of them book-length, four of them published before Fracastoro's. See references to "Syphilis—Poetry" in Alden's Index.

8. It would be more precise to call *De Syphilis* the first *original* "poem of the New World." Giuliano Dati published a verse paraphrase of Columbus's *Letter to Sanchez* in 1493, which ran to several editions.

9. See Abraham's introduction to the Wynne-Finch edition of *Syphilis*.

10. Again, this is not only metaphorical. Minerals were still understood to be generated and nourished to maturity in the earth. Alchemical procedures were designed to mimic and speed up this process; both Fracastoro and Bembo were alchemical amateurs.

11. The radical degree of romancification in *De Syphilis* is most quickly appreciated by comparing this description of the first mercury treatment with a description by the Tudor surgeon William Clowes: "A great and inordinate flux of vicious and corrupt humors passed out of his mouth, with much acrimony, burning heat and sharpness, by reason of the putrefaction of his gums, with a horrible stinking savour and a fever accompanying the same" (quoted in Crosby 1972: 154).

12. Wynne-Finch's translation of "bene olentibus heracleis" [III, 458]. Eatough has "sweet scented lilies" and a note identifying the plant as Pliny's *nymphaea*, which if ingested could erase sexual desire for forty days.

13. The spiral *reductio ad absurdum* linking the New World, guaiacum, the Fuggers, von Hutten, and profit may lie behind Crosby's suggestion that the popular assumption of American origin for syphilis emerged from the American origin of the guaiacum remedy. Alden accounts as follows for the popularity of that remedy (denounced by Paracelsus as early as the 1530s): "Not in fact without valid therapeutic uses, its popularity as a specific remedy owes much more to the press-agentry of Ulrich von Hutten and Lorenz Fries than to its actual merits, and offers a curious footnote to history. To compensate the great Augsburg family of international merchant bankers, the Fuggers, who had provided funds to help purchase his election as Holy Roman Emperor, Charles V granted them a monopoly for the importation of Guaiacum from the Spanish Indies. In turn the family set up 'hospitals' utilizing it to treat syphilis, at the same time commissioning von Hutten (better known as a poet and theologian) to write his *De Guaiaca medicina* (1519) advocating its use, a work widely reprinted and translated" (Alden 1980: 19).

14. This angry and farseeing bird is later referred to as the "messenger of Apollo" (*interpres Phoebi*)—in a phrase which sets up an odd identity between the bird and the reluctant poet/healer who invented it.

15. The derivation of Siphilus is complicated. The name itself comes from one of the sons of Niobe, but the parallel is between Niobe herself and

Fracastoro's Siphilis, since in Ovid's tale Niobe is the character who defies the power of a god in preference for a human power (her own fertility) and is stricken with calamity by Apollo in revenge. His revenge, of course, is the slaughter of her children, including Sipylus, by mysterious arrows from the clouds (see Book VI of the *Metamorphoses*).

16. See Bal (1985) for more on the linguistic play with gender and gendering in the Hebrew text.

17. The tendency to think of syphilis as a male disease contracted from a female source was not, of course, restricted to topographical expression. Martin Luther is as explicit as Tate's friend: "If I were judge, I would have such venemous syphilitic whores broken on the wheel and flayed because one cannot estimate the harm such filthy whores do to young men (1955: 293).

18. Cf. Greenblatt on Guyon's destruction of Acrasia's Bower of Bliss: "Acrasia offers not simply sexual pleasure . . . but self-abandonment, erotic aestheticism, the melting of the will, the end of all quests" (1980: 173). "In Guyon's destructive act we are invited to experience the ontogeny of our culture's violent resistance to a sensuous release for which it nevertheless yearns with a new intensity. The resistance is necessary for Spenser because what is threatened is 'our Selfe, whom though we do not see, / Yet each doth in himselfe it well perceiue to bee' (*Faerie Queene* 2.12.47). We can secure that self only through a restraint that involves the destruction of something intensely beautiful; to succumb to that beauty is to loose the shape of manhood and be transformed into a beast" (175). "Were [Acrasia] not to exist as a constant threat, the power Guyon embodies would also cease to exist" (177).

19. This gift exchange is historically accurate: it is a familiar but insufficiently analyzed fact that Europeans tended to bring to the Americas as gifts jewelry, clothing, and mirrors—the props of civilized eros.

20. Consider Fracastoro's language in his discussion of the harsh remedy of mercury: "for this savage plague is especially tenacious, and vigorous with plenty to nurture it, so that so far from allowing itself to be suppressed by gentle mild methods, it refuses treatments and resists having its severity tamed" (II, 256–59).

21. Estimates of American depopulation during the sixteenth century vary widely from scholar to scholar, although all have risen in recent years. I have chosen mine from the upper middle range. See for starters Cook and Borah (1971) and bibliographical notes in Crosby (1972) and McNeill (1976).

References

Alden, John L. 1980. *European Americana: A Chronological Guide to Works Printed in Europe Relating to the Americas, 1493–1776.* 2 vols. New York: Readex Books.

Bal, Mieke. 1985. "Sexuality, Sin and Sorrow: The Emergence of Female Character (A Reading of Genesis 1–3)." *Poetics Today* 6.

Baumgartner, Leona, and John F. Fulton. 1935. *A Bibliography of the Poem 'Syphilis Sive Morbus Gallicus' by Girolamo Fracastoro of Verona.* New Haven: Yale University Press.

Benjamin, Jessica. 1983. "Master and Slave." In *Powers of Desire: The Politics of Sexuality,* ed. Anne Snitow, Christine Stansell and Sharon Thompson. New York: Monthly Review Press.

Boose, Linda. 1987. "The Family in Shakespeare Studies." *Renaissance Quarterly* 40:707–42.

Camoëns, Luis vaz de. 1952. *The Lusiads.* Trans. William C. Atkinson. Harmondsworth: Penguin Books.

Chapman, George. 1596. "De Guiana, carmen epicum." In Keymis, *A Relation of the Second Voyage to Guiana . . . .*

Columbus, Christopher. 1930–1933. *Select Documents Illustrating the Four Voyages of Columbus.* Trans. and ed. Cecil Jane. 2d ser., 65 and 70. London: The Hakluyt Society.

Cook, Sherburne, and Woodrow Borah. 1971. *Essays in Population History: Mexico and the Caribbean.* Vol. 1. Berkeley: University of California Press.

Crosby, Alfred W. 1972. *The Columbian Exchange: Biological and Cultural Consequences of 1492.* Westport, Conn.: Greenwood Press.

de Bry, Theodor and Sons. 1590–1634. *The Great Voyages.* Frankfurt.

Donne, John. 1966. *John Donne's Poetry.* Ed. A. L. Clements. New York: W. W. Norton and Co.

Fracastoro, Girolamo. 1686. *Syphilis.* Trans. Nahum Tate. London: Jacob Tonson.

———. [1686] 1935. *De Syphilis sive Morbus Gallicus.* Ed. and trans. Heneage Wynne-Finch. Intro. James Johnston Abraham. London: William Heinemann.

———. [1686] 1984. *Fracastoro's 'Syphilis': Introduction, Text, Translation and Notes.* Trans. Geoffrey Eatough. ARCA: Classical and Medieval Texts, Papers, and Monographs 12. Liverpool: Frances Cairns.

Greenblatt, Stephen J. 1980. *Renaissance Self-Fashioning: From More to Shakespeare*. Chicago: University of Chicago Press.

Hakluyt, Richard, ed. 1582. *Divers Voyages Touching the Discoverie of America* . . . . London.

Hutten, Ulrich von. 1519. *De Guaiaci medicina*. Mainz.

Keymis, Lawrence. 1596. *A Relation of the Second Voyage to Guiana* . . . . London.

Las Casas, Bartolomé de. 1583. *The Spanish Colonie, or Briefe Chronicle of Actes and gestes of the Spaniardes in the West Indies [Brevissima Relacion . . . .]* Trans. M. M. S. London.

Luther, Martin. 1955. *Luther's Letters of Spiritual Counsel*. Trans. and ed. Theodore Tappert. Library of Christian Classics 17. Philadelphia: Westminster Press.

McNeill, William H. 1976. *Plagues and Peoples*. Garden City, N.Y.: Anchor Press/Doubleday.

Merchant, Carolyn. 1980. *The Death of Nature: Women, Ecology and The Scientific Revolution*. San Francisco: Harper & Row Publishers.

Montrose, Louis. 1986. "The Elizabethan Subject and The Spenserian Text." In *Literary Theory/Renaissance Texts*, eds. Patricia Parker and David Quint. Baltimore: The Johns Hopkins University Press.

Neely, Carol Thomas. 1988. "Constructing the Subject." *ELR* 18:5–18.

Nerlich, Michael. 1987. *Ideology of Adventure: Studies in Modern Consciousness, 1100–1750*. Vol. 1. Theory and History of Literature 42. Minneapolis: University of Minnesota Press.

Olson, Glending. 1982. *Literature as Recreation in the Later Middle Ages*. Ithaca: Cornell University Press.

Ortner, Sherry. 1974. "Is Female to Male as Nature Is to Culture?" In *Woman, Culture and Society*, eds. Michelle Zimbalist Rosaldo and Louise Lamphere. Stanford: Stanford University Press.

Ovid. 1984. *Metamorphoses*. Vol. 1. Trans. Frank Justus Miller. Loeb Classical Library. Cambridge: Harvard University Press.

Pollak, Ellen. 1988. "Feminism and the New Historicism: A Tale of Difference or the Same Old Story?" *The Eighteenth Century: Theory and Interpretation*. Vol. 29. Lubbock: Texas Tech. Press.

Ralegh, Sir Walter. [1590] 1790. *The Discoverie of the Large, Rich and Bewtiful Empire of Guiana* . . . . London, reprint for the Hakluyt Society. Ed. Robert H. Schomburg. 1848. Reprint. New York: Lenox Hill.

Skura, Meredith Anne. 1988. "Discourse and the Individual: The Case of Colonialism in *The Tempest*." *Shakespeare Quarterly* 40 (1):42–69.

Todorov, Tzvetan. 1984. *The Conquest of America: The Question of the Other.* Trans. Richard Howard. New York: Harper & Row Publishers.

Waldseemüller, Martin. 1507. *Cosmographiae introductio . . .* St. Die.

Waller, Marguerite. 1987. "Academic Tootsie: The Denial of Difference and the Difference It Makes." *Diacritics* 17:2–20.

2

Captivity in White and Red

Convergent Practice and Colonial Representation on the
British-Amerindian Frontier, 1606–1736

Pauline Turner Strong

Introduction: Books Written in Blood

One of the few Indians known to the proverbial American school-
child is Squanto, who brought seeds of maize to the starving Pilgrims
and taught them how to cultivate it. The hospitality of Squanto and
Native Americans more generally is acknowledged each year at the
Thanksgiving table, at once a representation of salvation, peaceful
communion, and legitimate occupation of a plentiful land. A comple-
mentary role in Anglo-American origin myths is played by Pocahontas, the "Indian princess" who represents salvation, communion, and
colonial legitimacy in a distinctly female, distinctly Southern way. As
John Smith's savior, a convert to Christianity, the mediator between
Powhatan's chiefdom and the colonists at Jamestown, the wife of
tobacco planter John Rolfe, and the mother of Rolfe's child, Pocahontas personifies the commingling of American and English "blood,"
the Christian "salvation" of the American heathen, and colonial appropriation of American abundance.[1]

Squanto and Pocahontas are all the more appropriate as legend-
ary figures in the dominant Anglo-American charter because they
are tragic heroes—early personifications of the noble, but vanishing,
Indian (Washburn 1988: 522–616; Berkhofer 1978). Neither Squanto
nor Pocahontas lived long after helping to ensure the survival of the

fledgling English colonies: Squanto dying in lonely exile in his own land; Pocahontas, in England aboard a ship bound for Virginia. Considerably less well known is another tragic dimension of the lives of Squanto and Pocahontas: both were captives among the English before they became valuable allies.

That Squanto and Pocahontas were prisoners as well as saviors and converts of the English is suppressed in Anglo-American mythology not only because it is inconsistent with their personification of peaceful communion between native and colonial peoples. More, their captivity conflicts with another dominant representation of the relations between Euro-Americans and Native Americans: the captivity of colonists among Indians, of "White" among "Red."[2] Like the Squanto and Pocahontas legends, the captivity of colonists among Indians represents a kind of communion between Indians and colonists, but one that is involuntary, achieved through violence, and generally repudiated. John Smith is the most famous of the White captives, but as we shall see, as a male saved from execution by a woman, Smith is an unusual captive. Indeed, no single figure personifies the complex captivity tradition—one which for more than three centuries has served as an extraordinarily potent and resilient vehicle for representing the European Self confronting the alien power of indigenous America.

This essay considers the practice and representation of captivity across cultural boundaries in the first century and a third of British colonization in North America. In contrast to the now familiar litany of material influences of Native Americans upon Europeans—Squanto's corn, Pocahontas's tobacco—we will consider one dimension of the less acknowledged, more controversial ideological influence. Over the last two decades, the ideological influence of Native Americans upon Europeans and Euro-Americans has been the subject of renewed debate, particularly with regard to personal liberty and equality (Honour 1975; Axtell 1975, 1981; Chiapelli et al. 1976; Brandon 1986; Mariani 1987), representative democracy (Tooker 1988; Barreiro 1988), and spirituality (Gill 1987, 1988, 1990; Jaimes 1988; Churchill 1988). Scholarly controversies over the Western appropriation of Native American cultures in Montaigne and Rousseau, the

American and French Constitutions, the Communist Manifesto, the ecology movement, and the curriculum are one context in which the lineage, boundaries, and permeability of the American or Western Self (and its Native American Other) are delineated and contested. Captivity among Indians has constituted a similar, but more popular and more persistent, context for the construction of a White (vs. a Red) American identity.[3]

For a revealing initial example of the Anglo-American representation of captivity among Indians, there is no better source than the prominent Boston minister Cotton Mather. Among the numerous occasions during which Mather employed representations of captivity was his sermon "Observable Things," delivered on a public fast day in 1698 commemorating the close of King William's War, an eight-year struggle against the French and their indigenous allies. The grueling events of this war, declared Mather, should be understood as "a sort of Book put into our Hands; a Book indeed all written in Blood; a Book yet full of Divine Lessons for us" (C. Mather [1699] 1978: 201–2). Reading that bloody book was properly the work of the clerical elite, he insisted, for only they could discern the hand of Providence behind the events of the war.[4]

Prominent in Mather's providential interpretation of the war was the captivity of English women and children, portrayed in one vivid passage as the defenseless prey of carnivorous beasts:

> How many *Women* have been made a *prey* to those *Brutish men*, that are *Skilful* to *Destroy*? How many a *Fearful Thing* has been suffered by the *Fearful Sex*, from those *men*, that one would *Fear* as *Devils* rather than men? Let the *Daughters* of our *Zion* think with themselves, what it would be, for fierce *Indians* to break into their Houses, and brain their *Husbands* and their *Children* before their Eyes, and Lead them away a Long Journey into the *Woods*; and if they begin to *fail* and *faint* in the Journey, then for a Tawny Salvage to come with Hell fire in his Eyes, and cut 'em down with his Hatchet; or, if they could miraculously *hold out*, then for some *Filthy* and ugly *Squaws* to become their *insolent Mistresses*, and insolently to abuse 'em at their pleasure a thousand inexpressible ways; and, if they had any of their *Sucking Infants* with them, then to see those Tender Infants handled at such a rate, that they should beg of the *Tygres*, to dispatch 'em out

of hand. Such things as these, I tell you, have often happened in this Lamentable *War*. (220–21)

Even more distressing to Mather than the fate of Puritan good-wives was the fate of their children, figured in the sermon as the prey of wild but seductive devourers:

> Our Little *Boys* and *Girls*, even these Little *Chickens*, have been Seized by the *Indian* Vultures. Our Little *Birds* have been Spirited away by the Indian Devourers, and brought up, in a vile Slavery, till some of them have quite forgot their *English Tongue*, and their *Christian Name*, and their whole *Relation*. (222)

In "Observable Things" this master of Puritan rhetoric developed a compelling and influential representation of the vulnerability of Christian civility in a wild and threatening New World.[5] Declaring a clerical monopoly over interpretation and utilizing systematic oppositions in ethnicity, gender, and Christian civility, Mather portrayed the English colonists as weak and innocent victims of brutish, demonic Indian captors. Today, in a considerably less vulnerable America, the representation of savage brutes destroying domestic tranquility and seizing, abusing, even devouring the most frail and innocent representatives of Christian civilization remains remarkably familiar and powerful. In the three centuries since Mather's time, the capture of vulnerable frontier settlers by Indians has been prominently featured in Anglo-American folklore and popular media. The representation has expanded from sermons, political oratory, and historical narratives to fiction, drama, public sculpture, textbooks, children's games, cinema, and television, remaining today a model for conceptualizing American relations with currently more threatening Others.[6]

While Mather's representation of captivity is complex and requires extensive analysis, we may begin by noting that it relies upon three kinds of symbolic oppositions between Indian predators and their English prey. Of the three, it is mainly the opposition between a vulnerable female captive and her brutish male captor that would come to dominate subsequent representations of captivity. Granted, the other two oppositions employed by Mather had considerable rhetorical power. The opposition between a fearful female captive and

Figure 2-1. John Vanderlyn, *The Murder of Jane McCrea*, 1804. Oil on canvas. (Wadsworth Atheneum, Hartford. Purchased by Subscription.)

Figure 2-2. 1853. Horatio Greenough, *The Rescue*. Located on the East Front of the U.S. Capitol, 1853–1958. (Architect of the Capitol)

her insolent and abusive "mistress" portrays captivity as a double violation (in both gender and ethnicity) of colonial patterns of domination. And the polarity between "little chickens" and the "Indian vultures" who consume them encapsulates the colonial fear of a fragile Christian civility being consumed by the dark and demonic forces of the Wild. Still, as the dominant representation of Anglo-American captivity developed, these two symbolic oppositions became subordinated to that between a vulnerable White female and her Red male captor. Again and again in representations of captivity—and visual iconography makes this particularly clear—the relationship between Captive and Captor maintains (and symbolically employs) male dominance over women while reversing the ethnic power relations that were established through conquest (see figures 2-1, 2-2, 2-3).[7] Red males threaten and prevail over their vulnerable White female victims. This is not to say that Red ultimately prevails over White, for the Captive is generally rescued by Providence or His representative, a White male Redeemer. The Redeemer, through a violence that is both heroic and redemptive, reestablishes the dominance of White over Red (Slotkin 1973).

So familiar and so removed from historical context is the dominant representation of captivity that even contemporary scholarship often fails to acknowledge the extent to which it is a highly selective rendering of a long and complex course of intercultural encounters. This paper is an attempt to recapture some of the complexity of captivity across the colonial frontier, both as historical practice and as symbolic representation. Our consideration is confined to the English colonies (and mainly to New England) in the seventeenth and early eighteenth centuries, an important early period in the development of both the practice and representation of captivity. As we shall see, the consistency in the typifications of red male Captor and white female Captive, together with the frequent appearance of a white male Redeemer, has considerably less to do with captivity as a historical practice than with the ideological potency of co-occuring oppositions in ethnicity, gender, Christian civility, and power—the very oppositions utilized so successfully by Cotton Mather.

The use of three terms thus far—"dominant representation,"

"typification," and "opposition"—reveals several somewhat disparate sources of theoretical inspiration for this analysis. Perhaps most significantly, my approach to the representation of captivity is influenced by the Gramscian concept of cultural hegemony (Gramsci 1972, R. Williams 1977). Control over the production of meaning is a significant part of a ruling class's hegemony, as Cotton Mather and his fellow clergymen understood so well (hence Mather's insistence that only the clergy could properly read the divine lessons contained in the bloody text that was King William's War).[8] The dominant representation of captivity may be considered an "element of a hegemony" (Williams 1977) insofar as it is part of the process through which a dominant social group legitimates its power through grounding it in a set of authoritative, taken-for-granted understandings that permeate and structure lived experience. That is, to appropriate Mather's title, relations of domination are legitimated as "observable things." More specifically, the hegemonic representation of captivity is a "tradition" in Raymond Williams's sense: "an intentionally selective version of a shaping past and a pre-shaped present, which is then powerfully operative in the process of social and cultural definition and identification" (1977: 115).

Another theorist of the "natural attitude" of everyday experience, the phenomenologist Alfred Schutz (1964–1973), has called such taken-for-granted understandings "typifications," a more felicitous term for my purposes than Williams's "hegemonic element."[9] The usefulness of the Schutzian concept for analyzing typifications of Others is indicated by Basso's (1979) study of Western Apache typifications of "the Whiteman," which analyzes how Western Apache jokes typify or "epitomize" the Whiteman through highlighting the oppositions between Anglo-American and Apache behavior. When the concepts of structural opposition and typification are embedded within an analysis of cultural hegemony, we are able to consider the construction of otherness as a more complex process than is revealed by structural, phenomenological, or ideological analysis taken alone.

As we shall see, typifications of Indian captors highlight oppositions between White and Red, but they also involve a subtle identification between captive and captor, White and Red. I take this counter-

Figure 2-3. John Mix Stanley, *Osage Scalp Dance*, 1845. Oil on canvas. Included in the Columbian Quincentenary exhibit, "The West as America: 1820–1920," National Museum of American Art. (National Museum of American Art, Smithsonian Institution, gift of the Misses Henry, 1908.)

point between opposition and identification to be a general feature of representation of Others, one that has been insufficiently appreciated in most analyses of otherness or alterity.[10] More specifically, the eclectic approach taken here highlights the following issues: the relationships among the typifications of white female Captive, red male Captor, and white male Redeemer; the social process and cultural forms through which these typifications achieved and maintained ideological dominance; the relationship between the captivity tradition and captivity as an intercultural practice; and, finally, the relationship between the hegemonic representation of captivity and alternative or oppositional representations, such as that featuring Pocahontas, the Redeemer—who is neither white nor male—of a captive (John Smith) who is male and only temporarily vulnerable.[11]

In Mather's "Observable Things" and more generally, the rhetorical power of the hegemonic representation of captivity relies in large part upon decontextualizing captivity from European colonial expansion and aggression—thus portraying colonial captives as innocent prey of marauding and aggressive beasts. The decontextualization of captivity is found in scholarship as well. Under the spell of the dominant representation or an equally decontextualized synchronic theory of culture, scholars until recently have neglected the extent to which the warfare, captivity, and diplomatic practices among Native American peoples were transformed by their engagement with European colonial powers. More specifically, scholarship, like the hegemonic representation, has generally presented captivity on the colonial frontier as a distinctively Indian practice—as an indigenous cultural trait or pattern—rather than as a complex historical phenomenon affected in significant ways by the European colonial enterprise.

Fortunately, over the last two decades ethnohistorians have begun to demonstrate the extent to which Native American patterns of warfare, captivity, and diplomacy were transformed as they met the demographic, political, economic, and cultural challenges imposed by European colonial expansion. As a result, those captivity practices coded as Red in the hegemonic representation can be seen instead as a "convergence" (Vaughan and Richter 1980) of multiple captivity practices, both indigenous and European.[12] The nature of this convergence, I believe, is illuminated by considering captivity across the British colonial frontier as a "structure of the conjuncture" in Sahlins's (1981, 1985) sense of the term. Like the Hawaiian capture and sacrificial incorporation of Captain Cook that to some extent they resemble, Native American captivity practices involved a conjuncture of distinct cultural categories deployed by socially situated (thus differentially interested and empowered) actors. While Sahlins is particularly concerned with the transformative effect of the conjuncture upon indigenous social relations, I consider how the conjuncture of captivity practices across the British-Amerindian frontier entailed transformations in both colonial and indigenous societies, at the same time that it structured relations among them.[13]

This paper, then, views captivity both as "structure of the conjuncture" and as "hegemonic representation." Combining a structural approach to history with a cultural approach to hegemony provides a way to conceptualize the dialectical relationship between captivity as historical practice and captivity as symbolic representation, and, further, the embeddedness of both practice and representation in structures of domination. More specifically, this combination of approaches provides a way to bring together the strengths of two largely separate traditions in the study of captivity among Indians (and in the study of Indian-White relations more generally): intellectual or cultural history, which focuses upon relationships among literary texts,[14] and ethnohistory or social history, which provides detailed historical and sociocultural contextualization.[15] Like several recent works (including Vaughan and Clark 1981b, and to a lesser extent, Ulrich 1982), I try to attend both to textual analysis and to social and cultural context. In doing so, I aim to bring the subject of captivity and its representation into the comparative framework offered by contemporary analyses of colonial discourse, modern structures of domination, and the construction of national identity.[16]

Captivity across the colonial frontier and its representation has a history as long as the European presence in North America. The years considered here include the first and most devastating Native American war of resistance against the English (King Philip's War of 1675–76) as well as the first two of four intercolonial wars between Britain and France (King William's War of 1689–97 and Queen Anne's War of 1702–13). The most significant vehicle for representing captivity during these years and into the nineteenth century were narratives written or dictated by captives upon their return to colonial society. The narratives are considerably more complex and variable than the hegemonic representation that is their legacy, so they enable us to begin to analyze the development of a captivity tradition out of a complex set of historical encounters and a multiplicity of representations.

We shall proceed from the general and speculative to the more determinate. The captivity tradition to the contrary, by far the largest number of captives on the British colonial frontier were Native Americans, an important point to emphasize if we are to understand what the representation of captivity suppresses. To this end we begin with a consideration of the earliest Indian captives of the British, exemplified by Squanto. This is followed by a general review of indigenous captivity practices and a brief discussion of their transformation in the colonial situation. Given this minimal historical and cultural context, we turn to the earliest accounts of English captives among North American Indians, concentrating (after a glance at Jamestown) on the New England colonies because it was there that captivity first took on ideological significance. The major texts we consider include the four earliest and most influential narratives of captivity published in the English colonies—those of Mary Rowlandson [1682], John Williams [1707], Hannah Swarton [1697], and Hannah Dustan [1697], the latter two narratives "improved" and published by Cotton Mather. All four narratives derive from the period of heightened warfare in New England that extended intermittently from 1675 through 1713. My conclusions regarding the development of a captivity tradition also take into account the remainder of the dozen narratives of captivity published in the English colonies during the half century between 1682 and 1736, the publication date of the last account by a captive taken during the first two intercolonial wars.[17]

European Devourers and Their Prey

In an intriguing legend of the Wampanoags, the Algonquian-speaking inhabitants of southeastern Massachusetts, Cape Cod, and the islands,[18] Europeans were first encountered riding a gigantic bird up the Taunton River (see map, figure 2-4). The newcomers seized several Wampanoags, holding them captive on the giant bird. The Wampa-noags attacked the bird when it stopped at a spring for water, man-aging to rescue its human prey despite the barrage of thunder and lightning with which the bird defended itself (Simmons 1986: 70).

Our only source for this revealing native construction of a first encounter with Europeans is a skeletal fragment of local history col-lected in the early nineteenth century. With the exception of the refer-ence to captivity, this legend resembles a number of other northeastern woodland legends that assimilate European ships to floating islands or the powerful Thunderbird of indigenous cosmologies (Hammell 1987). For example, in the seventeenth century an English colonist collected a Wampanoag account of their first encounter with Euro-peans, which reads: "They took the first ship they saw for a walking island, the mast to be a tree, the sail white clouds, and the discharg-ing of ordnance for lightning and thunder, which did much trouble them, but this thunder being over and this moving-island steadied with an anchor, they manned out their canoes to go and pick straw-berries there" (Simmons 1986: 66). This idyllic version, like many other northeastern Indian tales of floating islands or Thunderbirds bearing White newcomers, presents European ships as rich sources of spiritual wealth (for strawberries, like trade beads, were associated with physical and spiritual well-being) (Miller and Hammell 1986, Hammell 1987).

The cannibal bird story, for its part, emphasizes the dangers asso-ciated with the newcomers, assimilating early encounters with Euro-peans to the most fearsome cultural model available of a kidnapper and human devourer (Simmons 1986). A huge cannibal bird, called Gul-luoa by Abenakis of Maine (Gyles [1736] 1981: 115–16), figures promi-nently in Algonquian mythology across the Northeast (cf. Morrison 1979). The cannibal was described by a nineteenth-century folklorist as "a great bird whose wings were the flight of an arrow wide, whose body was the length of ten Indian strides, and whose head when he stretched up his neck peered over the tall oak-woods" (Simmons 1986: 189). In Wampanoag lore, the winged cannibal would seize children in its talons and carry them to its nest on Nantucket or Martha's Vineyard, where it feasted upon them, discarding their bones in heaps on the ground below.

That Wampanoags would represent the earliest European invaders as kidnappers and potential devourers of their people is striking as a reciprocal construction to Cotton Mather's representation of Indians as vultures who preyed upon European children. It is also consistent with accounts by English explorers, traders, and fishermen of their earliest forays along the eastern coast of North America. Following European precedents reaching as far back as Columbus's kidnapping of ten Arawaks on his first voyage, English expeditions habitually abducted a few, and occasionally scores, of the natives they encountered, often luring them aboard ship with trade goods. Unlike the Wampanoags rescued from the giant cannibal bird, most abducted Indians were forever lost to view.

Judging from accounts concerning those few captives who survived the journey to England, the abductions had various motivations. Captives taken in large groups—such as about two dozen Wampanoags, including Squanto, who were kidnapped in 1614— were generally destined for slavery. Individual captives, in contrast, were often displayed as exotic curiosities and further captured in drawings in order to prove their captors' claims of discovery and to arouse interest in further expeditions. Among the earliest were several Baffinland Inuits kidnapped by Martin Frobisher in 1576 and 1577 (figure 2-5), whom the expedition's chronicler, George Best, described baldly as "new prey" and "tokens from thence" (Sturtevant and Quinn 1987:69–70). In more contemporary parlance, these captives might be considered "tokens of Otherness" (Mullaney 1983), but rarely, if ever, were they treated as irreconcilably other. Rather, captives from the New World were pressured for information regarding their homeland, exposed to English life and power in an effort

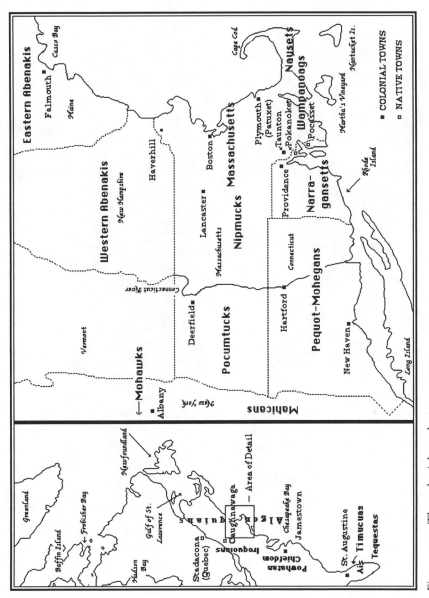

Figure 2-4. The colonial northeast, c. 1700.

Figure 2-5. John White, Inuit man and Inuit woman and baby, 1577. Original watercolors of Frobisher's captive Baffinland Inuits. Reprinted from *The American Drawings of John White 1577–1590*, by Paul Hulton and David Beers Quinn. © 1964 The University of North Carolina Press. Color plates © The British Museum. Used by permission. (Photographs courtesy of the Newberry Library, Chicago.)

to win their allegiance, groomed to serve as guides, interpreters, and emissaries, and occasionally converted to Christianity.

A rare exception to the anonymity of most indigenous captives and one of the few captives whose allegiance was won through the dubious strategy of abduction is Squanto, whose Algonquian name, Tisquantum, likely refers to the spiritual power he gained in a vision quest (Simmons 1986: 39–43). Despite his widespread fame, it is not generally known that Tisquantum's ability to communicate with the Pilgrims derived not only from his unusual resourcefulness, but from five years of involuntary exile in Spain, England, and Newfoundland. Tisquantum was among twenty-seven natives of the Wampanoag towns of Patuxet and Nauset who were kidnapped in 1614, against orders, by Captain John Smith's lieutenant, John Hunt. These captives were taken to Málaga, Spain, where apparently some were sold into slavery while others were claimed by the Church.

After a period of slavery or apprenticeship in the Church, Tisquantum surfaced in London, where by 1617 he was lodging with the treasurer of the Newfoundland Company. Later, in Newfoundland, he encountered Thomas Dermer, who had served John Smith on the expedition which kidnapped Tisquantum. Dermer, now working for the commander of Plymouth Harbor, Ferdinando Gorges, introduced Tisquantum to his employer. Gorges had attempted to use Indian captives to promote various colonization schemes since 1605, when explorer George Waymouth turned over to him five Abenaki captives.

The abductions that Gorges encouraged created lasting enmity against the English among coastal Algonquians. Most notably disastrous was Edward Harlow's kidnapping in 1611 of six natives, including Epenow, a sachem (headman) on Martha's Vineyard. Gorges pinned his colonial ambitions upon Epenow, who learned English well, impressed would-be financiers with his noble bearing, and told intriguing tales of gold in New England. Epenow, however, proved disappointing upon his return to Martha's Vineyard in 1614, when he escaped from the gold-seeking expedition he was expected to guide. Thereafter Epenow was a leading opponent of the English.

Tisquantum proved to be more enduringly useful to the English than Epenow, probably because by the time he managed to return to Patuxet with Dermer, in 1619, his village had been completely deserted. During Tisquantum's absence, the people of Patuxet had almost all been extinguished by a European disease to which the Indians had not developed immunity. The epidemic had claimed seventy-five to ninety percent of the coastal Algonquians living from southern Maine to Cape Cod, opening prime agricultural land to European settlement.[19] Characteristically, the Pilgrims attributed the devastation of Tisquantum's people to Providence, who "would destroy them, and give their country to another people" (Crosby 1978).

Tisquantum facilitated contacts between Dermer's party and the leaders of several Wampanoag towns, an ability which suggests that Tisquantum had been trained as a *pniese* or shaman, an office with political and military as well as religious significance among the Wampanoags (Salisbury 1981; Simmons 1986). But Tisquantum's efforts to forge an alliance between the English and the semi-autonomous Wampanoag sachems were not able to prevail over the hostility created by earlier English visitors. Tisquantum was captured once again, this time by Gorges's former protegé, Epenow.

Tisquantum soon found himself in the hands of Massasoit, the paramount sachem of Pokanoket. Once the most powerful Wampanoag village, Pokanoket had been severely weakened by the epidemic, forcing Massasoit into a tributary relationship to his inland enemies, the Narragansetts. When the Pilgrims arrived in 1620, establishing Plymouth on the abandoned site of Patuxet, Massasoit decided that an alliance with the English would be superior to his present subordination to the Narragansetts. As emissaries to Plymouth he sent an Abenaki sachem named Samoset (himself likely a former captive of the English) and the captive Tisquantum. The latter won his freedom from Massasoit through successfully negotiating a treaty with the Pilgrims. Living on the site of his ancestral home as an interpreter and intermediary for Massasoit, Tisquantum helped Plymouth extend its influence over several Wampanoag towns, ensuring a reliable supply of corn and pelts. He also taught the English how to gather native foods and cultivate corn, planting it in hills fertilized with whole fish. Ironically (but consistent with the complexity of colonial-indigenous cultural exchanges), the use of fish as fertilizer may not have been an

indigenous Algonquian practice but, instead, a product of Tisquantum's exile in Newfoundland (Ceci 1975, 1990).

Then as now a prominent symbol of alliance between natives and
colonists, Tisquantum suffered one more period of captivity among
Wampanoag opponents of an alliance. This time his captor was Corbitant, the leading sachem of the Pocassets. Tisquantum was rescued
by Plymouth's Captain Miles Standish from this, his third captivity,
and spent the next (and last) year of his life attempting to establish
himself as an independent political leader. Thus arousing the enmity
of Massasoit, Tisquantum was forced to live under the protection of
his English friends, who considered him a special instrument of God
(Humins 1987; Sanders 1978). Soon after Massasoit called for his execution, Tisquantum died. Bereft of kinsmen and branded a traitor by
Massasoit, Tisquantum requested conversion to Christianity upon his
deathbed.

Few cases of captivity among the English are as well documented
as Tisquantum's, so the extent and outcome of English abductions of
Indians is difficult to assess, especially prior to colonization. To gen-
eralize, the English abducted the native inhabitants of North America
more often than did the French, though less frequently than the Spanish and Portuguese, who preceded the English in slave raids as well
as in kidnappings along the North American coastline. English enslavement of Indians became especially significant during the colonial
period, particularly in two regions: Carolina, Georgia, and northern
Florida, where a flourishing trade supplied thousands of slaves for the
West Indies; and New England, where Indian slaves or indentured servants were imported from the West Indies and, in greater numbers,
captured from local tribes during periods of hostility.

In contrast both to the English and the Iberians, Frenchmen more
often obtained consent before transporting Indians across the ocean,
hoping to win persons of influence over to the cause of the Crown and
the Church. The most notorious exception is revealing in its conspicuous breach of native expectations regarding hostages. Upon meeting
a party of fishermen from the Iroquoian village of Stadacona (at the
site of Quebec) in 1534, Jacques Cartier abducted two teenage sons or
nephews of Donnacona, the headman. Cartier returned to Stadacona

two years later with the boys, Domagaya and Taignoagny, both now able to serve as interpreters, but highly suspicious of Cartier.

Iroquoians would have understood Cartier's motivations for training interpreters, but would have expected him to leave French boys in their place, following an indigenous pattern of creating kinship ties between trading partners through temporary child-exchange. Indeed, Donnacona entrusted Cartier with several Stadaconan children as a token of alliance on his second visit. Although Europeans of the sixteenth century had their own conventions of hostage-exchange, Cartier did not reciprocate; rather, wishing to impress his King with the Stadaconans' knowledge of precious metals (probably native copper), Cartier abducted Donnacona himself, two additional headmen, and, once again, the two interpreters. Neither these captives nor the children were ever seen again in Stadacona. By 1541, when Cartier established a short-lived settlement west of Stadacona, only one of the captives remained alive. She was not allowed to return to her people, lest she reveal the sad fate of her compatriots.[20]

Indigenous Captives: Hostages, Kin, Sacrificial Victims

As the vignettes regarding Tisquantum and Donnacona suggest, both the captivity of enemies and hostage-exchange among allies were known indigenously among the Algonquian and Iroquoian peoples of the northeastern woodlands.[21] Indeed, at least among Iroquoians, the taking of captives was a primary goal—perhaps *the* primary goal—of indigenous warfare. In what have been aptly characterized as "mourning wars" (Smith 1951), an Iroquoian woman whose grief remained unassuaged after a series of condolence rituals (involving, most centrally, gifts of wampum) might influence the sons of her male clansmen to "set up the war kettle," that is, send out a war party. In this matrilineal society, it was the responsibility of those whose fathers belonged to the bereaved clan to console the members of that clan (their *agadoni*) by obtaining a captive from among traditional enemies. The captive would be treated in a highly ritualized fashion in order to revitalize the bereaved lineage and "dry its tears." First, the mourners would generally vent their rage against captives as they "ran the gauntlet," that is, ran into the town through two lines of villagers who administered physical and verbal abuse. At the behest of the bereaved women of the lineage, the gauntlet might be followed by further torture. Then a captive would be incorporated into the lineage through adoption. If the captive was a woman or child, she would most often be welcomed as a valuable addition to the lineage, her cultural identity transformed through a variety of institutionalized inducements and punishments. A male captive, however, was considered less malleable and compliant, and he would often be further tortured, executed, and ritually ingested.

The adoption of a captive filled the vacant social position left by the deceased and, additionally, was thought to replenish the spiritual power of the lineage. Spiritual power might also be replenished symbolically through ritual cannibalism—perhaps especially when the captive had exhibited particular bravery during torture. In the absence of a captive, spiritual power would be garnered through performing an adoption ceremony over a dead enemy's scalplock, considered the seat of the soul. Torture and scalping also were offered as sacrifices to Agreskwe, the spirit responsible for success in war.

The Iroquoian "mourning-war" or "war trophy" complex has received penetrating analysis as a cultural pattern by anthropologists, historians, and linguists.[22] Especially well known are the eloquent rites of condolence that developed as a means of establishing and maintaining peace, for these formed the basis of colonial diplomacy. In these rites, the bereaved were condoled by gifts of wampum, furs, or other valuables in place of a captive or enemy scalp.

Recent scholars have demonstrated the importance of greater historical contextualization of Iroquoian warfare and captivity practices (e.g., Jennings 1975, 1984; and Richter 1983). Our major source on Iroquoian warfare and treatment of captives, the *Relations* of the French Jesuits, documents events in the mid-seventeenth century when warfare and captivity had reached an unprecedented intensity in response to the European presence. In contrast to seventeenth-century warfare, indigenous warfare had been limited in scale, in large part due to the goal of taking captives without sustaining casualties (since any additional casualties among the raiding party would require the mounting of still another raid). War, therefore, consisted mainly of isolated ambushes, conducted with a restraint and caution that was as ludicrous to Europeans as the European practice of total war was horrifying to Indians. Following sustained contact with Europeans in the 1620s, however, Iroquoian peoples suffered a demographic crisis of unparalleled proportions—a crisis that dramatically intensified their search for captives or scalps to restore the demographic and spiritual power of the population.[23]

The serious decrease in population that Iroquoian villages suffered in the early seventeenth century had a number of related causes: devastating European epidemics; depletion of fur-bearing animals due to the European trade; an intensification of warfare from the 1640s through the 1670s due to the introduction of firearms and the struggle to control the colonial fur trade; and the emigration of large numbers of converted Iroquoians to mission villages in Canada. Increasingly, Iroquoians adopted non-Iroquoian captives, formerly spurned because of the difficulty of integrating them into the society. So many war prisoners and refugees were adopted that by the 1660s, according to French missionary estimates, they outnumbered natives in many Iroquoian villages. Even so, massive adoptions could not offset Iroquoian losses to disease, the missions, and warfare, losses augmented by serious conflicts with the French after 1674. In the early eighteenth century the Five Nations of Iroquois (namely, Mohawks, Oneidas, Onondagas, Cayugas, and Senecas) turned increasingly to peacefully assimilating entire peoples, most notably the Tuscaroras (after which the League became known as the Six Nations).

In sum, scalping, torture, human sacrifice, ritual cannibalism, and the adoption of captives were central to indigenous Iroquoian cultures, as was the use of wampum as an equivalent for all of these. In the seventeenth century, Iroquoian captivity practices were affected in significant ways by the European presence. The taking of captives and scalps increased greatly in scale among the Iroquois, and the potential pool of adoptive kin was broadened from Iroquoian to non-Iroquoian Indians. A significant proportion of the adoptees were Algonquians, which led to a commingling of populations that likely contributed to a

convergence of Iroquoian and Algonquian captivity practices. Algonquians adopted elements of the Iroquoian condolence complex that
were formerly foreign, even repugnant to them. In turn, the Iroquoians may have learned a less ceremonial, more instrumental approach
to captivity from the Algonquians—one that proved to be compatible
with the warfare practices Europeans imported to America.[24]

The nature of the convergence between Iroquoian and Algonquian
captivity practices remains a matter of conjecture because indigenous
Algonquian practices are much more poorly documented than those
of their Iroquoian neighbors. Too often, scholars have generalized
from the Iroquois across eastern North America, despite considerable evidence to the contrary. A careful consideration of the evidence
suggests that captivity lacked the central role in indigenous religion
and social structure among Algonquians that it had among the Iroquois, with the possible exception of those groups heavily influenced
by the Iroquois such as the Montagnais, Mahicans, and Delawares.
Algonquians apparently lacked a sacrificial motivation for torture, re-
serving it for revenge against those enemies who practiced it, both
Iroquoian and European. Individual captives were not a major objective of Algonquian warfare; rather, Algonquian warfare was directed
at obtaining the heads or scalps of enemies, which were utilized as
sacrificial offerings, at least among the more southerly coastal peoples.
Algonquians augmented their populations less through adopting individual captives than through subjugating their enemies by military
means and adopting the refugees collectively.

In indigenous Algonquian societies, then, captives were not utilized to replenish population or spiritual power. Rather, it seems that
Algonquian peoples primarily took captives for instrumental reasons,
for example, to neutralize a political enemy such as Tisquantum, or
to extort wampum or other ransom settlements. The Algonquian
practice of using wampum to ransom captives was first revealed to
Europeans in 1622 when a Dutch trader kidnapped a Pequot sachem
for ransom. The Pequots responded with more than 140 fathoms of
wampum—a striking revelation to the Dutch of the value of these
strings of purple and white shell beads (Salisbury 1982a: 148–49).[25]
Instrumental captivity and redemption practices were readily incor-

porated into colonial modes of warfare: for example, seventeenth-
and eighteenth-century Algonquian and Iroquoian war parties took
captives, heads, and scalps both in order to fulfill conditions of alliance imposed by colonial officials and to obtain from them ransom or
bounty payments. At the same time, the Indian allies of the English
or the French insisted on utilizing captives, refugees, or scalps in
purely indigenous ways, adopting captives or refugees to replenish
their numbers and spiritual power, and offering captives and scalps as
sacrifices.

In sum, what has been called the mourning-war or condolence
complex in the eastern woodlands was extended and transformed in
important ways by the colonial encounter. In their intercultural scope,
their expanded scale, and their responsiveness to demographic, political, and economic changes, the Native American captivity practices
of the colonial period were a complex "structure of the conjuncture."
The remainder of this paper discusses in more detail the convergence
and transformation of captivity practices during the seventeenth and
early eighteenth centuries (especially during the conflict-laden years
between 1675 and 1713), as well as the manner in which the European contribution to captivity is denied in the English representations
of captivity developed during this period. The bulk of my discussion concerns New England, where the dominant Anglo-American
representation of captivity developed. However, no discussion of the
captivity of White among Red can neglect to mention the earliest and
most famous English captive among Native Americans, John Smith.

Captivity and its Representation in the
English Colonies, 1607–1682

For the most part, the captivity of English settlers among Indians as
well as its representation in colonial accounts dates to the last quarter of the seventeenth century. An apparent exception is John Smith's
famous account of his imprisonment by Powhatan in 1607 and his
timely rescue from execution by that chief's daughter, Pocahontas (see
figure 2-6; Barbour 1986: 9–15; Levernier and Cohen 1977). While the
rescue may well have been an adoption ritual, there is some reason to

The Countrey wee now call Virginia beginneth at Cape Henry distant from Roanoack 60 miles, where was S.r Walter Raleigh's plantation: and because the people differ very little from them of Powhatan in any thing, I have inserted those figures in this place because of the conveniency.

King Powhatan comands C. Smith to be slayne, his daughter Pokahontas beggs his life his thankfullnes and how he subiected 39 of their kings. reade ý history.

printed by James Reeve

Figure 2-6. Robert Vaughan, "King Powhatan commands Capt. Smith to be slain; his daughter Pocahontas begs his life," 1624. Part of an engraving for John Smith, *The Generalle Historie of Virginia, New-England, and the Summer Isles* (London). (Courtesy of the Newberry Library, Chicago.)

question Smith's veracity, partly because he was silent on the matter until after Pocahontas had been held hostage by the English, married John Rolfe, become famous as a convert to Christian civility, and died in England. A further reason to refrain from taking Smith's account at face value is that rescue from captivity by a native maiden is a conventional motif in travel narratives, a motif utilized previously by Smith himself, and featured prominently in one of the two previously published accounts of Europeans taken captive in North America: Juan Ortiz, a sixteenth-century explorer captured and adopted by the Timucuas of Florida, reported that he had twice been saved from sacrifice through the intercession of his captor's daughter (Levernier and Cohen 1977: 3–11; cf. Barbour 1964, 1970, 1986).

Whatever the historical status of Smith's account, Pocahontas the merciful Redeemer unquestionably stands as a mythical heroine in Anglo-American culture (though Pocahontas the Captive does not). However, it was two centuries before Pocahontas would play a prominent role in Anglo-American captivity imagery.[26] By then (the early nineteenth century), hopes for peaceful alliance between Red and White had largely been consigned to the realm of myth, and captivity had long been established as a representation not of alliance and acculturation but of the struggle of Christian civility against savagery in the American wilderness. That is, a tradition of captivity had developed in New England in the late seventeenth and eighteenth centuries in which Divine Providence, not Indian mercy, served as the agent of salvation.

The dominant Anglo-American representation of captivity took its form during the extended series of wars beginning in 1675 during which Algonquians and English colonists—soon joined by Iroquoians and the French—struggled for control over northeastern America. Only one earlier captivity among Indians was recorded in New England, involving three young women who were seized in 1637 when Pequots attacked the new settlement of Wethersfield, Connecticut, as a protest to English expansion and treaty violations. Two of the three English girls were returned safely after showing themselves unable to make gunpowder. Following this incident, hostilities between the Pequots and Connecticut intensified, culminating in the destruction of the Pequots' major village on the Mystic River. Some three to seven hundred inhabitants of the village were burned alive or shot while attempting to escape. The refugees were hunted down by colonial forces and their Mohegan allies, who were offered a bounty for severed Pequot heads. Over the next several months, most Pequot refugees were captured and either executed or enslaved. Four to fifteen hundred Pequot refugees were assigned to colonists or their Mohegan and Narragansett allies, while a small group, including fifteen boys and two women, were shipped to the West Indies. Those distributed among Indians were generally adopted and supplied with houses and fields according to indigenous custom. The English, however, counted the refugees as slaves, and required the Mohegans and Narragansetts to pay an annual tribute payment for each adopted Pequot.[27]

It was not until the next major Puritan-Algonquian conflict over land and political sovereignty, some four decades later, that other colonists were taken captive. "King Philip's War" of 1675–76 pitted the United Colonies (Massachusetts Bay, Connecticut, Plymouth, and New Haven) and their Christian Indian allies against Wampanoag and (later) Narragansett forces led by Philip (or Metacomet) of Pokanoket, the son of Plymouth's ally, Massasoit. In this war, unprecedented in scale in the English colonies, the English put an end to Algonquian resistance to colonial expansion in southern New England. The cost of victory, however, was high: some twenty frontier towns were destroyed, the colonial male population was literally decimated, and at least forty-two colonists were abducted from frontier settlements. Like the girls from Wethersfield, these colonists seem to have been captured primarily for economic and political reasons, namely, the ransom payments and political concessions they might bring. The captives shared the hardships of their captors, who were short of food and in constant movement to escape colonial forces. Slightly over half of the captives were eventually ransomed; most of the remainder were killed in captivity or died from wounds or illness. One case of torture was reported, involving an uncooperative pregnant woman and her child.

The English, for their part, likewise captured, enslaved, scalped, and tortured their opponents during King Philip's War and its aftermath—all practices that would subsequently be coded as typically Indian in the representations of captivity developed by the clerical elite. Much as Connecticut had done during the war against the Pequots in 1637, that colony and Massachusetts Bay offered a bounty for enemy heads or scalps to their Narragansett allies. Despite the bounty, most Narragansetts attempted to maintain neutrality in the conflict, and soon the two colonies extended the bounty payments to colonial soldiers, who received thirty shillings for each enemy head. Narragansett neutrality soon foundered on the issue of Wampanoag refugees: the Narragansetts refused to turn them over to the English, instead preferring to assimilate the Wampanoags as they had the Pequots. The English response was a massive attack on the major Narragansett village, during which some three to six hundred Narragansetts and Wampanoags were killed. Massachusetts alienated other Indian allies—the Christian inhabitants of missionary "praying towns"—by incarcerating some five hundred of their number on Deer Island in Boston Harbor, where they suffered from starvation, disease, and exposure.[28]

After achieving victory the colonists quickly consolidated their gains, appropriating Wampanoag and Narragansett lands and dispersing or destroying the former inhabitants. Philip and other Algonquian leaders were executed for treason, Philip being tortured as well. Like domestic traitors, he was drawn, quartered, and decapitated. Cotton Mather, a youth at the time, himself disengaged Philip's jaw from the rest of his skull (Silverman 1984: 20). Philip's head was displayed on a pole in Plymouth for twenty years thereafter, while the head of his sister-in-law and ally, the "squaw sachem" Wetamo, was likewise displayed at Taunton. At least one additional Indian captive was tortured by the English during the war, a woman whom the Hatfield court ordered to be torn to pieces by dogs. Philip's wife and nine-year-old son, together with at least one thousand captives or refugees, were sold into foreign slavery, while hundreds of others were sold to colonists as slaves or indentured servants. The remainder were forced to live on small reservations for "praying Indians" or to take refuge in New York or Canada.[29]

The English, true to their providential hermeneutics, discerned

God's hand in both the Indian challenge to New England's expansion and in the Indian defeat. Providential interpretations of the war were developed in fast-day sermons, histories (e.g., I. Mather [1676]) and, most compellingly, in a personal narrative published six years after the war, entitled *The Sovereignty and Goodness of God, together, with the Faithfulness of His Promises Displayed: Being a Narrative of the Captivity and Restoration of Mrs. Mary Rowlandson* [1682]. One of only four works by women published in seventeenth-century New England, Mary Rowlandson's narrative was among the most widely read colonial works of her century and the next. A clergyman's wife, Mrs. Rowlandson adapted the Puritan genre of spiritual autobiography to the New World experience of captivity among Indians, interpreting as a personal spiritual trial and opportunity for redemption her hardships during three months as a captive of the squaw sachem Wetamo of Pocasset and her Narragansett husband.[30]

Beginning with a vivid description of a seemingly unprovoked attack upon the frontier settlement of Lancaster, Massachusetts, Mary Rowlandson's narrative continually situates her captivity in the context of spiritual, rather than political conflict. Structurally the narrative consists of twenty "removes . . . up and down the wilderness" (Vaughan and Clark 1981b: 35), a formulation reminiscent of the stages of Christian's pilgrimage "through the wilderness of this world" in Bunyan's *Pilgrim's Progress*, published in 1678, four years prior to Rowlandson's work (Hambrick-Stowe 1982). Rowlandson's description of these "removes" farther and farther from home—these separations from previous experience—is coupled throughout with observations on her parallel spiritual journey. The Indian attack came at a time of personal prosperity, complacency, carelessness, and vanity, Rowlandson declared, when she was almost wishing for God to submit her to trial in order to test and strengthen her faith. "Affliction I wanted and affliction I had, full measure," she reflected, seeing her captivity as a trial analogous to the captivities of God's chosen people in the Old Testament (Vaughn and Clark 1981b: 75). In captivity, Rowlandson finds herself stripped of the comforts of domestic life; isolated from her family and the supports of Christian existence; reduced to a near-bestial state exemplified by her "wolfish" appetite; and forced to abandon herself and her children into the custody of masters and, worse, a mistress who themselves served the Devil. Most poignantly, she endures the death of her six-year-old child from a bullet wound sustained during the attack. Returned to her essential human condition of isolation and vulnerability—figured as nakedness—Rowlandson at last abandons all vanity and complacency, acknowledging her utter dependence upon God's power. When she is returned to her husband through a ransom agreement facilitated by praying Indians, she feels herself to be spiritually as well as physically redeemed.

Reading her experiences as evidence of the workings of Providence, Rowlandson portrays her captors as instruments of God whose actions, whether abusive or merciful, were ultimately oriented to her own spiritual condition rather than to any Indian values, grievances, or interests. When "wild, ravenous beasts," the Indians were serving as scourges of God; when kind, they were restrained in their furious lust and rage by the hand of God. The narrative abounds in vituperative epithets characterizing her captors as bestial and diabolical: they are "bloody" and "merciless heathen"; "barbarous creatures"; "hell hounds"; "black creatures in the night." However, Rowlandson's descriptions of individual Indians are considerably more varied. She knows the names of many of her captors: indeed, among those most despised by Rowlandson are former inhabitants of the nearby praying town of Marlboro. Rowlandson describes as her primary antagonist the squaw sachem Wetamo, who apparently took delight in taunting her captive and depriving her of food, fire, and shelter.

Indeed, the squaw sachem Wetamo appears to be a model for Cotton Mather's "filthy and ugly squaws" who act as "insolent mistresses," abusing captives "at their pleasure a thousand inexpressible ways." Yet Rowlandson's portrait of Wetamo is more complex than this, for foremost among the traits in Wetamo that she criticizes is her pride and vanity—two of the very same traits Rowlandson criticizes in herself. Wetamo, it seems, serves her captive not only as a scourge but as a spiritual object lesson—possible only because of the qualities she shares with her captive.

In contrast to her antipathy towards Wetamo, Rowlandson thanks God for the kindness of Wetamo's husband, Quanopin, who "seemed to me the best friend that I had of an Indian both in cold and hunger" (51). Quanopin often protected the captive from the abuses of his wife and reassured Rowlandson that he would return her to her husband for a ransom payment. One wonders if Wetamo and Quanopin were taking alternative, perhaps gender-coded stances towards their captive: Wetamo seeking revenge through mild torture, Quanopin more interested in Rowlandson's political and economic value. It is perhaps more significant, however, that Wetamo (perhaps the daughter of Corbitant, the anti-English sachem who captured Squanto) was one of Philip's major allies, while Quanopin (a new husband) was of the once neutral Narragansett. In addition to Quanopin's kindness, Rowlandson also remarked upon the kindness of Philip himself and at the numerous "common mercies" shown to her by total strangers.

Rowlandson's well-nuanced descriptions of her captors comprise one aspect of her general attentiveness to the details of her experience, all of which were significant in the context of a spiritual autobiography. Also appropriate to the genre of spiritual autobiography is Mary Rowlandson's prose—simple, direct, vivid—and her highly personal viewpoint. Apart from certain passages near the close of the narrative that, like a jeremiad, censure her society's shortcomings, Rowlandson's descriptions of her experiences are mainly concerned with the condition of her own soul under adversity. Her interpretations are closely intertwined with the course of events she relates, and her references to Scripture occur in relation to her need for comfort or instruction at particular times. In sum, although Scripture was essential in sustaining her, in true nonconformist fashion the narrative presents experience as the *sine qua non* of knowledge.

The creative blend of experience and interpretation found in Mary Rowlandson's narrative makes it an exceptional captivity narrative, just as Mary Rowlandson, a minister's wife, was an exceptional captive. Here I depart from the scholarly consensus, which treats *The Sovereignty and Goodness of God* as an archetype for an indigenous Anglo-American captivity genre (e.g., Pearce 1947, [1953] 1965; Slotkin 1973). However, in contrast to Rowlandson's first-person interpretation of captivity, other captivity narratives published in New England for half a century were written or edited by clergymen, including Increase Mather, his son Cotton Mather, and John Williams, a minister related by marriage to the Mathers who was himself taken captive in 1704. These narratives by the Puritan clergy tend to subordinate immediate experience to dogmatic interpretation, presenting captivity less as a personal spiritual trial than as a divine lesson to an unregenerate society. In clerical hands, captivity narratives depart from the form of spiritual autobiography and become jeremiads, taking a form that explicitly reinforced clerical authority.

Even Rowlandson's narrative—internally free of clerical "improvements"—is framed by clerical interpretations. Preceded by an anonymous preface, the narrative is followed in early editions by an outline of the last sermon Joseph Rowlandson, Mary's husband, preached before his death. The preface, written in the literary style of the clergy in contrast to Rowlandson's truly "plain style," was probably written by the foremost minister of the time, Increase Mather, whose congregation provided a house for the Rowlandson family after Mary's return from captivity.

The preface, even while establishing Mary Rowlandson's authority as a writer, undermines that authority in two ways. First, the narrative is commended less as a record of inner spiritual trial and redemption than for "particularizing" instances of divine providence in outward events. Indeed, this is the use Increase Mather himself made of captivity in publishing, in 1684, the narrative of Quentin Stockwell as an "illustrious providence" (Mather [1684] 1977; Vaughan and Clark 1981b: 77–89). The preface summarizes the particular knowledge Rowlandson's narrative imparts:

> as none knows what it is to fight and pursue such an enemy as this, but they that have fought and pursued them: so none can imagine, what it is to be captivated, and enslaved to such Atheistical, proud, wild, cruel, barbarous, brutish, (in one word) diabolical Creatures as these, the worst of the heathen; nor what difficulties, hardships, hazards, sorrows, anxieties, and perplexities, do unavoidably wait upon such a condition, but those that have tried it. ([1682] 1977, n.p.)

Ironically, Rowlandson's narrative becomes reduced here to a general account of sufferings among a diabolical enemy. The "particular" nature of Rowlandson's portrayal of her sufferings—the imaginative

correlation of her inner and outward "removes"—as well as Rowlandson's "particular knowledge" of her various captors are elided.

A second manner in which Mary Rowlandson's authority is
undermined is that the narrative is introduced and its publication justified largely by reference to "that Reverend servant of God, Mr. Joseph
Rowlandson." In contrast to the narrative, the Indians' attack appears
in the preface through the eyes of Joseph Rowlandson, who returned
home after seeking aid for the defense of Lancaster only to find his own
house in flames and "his precious yoke-fellow, and dear Children,
wounded and captivated . . . by the cruel, and barbarous Salvages."
Although other inhabitants of Lancaster were captured or killed, the
preface presents the catastrophe that befell the Rowlandson family as
"the most solemn and remarkable part of this Tragedy" because it
occurred to "God's precious ones." Mary Rowlandson was herself a
Saint, but her afflictions and deliverance were all the more of public
concern "by how much nearer this Gentlewoman stood related to that
faithful servant of God" ([1682] 1977, n.p.).

The preface, in sum, defines Mary Rowlandson primarily by her
relationship to her husband and justifies the publication of her narrative by virtue of her marriage to a legitimate spokesman of Puritan
society. *The Sovereignty and Goodness of God* was only the second work
by a woman to be published in seventeenth-century New England
(following Anne Bradstreet's poetry), and Mrs. Rowlandson's affinity
to the clergy provided the requisite justification for allowing her
words to enter the public realm of elite males. Still, her character
needed protection, and the preface dwells on her modesty and her
status as a Saint, assuring the reader, as does the title page, that the
narrative was written for the author's "private Use," and was only
"made public at the earnest Desire of some Friends."

Despite the emphasis upon Joseph Rowlandson's perspective on
Mary's captivity in the preface, no reference to that or to any captivity appears in the appended outline of his 1678 fast-day sermon
(Rowlandson [1682] 1977: 35–46). Still, Joseph Rowlandson's sermon,
entitled "The Possibility of God's Forsaking a People that have been
near and dear to him," is congruent with Mary's captivity narrative in
an intriguing way. Warning God's chosen people that they must stop

forsaking God lest they be forsaken, Joseph Rowlandson makes use of a common Puritan trope: the proper relationship of a wife to her husband exemplifies the Saint's relationship to God.[31] Like the faithful wife who retains good and respectful thoughts towards her husband, even in his absence, the Saint remains faithful to God even when seemingly being forsaken. The sinner who forsakes God in this situation is likened to an adulteress; the sinner who, in response, is utterly forsaken by God is like a widow. Although the outline gives no clue as to how Joseph Rowlandson developed this analogy in his sermon, when it is juxtaposed to the captivity narrative, Mary Rowlandson emerges as doubly faithful in her captivity: both to her husband in his absence, and to God, who seemingly had forsaken her.

These correspondences between the faithful wife, the faithful saint, and the faithful captive are what Cotton Mather would play upon more explicitly in developing the female captive as the typification of colonial vulnerability. Unlike Mary Rowlandson, who was able to maintain her faith, although with difficulty, when removed from the influence of her husband and the clergy, weaker captives were liable to forsake family, community, and God. Like the adulteress, they would fall prey to the seduction of Satan and his worldly servants; like the widow, they risked being utterly forsaken.

Indeed, when Rowlandson's narrative was published in 1682, the clergy was particularly concerned over what it perceived as faithlessness, spiritual vulnerability, and foundering identity. The death of the first generation of Puritan emigrants had deprived their descendants of a direct link to England. Millennial expectations had been dashed with the restoration of the monarchy in England, church membership in New England was declining, and the vacated lands won in King Philip's War were enticing settlers away from the authoritarian confines of the older towns. Meeting in 1679 under the leadership of Increase Mather to consider spiritual degeneracy, a clerical Synod deplored the colonists' "insatiable desire after Land, and worldly Accomodations, yea as to forsake Churches and Ordinances, and to live like Heathen, only so that they might have Elbow-room enough in the world" (Hambrick-Stowe 1982: 256–65).

The clergy feared that frontier settlers were succumbing to what missionary John Eliot called "wilderness temptations" (Nash 1982: 102), willingly abandoning the lawful and godly order of Puritan settlements and embracing the individualistic anarchy presumably characteristic of Indian life. One significant manifestation of this anarchy was the lack of hierarchical relations taken to be natural and ordained by God: the subordination of women to their husbands, children to their parents, servants to their masters, and laity to the clergy. Such a subordination of the weak, wild, and spiritually vulnerable to their natural masters, who were stronger, more reasonable, and more godly, was central to Puritan notions of domestic and civic order (Morgan 1966, Koehler 1980). Just such notions of the natural subordination of wife to husband were at the base of Joseph Rowlandson's sermon when he used the proper husband-wife relationship as a model for that between God and the Saint. And just such notions of the natural vulnerability of women and children were called into play in the representation of captivity developed by Cotton Mather. In either case, a woman and her children were easy prey to physical assaults and spiritual seduction in the absence of the master of the house.

Captivity in the Early Intercolonial Wars and Its Representation, 1689–1707

The Synod's fears of the disastrous consequences of the search for "elbow room" seemed to materialize around the turn of the century. The new English settlements on the northern and western frontiers were vulnerable to intermittent attacks by Algonquians and Iroquoians from across the Canadian border, many of whom French Jesuits had converted to Catholicism. Hostilities intensified from 1689 through 1697 (King William's War) and again from 1702 through 1713 (Queen Anne's War), when England and France were engaged in European power struggles that in the colonies took the form of contests for control over northeastern North America.[32] During these two early intercolonial (or "French and Indian") wars, parties of Canadian Indians commanded by French officers attacked frontier settlements, taking some six hundred captives for adoption, occasional use as victims in torture rituals, and for sale to the French for bounty payments. The French, like the English, also offered a bounty for enemy scalps, European as well as Indian, but they paid more for captives, owing to their desire for an increased population. A large number of ransomed captives remained in Canada, converting to Catholicism, although many others were eventually returned to English officials for ransom or exchange.

In the context of its concerns over the colonies' spiritual vulnerability, the clergy interpreted the intercolonial wars primarily as spiritual battles against the heathenism of Rome and America alike, expanding the captivity metaphor to encompass a redemptive experience not only for captives, but for the community as a whole. Captivities—taken as signs of God's displeasure with the Puritans for their collective unfaithfulness—were seen as God's way of evoking a renewed acknowledgment of His power while confirming the Puritans' identity as His chosen people. Three prominent clergymen—Increase Mather, his son Cotton Mather, and his niece's husband, John Williams, himself a captive in the second intercolonial war—developed this interpretation between 1684 and 1707, presenting captivity as a divine punishment for internal degeneration.

Such an interpretation of captivity largely excluded a reexamination of British colonial relations with native peoples or the French, since captivity was seen as a punishment for internal degeneration rather than a consequence of political relations. Puritan identity had become so dissipated on the frontier, went the logic, that Puritans were doubly vulnerable: both to physical attack and to the spiritual onslaughts of Catholic Indians and Jesuits. As we have seen, Cotton Mather's "Observable Things," delivered at the close of King William's War, underscored the vulnerability of New England through his typification of young and female captives. These captives, although a minority of those taken during the intercolonial wars, were the most likely to be assimilated into Indian or French society. Mather's concern with assimilation is perhaps most forcefully expressed in the image of Indian vultures devouring English chicks, but it was more fully developed in the most extensive captivity narrative he published, that of Hannah Swarton, which appeared first as an appendix to a jeremiad, "Humiliations follow'd with Deliverances" ([1697] 1977) and again in his major work of providential history, *Magnalia Christi Americana* ([1702] 1977).[33]

Swarton's narrative, written in the first person although undoubtedly edited by Mather, presents her five and a half years of captivity among Catholic Indians and then the French as a personal trial and opportunity for spiritual rebirth. Her perceived failings, however, differ greatly from the vanity and complacency of Rowlandson, the pastor's wife: Swarton's involve abandoning an established Puritan settlement in pursuit of worldly goods in the frontier community of Falmouth, Maine. Hannah Swarton, then, is the personification of those Puritans so deplored by the Synod of 1679 who "lived like heathen" on the frontier. In this context, Swarton's captivity in 1690 and the loss of several family members become exaggerated versions of the independence that she herself had sought on the frontier; the spiritual temptations of French Canada, likewise, exaggerations of those temptations she had courted at home. Like Rowlandson, Swarton presents captivity as a profound isolation from all that had sustained her, here figured not as nakedness but as bereavement. She emerges from captivity with a renewed appreciation for God's power and with a revelation concerning her identity: indeed, her repentance over her past inattention to her spiritual needs and those of her children assume the quality of a conversion experience.

Despite its message of spiritual redemption, Swarton's narrative lacks much of the experiential immediacy that makes Rowlandson's so effective. Passages from Scripture are less fully integrated with experience, and Indians are portrayed as generically satanic, notable mainly for the conjunction of brutality and Catholic piety. This characterization serves Mather well in both his denigration of Catholicism and his censure of growing Puritan worldliness. Ironically, the Indians, though "idolaters," are more faithful than Swarton; it is they who first offer a providential interpretation of the captivity, reminding the despairing captive that her fate is in the hands of God. Like Wetamo, the Wampanoag squaw sachem who shares the vanity Mary Rowlandson comes to repudiate, Swarton's captors serve as object lessons, exemplifying the piety Swarton has lacked—albeit Catholic piety. Mather's version of Swarton's narrative, in sum, moves toward a more abstract presentation of captivity, one that emphasizes the Catholic assault upon what Swarton calls her "inward man" over the sufferings of her "outward man" among the Indians, themselves characterized abstractly.

The narrative of another Hannah, the most famous of Mather's exemplary captives, moves toward abstraction from experience and typification of Indians in a different way, through telling the story in the third person. Hardly an example of feminine vulnerability, Hannah Dustan, of Haverhill, New Hampshire, murdered and scalped her captors in their sleep, turning in the scalps of two men, two women, and six children to the colonial government for a ransom payment. Hannah Dustan would thus seem to lie completely outside the representation of captivity that Mather develops elsewhere. However, as we shall see, Mather manages to contain her within that representation, for his own generation at least.[34]

Mather first told Dustan's story in his jeremiad, "Humiliations follow'd with Deliverances," which he preached shortly after she returned from six weeks as a captive of a small Abenaki band. Pointing to Dustan, sitting in the congregation, as a woman who had been humiliated but subsequently delivered through God's providence, Mather told her story in his own inimitable style. When the Dustan house was attacked, Mr. Dustan escaped with seven of their children, leaving Mrs. Dustan, her week-old infant, and their nurse behind. After seeing "the raging dragons rifle all that they could carry away and set the house on fire," the three captives were led away by the Indians, "but ere they had gone many steps they dashed out the brains of the infant against a tree." In vengeance for the infant's death and fearful of being "stripped and scourged" when they arrived at the "rendezvous of savages which they call a town," Hannah Dustan resolved "to imitate the action of Jael upon Sisera." One night, she awakened her nurse and an English youth held captive with them, convincing the latter to help her kill all but two of the twelve members of her captor's family, making use of the Indians' own tomahawks. The Indians "bowed, they fell, they lay down," in Mather's telling, echoing the Book of Judges (5:27); "at their feet they bowed, they fell where they bowed; there they fell down dead" (Vaughan and Clark 1981b: 162–64).

Mather's account justifies the axings both through Biblical references and, implicitly, through formulaic typifications of the Indians as "raging dragons," "those whose tender mercies are cruelties," "formidable savages," and "furious tawnies." Yet, acknowledged Mather, these captors, like Swarton's, put many an English family to shame in their regular observance of prayer. Indeed, Dustan's master, like Swarton's, gave his captive a lesson in spiritual resignation, asking " 'What need you trouble yourself? If your God will have you delivered, you shall be so.' " To which Mather added, "And it seems our God would have it so to be." Still, Mather seems to suggest in his "improvement" upon the narrative, Hannah Dustan's deliverance may have been too easy. He admonished Dustan and her companions to guard against undue pride, against the temptation of believing that their deliverance was testimony to their righteousness. They must "make a right use of the deliverance," he insisted, repenting and humbling themselves before God. Warned Mather: "You are not now the slaves of Indians, as you were a few Days ago; but if you continue unhumbled, in your sins, you will be the slaves of Devils; and, let me tell you, a slavery to Devils, to be in Their hands, is worse than to be in the hands of Indians!" (Mather [1699] 1978: 47–50). Perhaps it was as an example of the desired humility that Mather appended to the sermon upon its publication the narrative of the more humble and vulnerable Hannah Swarton.

Mather published and interpreted the narratives of a number of other captives in his sermons and histories, all third-person accounts. None of these accounts is as significant or as divergent as those of the two Hannahs, and all of these accounts serve the same interpretive end. Captivity was a work of Divine Providence designed to humiliate and chastise God's people, to call attention to their collective lack of piety and subservience to the clergy. Within this interpretation, Indians were God's instruments, even in their pious "idolatry." Mather's interpretation is supported through an abstraction from individual experience and a typification of Indians, greatly contrasting with the sharp and concrete detail of Rowlandson's spiritual autobiography.

Mather's level of abstraction and typification might be attributed to his lack of personal experience as a captive, were it not for the fact that these qualities are also found in the widely read captivity narrative of his colleague, the Rev. John Williams.

The pastor of the frontier town of Deerfield, Massachusetts, Williams was captured in 1704 along with his family and more than one hundred members of his congregation. Although he suffered severe personal losses and hardships during his captivity, including the death of his wife, Williams's *The Redeemed Captive Returning to Zion* [1707] is preoccupied with his efforts toward countering the spiritual "seduction" of the French Jesuits, who successfully converted some of his flock, including his own son. Williams eventually convinced his son to return to the fold, but to his dismay completely lost his daughter Eunice, who was seven years old at the time of her capture. Eunice eventually married a Catholic Mohawk and remained in the community of Caughnawaga. She forever refused to return to New England, except for brief, highly publicized visits with her Indian husband and children, when she is said to have camped in her brother's apple orchard wearing buckskin and moccasins. For much of the first half of the eighteenth century Eunice Williams symbolized the fragility of English identity in the New World, personifying Cotton Mather's "little chickens . . . seized by Indian vultures, . . . little birds . . . spirited away by the Indian devourers." [35]

John Williams was the only Puritan captive to publish a full-length account of captivity between the Rowlandson narrative of 1682 and a narrative by John Gyles published in 1736. He is then, in a significant sense, the male counterpart of Mary Rowlandson. However, Williams's work is not a spiritual autobiography but a polemic against the French Jesuits. If Mary Rowlandson appears in her narrative as the isolated individual struggling to maintain her faith in the absence of her husband and community, John Williams appears as God's representative against Indian and French idolatry and as the mainstay of his congregation's faith. Indeed, *The Redeemed Captive*, despite its title, presents Williams less as a captive redeemed after undergoing spiritual trial than as himself a spiritual redeemer. That he was unsuccessful in Eunice's case underscored the vulnerability of the English colonists before the joint Indian and French threat.

To recapitulate and extend our analysis, we have traced a process of increasing abstraction of the captivity experience and increasing typification of Indians in four captivity narratives published over a quarter century: Mary Rowlandson's spiritual autobiography of 1682, Hannah Swarton's and Hannah Dustan's accounts as recounted in Cotton Mather's jeremiad of 1697, and John Williams's narrative of 1707. Rowlandson's narrative—the first extended interpretation of captivity to appear in the English colonies—is notable for its immediacy, its correlation of spiritual and physical experience, and, in comparison to the other narratives, its differentiated portrayal of individual Indians. However, despite its attention to concrete experience, Rowlandson's narrative abstracts the captivity experience from its nexus of political conflict, and typifies Indians both through dehumanizing epithets and through a providential interpretive frame. In other words, the narrative is highly univocal, in Bakhtin's sense: Indians serve as instruments of God to chastise, instruct, and deliver the captive, and are denied motivations, perspectives, and voices of their own.[36]

Although the narrative denies Indians a voice, hardly unusual in colonial New England, it is notable for articulating the experience of captivity through the voice of a female captive, with minimal clerical "improvements." This is no doubt due to Rowlandson's status as one of the elect and a clergyman's wife, but may also be because her own voice was extraordinarily effective in describing and interpreting the captivity experience. Still, the narrative is framed by clerical interpretations, and these provide strong indications of the dominant direction that the interpretation of captivity would take once the clergy claimed interpretive hegemony—as Cotton Mather did in "Observable Things," claiming that it was properly the work of the clergy to read these texts "all written in blood."

First, the experience as a whole would be read as a deliverance by Divine Providence from slavery to diabolical and idolatrous forces. Neither the concrete details of the captivity (as in Rowlandson's diary of her removes) nor concrete variations among Indians (as in her contrasting portraits of Wetamo and her husband Quanopin) were essential to establishing this interpretation. No such narrative structure as Rowlandson's parallel spiritual and physical "removes" are found in subsequent narratives. As regards Indians, general typifications substitute for description, and laudable characteristics among Indians are reduced to one: their misguided faithfulness in observing an idolatrous religion. In other words, Indians become typified as a demonic, idolatrous Other defined almost completely in opposition to the Puritan Self. While such oppositional typification is not absent in Mary Rowlandson, it is complicated by her observation of differences among her captors and similarities between herself and her captors. The narratives published by Cotton Mather and John Williams contain no such memorable figure as Wetamo, the proud and vain female sachem who seems to serve as Rowlandson's alter ego, to represent her own sins taken to the extreme.

Secondly, as the representation of captivity became more abstract, it was joined more explicitly to orthodox representations of feminine vulnerability and subservience. While Rowlandson's gender added poignancy to her captivity, one can imagine a male captive writing a similar spiritual autobiography, as John Bunyan had in another setting. Not so in the case of Hannah Swarton, Hannah Dustan, and Eunice Williams: the interpretations of their captivities are all highly dependent on their vulnerability as females to seduction and violation when removed from the paternal supervision of their husbands or fathers and the clergy. Dustan's apparently anomalous case is especially revealing: her decision to tomahawk her captors is attributed to fear of having to run naked through the gauntlet; she is compared to a female type from Scripture (Jael); and she is counselled to eschew any inappropriate pride in her act.

Appropriately, given the typification of the exemplary captive as female and the general oppositional logic, the gender of the Indian captor becomes coded primarily as male, though abstractly male. While the captor may be accompanied by "filthy," "ugly," "insolent" squaws, they are secondary and dispensable to the overall interpretation: captivity becomes an improper subservience to men who are themselves subservient to the Devil rather than to God.

In short, during the decade between 1697 and 1707, Cotton Mather and John Williams began to develop a representation of captivity that is highly condensed in the quotation from Mather's "Observable Things," the vivid sermon with which we began. In this clerical interpretation, the figure of the female captive represents the vulnerability of the English colonies in the New World, where they are preyed upon by the brutish and diabolical forces of the wilderness which destroy domestic and civil order and threaten to seduce or devour them. The opposition between a vulnerable female Captive and a male Captor unrestrained in his savagery is fundamental to this interpretation. Furthermore, a white male Redeemer seems to be prefigured in the person of John Williams—a less successful redeemer, to be sure, than his secular counterparts of the next century, Daniel Boone and Leatherstocking. To complete the configuration, the red female Captor—so prominent in Mary Rowlandson's narrative—is subordinated to her male counterpart.

Hegemonic and Alternative Representations of Captivity, 1682 to 1736 and Beyond

The clerical representation of captivity gained its influence from both social and cultural sources: it bore the authority of those who articulated it, the clerical elite, as well as the hegemonic system of assumptions regarding gender, savagery, and civility which it deployed. However, throughout the period under discussion—the half-century following the publication of Mary Rowlandson's narrative—there were certain challenges to the clerical representation. To begin with, Mary Rowlandson's spiritual autobiography continued to appear in new editions. Further, it was supplemented by three other full-length captivity narratives: two of them by male captives, two of them spiritual autobiographies written by Quakers.

The first of the Quaker narratives ranked in popularity with the Rowlandson and Williams narratives in the English colonies, and was published abroad as well, in Dutch and German as well as English editions. First published in 1699, the narrative was entitled: *God's Protecting Providence Man's Surest Help and Defense in the Times of the Greatest Difficulty and most Imminent Danger: Evidenced in the Remarkable Deliverance of Divers Persons, from the Devouring Waves of the Sea, and also from the more Cruelly Devouring Jaws of the Inhumane Cannibals of Florida amongst whom they Suffered Shipwreck.* This detailed journal records the experiences of Jonathan Dickinson, a prosperous merchant who was shipwrecked in Florida, together with his family and a famous Quaker missionary, Robert Barrow. This desolate party was captured by a little-known group of coastal Indians known as Ais or Tequesta.

Despite its exotic setting in comparison to other colonial captivity narratives, Dickinson's account is similar to Rowlandson's in its immediacy and its interpretation of captivity as a lesson in resignation to God's will, a lesson both articulated and exemplified by the missionary. The account contrasts with Rowlandson's narrative, however, in its highly stereotypical portrayal of Indians, a portrayal dominated by fear of the "cruelly devouring jaws" of these reputed cannibals. Indeed, it seems that the Dickinson narrative fleshes out the possibilities inherent in Mather's image of Indian vultures and devourers, using cannibalism to represent loss of self through a literal incorporation by the Other. This interpretation is supported by the nature of Dickinson's second overriding concern: that his infant son would survive his mother and father and be raised by the Indians. This remained a horrifying prospect despite the tenderness of the Indian women, who repeatedly nourished the starving infant at their own breasts. One wonders if Dickinson and his wife experienced this act of mercy as a threatening transformation of the infant's substance, as an alternative form of incorporation.[37]

The second Quaker account related the experiences of Elizabeth Hanson, a pacifist abducted by Algonquian allies of the French during one of the skirmishes that intermittently plagued the frontier between 1713 and the beginning of the third intercolonial war in 1744. Upon her return from captivity Hanson narrated her experiences to an English minister, who edited and published the account anonymously as a testament to God's power and a reminder of the importance of spiritual resignation. *God's Mercy Surmounting Man's Cruelty* [1728], as Hanson's narrative is titled, retains a providential interpretation of captivity, but lacks the oppositional typification of Indians found in Dickinson's and the Puritan narratives. Hunger is the focal condition in Hanson's account, plaguing captive and captors alike, and motivating both the cruelties of her master and the compassion of Indian women, who showed Hanson how to supplement her failing breast milk with a gruel of walnuts and corn. Hanson's willingness to identify to some extent with her captors includes religion: for example, she is willing to acknowledge a spiritual dimension to the scalp dance she witnessed upon the war party's return home.[38]

This move towards what, from a contemporary perspective, appears as nascent ethnographic curiosity and cultural relativism, is furthered in the final narrative published before the intercolonial wars resumed. *Memoirs of Odd Adventures, Strange Deliverances, etc. in the Captivity of John Gyles,* published in 1736, concerns Gyles's abduction in 1689, when he was ten years old.[39] Gyles, who spent six years among the Eastern Abenaki and three as a prisoner of the French, explicitly imparts material on ethnography and natural history, adding separate sections on these subjects to the chronologically-ordered narration of his experiences. For example, Gyles's section on "Indian fables" is one of our earliest sources on the Algonquian cannibal bird, "called gulloua," he writes, "who buildeth her nest on a high rock or mountain." As Gyles relates the Abenaki tale:

> A boy was hunting with his bow and arrow at the foot of a rocky mountain when the gulloua came diving through the air, grasped the boy in her talons, and though he was eight or ten years of age, she soared aloft and laid him in her nest, a prey of her young, where the boy lay constantly on his face but would look sometimes under his arms and saw two young ones with much fish and flesh in the nest and the old bird constantly bringing more, so that the young ones not touching him, the old one clawed him up and set him where she found him, who returned and related the odd event to his friends.
> (Gyles [1736] 1981: 115–16)

One wonders how greatly Gyles identified with the Indian boy who was taken captive but ultimately returned home to tell his tale. While Gyles does not explicitly identify himself with the gulloua's prey, he does devote considerable attention to the tale, locating the bird's nest at the top of a specific mountain, identifying the bird as a larger version of a speckled eagle, and comparing it to the "hungry harpies" in Dryden's *Virgil*.

Gyles's reference to harpies is only one of many classical references in the narrative, which departs from Puritan and Quaker precedents in identifying the captive with a classical hero, Odysseus, rather than with Hebrew prototypes. Like Odysseus, Gyles returned home transformed, and he put the extensive linguistic, cultural, and environmental knowledge he had gained to good use, serving as an interpreter and diplomat for the colonies after his release from captivity. Gyles's willingness to adopt certain Indian traits marks a strong departure from the Puritan preoccupation with maintaining an unsullied identity in the New World. Likewise a departure from earlier narratives is Gyles's emphasis not on spiritual redemption but on physical survival, which he attributes as much to his own human wit as to Divine Providence. Gyles survives the hardships of captivity and emerges to tell his tale, it seems, because his flexible identity incorporates knowledge of Abenaki culture while still remaining oriented primarily to colonial values. Although this narrative is among the least well known, the power of a partially acculturated identity, as Slotkin (1973) has shown, was to become a central theme in Anglo-American representations of captivity after the Revolution, embodied both in male captives such as Daniel Boone and in fictional characters such as Cooper's Leatherstocking.

Given the existence of, first, a more multivocal interpretation of the captivity experience in the Hanson and Gyles narratives and, secondly, narratives of two male captives, Gyles and Dickinson, who present themselves as vulnerable, at least to the dangers of torture, it is important not to overstate the extent to which the Puritan clergy dominated the interpretation of captivity in the English colonies during the period we are considering. The half century after Mary Rowlandson first explored the meaning of the captivity experience was a time in which a number of interpretations of captivity coexisted. However, the interpretation fashioned in the works of Increase Mather, Cotton Mather, and John Williams has left the most enduring legacy. Their interpretation of captivity—which justifies colonial domination and aggression as a response to savage threats to vulnerable civility—was developed in the voluminous captivity literature that began to appear during the third and fourth intercolonial wars (especially the latter, the Seven Years' or "French and Indian"

War of 1755–63). The hegemonic interpretation was further developed in narratives deriving from the Revolutionary War and the various frontier wars in which the nation engaged in the late eighteenth century and throughout the nineteenth century. Especially important in the development and dissemination of a hegemonic representation were illustrations of the captivity experience, which only began to appear in colonial editions in the 1770s; anthologies of captivity narratives and "Indian atrocities," which date to the 1790s; narratives included in children's readers and Sunday School literature, dating to the early nineteenth century; and fictional accounts, dating to the 1790s and appearing with ever greater frequency in the first half of the nineteenth century, when Cooper's influential Leatherstocking Tales appeared.[40]

We cannot consider these developments here, but must simply note that the twin processes of abstraction and typification noted in Mather's and Williams's interpretations of captivity are key to the further development of a hegemonic representation of captivity. The historical and cultural contexts of captivity are even more thoroughly suppressed, particularly the manner in which captivity on the colonial and, later, the national frontiers represented a convergence of Indian and European practices. Especially in visual and fictional versions of the captivity experience, the Captive becomes more completely typified as a vulnerable White female, the Captor as a threatening Red male (see figures 2-1 and 2-3). Meanwhile, the white male Redeemer becomes ever more prominent. Just as the clerical version carried the authority of the Puritan elite, the dominant representation in subsequent discourse carries the authority of local and national historians, school and church publication boards, the mass media, and especially in the case of public sculpture, representative government (see figure 2-2).

Finally, just as alternatives to the clerical version existed in the half century we have surveyed, significant alternatives to the dominant version continued to appear, such as the popular narrative of Mary Jemison, an adopted white captive, first published in 1824 (Seaver 1824), and the many literary and dramatic treatments of Pocahontas and King Philip that began to appear at the same time. These alternatives can be recognized precisely by the manner in which they transgress the oppositional logic upon which the hegemonic representation is built: Jemison is a "white squaw"; Pocahontas a red female Redeemer; Philip, a red male Captor-become-Captive. Rarely, however, do these alternatives function truly as counter-hegemonic representations, for they appear as romantic possibilities for contemplation, not as models for action.

Especially in Native American discourse, however, the oppositional power of alternative representations of captivity may emerge. The nineteenth-century Wampanoag legend of the European cannibal bird, for instance, counters the hegemonic representation of captivity with a representation in which the captors are White, the captives, Red. While the legend only survives in fragmentary form, it gives us a glimpse of Wampanoag attempts to retain their own definitions of their identity and their relations with the European invaders. These definitions have been crucial in the Wampanoags' struggle to maintain a way of life that remains, to some extent, oppositional to Anglo-American hegemony.

For a more fully developed example of oppositional representations of captivity we may return to the Pocahontas story, not as told by the descendants of John Smith, but as told by the descendants of Pocahontas. As Feest has recently shown (1987a), the Pamunkeys of Virginia have utilized their descent from Pocahontas as a major marker of their cultural identity. Countering the hegemonic forces that have attempted to define them as individual "persons of color" and to deprive them of the lands, the rights, and the dignity they hold as "tribal Indians," the Pamunkeys have vividly represented themselves in pageants, artifacts, and naming patterns as the rightful heirs of that Red captive, that Red redeemer, Pocahontas. Some might emphasize the irony that the Pamunkeys assert their separate cultural identity in terms that are largely hegemonic ("inauthentic"), and find little that is alternative or oppositional in their use of the captivity tradition. Quite to the contrary, I (like Feest) regard their appropriation of the Pocahontas legend as a creative and skillful utilization of the cultural resources available to them—one that has helped the Pamunkeys preserve a sense of corporate identity in the face of powerful forces that would destroy that identity. It is just such a sense of separate and valuable cultural identity that enables the Pamunkeys—and the Wampanoags, the Abenakis, the Iroquois—to assert some independence and to demand respect, reciprocity, and redress from the European vulture that continues its attempts to capture, confine, and incorporate them.

Notes

I am grateful to Daniel Segal and Harry Liebersohn for inviting me to participate in a most stimulating conference. The participants offered valuable comments upon my paper, as have audiences at Colby College, the University of Missouri-St. Louis, and the 1989 annual meeting of the American Society for Ethnohistory. I am indebted to Alfonso Ortiz for inspiration and guidance; Raymond Fogelson, George Stocking, Jean Comaroff, Neal Salisbury, Thomas Abler, and Barrik Van Winkle for careful readings of this and related papers; and John Lawrence, June Namias, and James Lewis for sharing works in progress. Barrik Van Winkle prepared the map and has furthered my research and writing in every conceivable way. More generally, I have been greatly influenced by my participation in scholarly communities at the University of Chicago (Department of Anthropology and Social Science Collegiate Division) and the Newberry Library. My research on this topic was facilitated by support from the Danforth Foundation, the National Science Foundation, the Phillips Fund of the American Philosophical Society, and the D'Arcy McNickle Center for the History of the American Indian at the Newberry Library. Working at the Newberry Library has been a special privilege, and I am deeply grateful for the help of present and past staff in Special Collections, Research and Education, and the D'Arcy McNickle Center. All those familiar with the Edward E. Ayer Collection will detect the aid of John Aubrey and Michael Kaplan behind these pages. For a fuller discussion of the sources and an expanded version of this analysis, see Strong (1992).

1. Green notes Pocahontas Saving Capt. John Smith and Squanto Helping the Pilgrims as national legends "spread primarily through print in educational institutions and reinforced by visualization" (1988: 588). If we take Hirsch (1987) seriously, the literate American is no longer familiar with Squanto (or maize or Thanksgiving, for that matter). Pocahontas, however,

is one of the few women included in Hirsch's list of literate Americans' "core knowledge." Only three other Native Americans are included, all war leaders: Geronimo, Montezuma, and Sitting Bull. Strangely, although maize (or "Indian corn") is absent from this list, "Indian file" and "Indian summer" are present. Further indicating the hegemonic representation of American Indians are the remaining Indian entries: the names of seven prominent native peoples (the Apache, Cherokee, Iroquois, Navaho, Shawnee, Sioux, and Eskimo); several phrases related to warfare ("on the warpath," "bury the hatchet"; the French and Indian Wars; the massacre at Wounded Knee); and two romantic Anglo-American texts ("Hiawatha" and *The Last of the Mohicans*). Captivity across the frontier is involved in several additional entries: John Smith, Daniel Boone, James Fenimore Cooper, and dime novels.

2. The coding of Indians as "Red" (connoting blood, war paint, and unrestrained passion, as in "blood lust" and "bloodthirsty") vs. Europeans as "White" (connoting purity and innocence) carries important symbolic significance in representations of captivity. However, the racial categories of White and Red were largely developed subsequently to the period considered here, in the mid to late eighteenth century (Vaughan 1982; Berkhofer 1988: 524–26; cf. Fogelson 1985). As the quotation from Cotton Mather's "Observable Things" indicates, seventeenth-century English colonists described Indians as "tawny" (or even "white"), and distinguished themselves from Indians not by color or other racial characteristics but by religion, nationality, and civility, calling themselves "Christians" or "English" (vs. "heathen," "pagans," "Indians," or "savages"). In his important article, Vaughan argues that it is anachronistic for scholars to project nineteenth-century racial categories back into the early colonial period. I agree, but find it useful to employ the terms here in reference to the hegemonic representation of captivity that developed between the late seventeenth century and the present. As we shall see, the opposition of savage passion to innocent purity was fundamental to the earliest representations of captivity, although it was not reinforced by color symbolism until the late eighteenth century. Color symbolism is especially important in visual representations; see, for example, John Vanderlyn's *The Murder of Jane McCrea* (figure 2-1; reproduced in color in Strong 1985) and John Mix Stanley's *Osage Scalp Dance* (figure 2-3).

3. More general treatments of Indian "gifts" or "contributions" to "civilization" include Weatherford (1988), Axtell (1981, 1985a, 1988), and classic works by Hallowell (1957a, 1957b). Clifton (1990) includes articles on a number of controversial issues; but see Strong (forthcoming). Axtell's works manifest a consistent and sophisticated concern for the reciprocal influence of Europeans and Indians. While Pocahontas's "gift" of tobacco is not prominent

in legend, Virginians remember that she assisted John Rolfe in his experiments with tobacco cultivation (Feest 1987a: 6). Her alleged contribution to the tobacco industry is represented in nineteenth-century statuary: one of the three major types of cigar-store figures features Pocahontas holding out a bundle of cigars or tobacco leaves (Green 1988: 594–97).

4. I have retained archaic spelling and punctuation in quotations because they are revealing and especially significant in the works of Cotton Mather. However, the titles of seventeenth- and eighteenth-century works are modernized, as they are highly variable and generally reflect decisions by the printer rather than the author. Mather published "Observable Things" in *Decennium Luctuosum* [1699], his history of King William's War, and again in his monumental providential history, *Magnalia Christi Americana* (1702). Mather ([1699] 1978) is a facsimile edition of the former; see also Lincoln (1913). Puritan providential history is discussed in Lowance (1980), Bercovitch (1972, 1978), and Murdock (1942, 1949, 1955). In addition, Clark (1979) and Daly (1977) discuss the Puritan reading of events as texts. The increasingly strident call for clerical authority among ministers of Mather's generation is discussed in Stout (1986).

5. The spiritual vulnerability and failure of the colonists was a standard theme of fast-day sermons. In "Observable Things" Mather meshed this theme with the threatening events of the war. For analyses of fast-day sermons see Miller (1953), Elliott (1975), Bercovitch (1978), and Stout (1986), who criticizes the conclusions of earlier scholars regarding fast-day and other occasional sermons on the basis of his study of unpublished regular sermons.

6. Bercovitch (1978) argues that Puritan rhetoric, including its providential mode of interpretation, has been persistently influential in the dominant American culture. On captivity as a conceptual model, see Slotkin (1973, 1987), Drinnon (1980), Jewett and Lawrence (1977, 1983, 1987), and Strong (1985).

7. John Lawrence's work in progress analyzes visual representations as, in part, do Strong (1985, 1992), Drinnon (1980), Berkhofer (1978), and Namias (1989). There remains a need for additional analysis of visual representations.

8. Bercovitch (1978) analyzes the hegemony of the Puritan elite; cf. Lears (1985), Denning (1986).

9. I use "typification" in referring to single elements in representations of captivity, e.g., the Captor, the Captive, the Redeemer. (Like White and Red, these are capitalized to indicate their nature as typifications; similarly Basso (1979) refers to "the Whiteman.") Schutz's concept extends the Weberian ideal type to lived experience. Although Schutz's use of the concept

does not highlight the structures of domination that make typifications authoritative, nor their nature as lived forms of domination and subordination, the concept is not incompatible with this Gramscian concern. It is more common to bring Gramsci into relationship with Lukács's concept of typification (R. Williams 1977: 101–3); however, I do not use it in this or in other Marxist senses. My use of "typification" is similar, rather, to Sahlins's use of 'type' and "category," as for example in his description of the Hawaiian perception of Cook's arrival: "The event thus enters culture as an instance of a received category, the worldly token of a presupposed type" (1981: 7). Going beyond Schutz (and the Puritan hermeneutics that his own language evokes), Sahlins stresses that events have their own dynamics and may transform, rather than reproduce, presupposed types. This is essential for understanding typification (and the hegemonic) as an historical process. Another analysis of European typifications of colonial Others is Strong (1986).

10. Works that have influenced my approach to the construction of Otherness include Todorov (1982), Greenblatt (1976, 1980, 1988), Boon (1982), Said (1978), Ohnuki-Tierney (1987), Babcock (1978), Bucher (1981), Fanon ([1952] 1967), Mannoni (1964), H. White (1976), Beauvoir (1953), and recent analyses of the ethnographic Other in Clifford (1988a), Clifford and Marcus (1986), Marcus and Fischer (1986), and Fabian (1983). The influence of Foucault (1965, 1979) is evident in my treatment of structures of domination.

11. R. Williams (1977: 108–14, 121–27) develops Gramsci's concept of alternative or oppositional hegemonies. These challenge the hegemonic, which itself attempts to incorporate and thus diffuse them. The complexity and dynamism of the concept 'cultural hegemony' resides in its recognition of the importance of alternative or oppositional hegemonies, as well as their dependence upon the hegemonic. Briggs (1988) analyzes the oppositional power of an extensive array of New Mexican Hispanic discourse forms; my conclusions are similar in some respects, though necessarily more speculative. I am indebted to Brackette Williams for encouraging me to clarify my use of 'alternative hegemony.'

12. Vaughan and Richter (1980: 77) refer to a convergence of practices between the two major language families in the Northeast, the Iroquoians and the Algonquians. I extend the term to include, in addition, the conjuncture of these (already complex) Native American practices with European practices.

13. Sahlins, differentiating his use of "structure of the conjuncture" from Braudel, writes that he refers not to structural relations of an intermediate duration, but to "a situational set of relations, crystallized from the operative cultural categories and actors' interests" (1985: 125n). For my purposes,

Sahlins's concept, used in combination with Gramsci, underscores the power of elites to exploit the colonial encounter and manage its interpretation—as well as certain significant limitations upon that power.

14. Slotkin (1973), Berkhofer (1978), and Kolodny (1984) have written landmark works in American Studies that deal in part with captivity among Indians. These and other students of images of Indians and the frontier have developed Pearce's (1947, [1953] 1965) pathbreaking inquiry into how an American identity has been defined through opposition to an imagined Indian. After a brief study of "authentic" captivity narratives (1947), Pearce turned his attention toward the interpretation of captivity in the classic American literature of Cooper, Hawthorne, Melville, and Thoreau ([1953] 1965). In general, literary analyses of captivity narratives provide minimal social or ethnographic contextualization. Absence of the latter is of particular concern, because inadequately contextualized scholarship on captivity tends, often unintentionally, to reproduce the hegemonic representation (Strong 1992). Levernier and Cohen's (1977: 277–78) bibliographic essay is a good introduction to literary studies of captivity; see also Vaughan and Clark (1981a), and Vaughan (1983).

15. In a series of works reaching back to Schoolcraft and Morgan, ethnologists and ethnohistorians have analyzed accounts of captivity as documents revealing ethnographic details and patterns of acculturation. A new generation of ethnohistorical research on captivity was initiated by Axtell (1975, 1981), who abstracted ethnographic details from a large and disparate group of narratives in order to analyze the attraction that Native American societies held for those assimilated captives who resisted repatriation. Vaughan and Richter's statistical analysis (1980) challenges Axtell's conclusions and is answered in Axtell (1985b). Axtell is notable for studying both Indian and European captives; see also Axtell (1988). Vaughan and Clark (1981b) and Vaughan (1983) provide bibliographies of the ethnohistorical literature on captivity.

16. See, for example, Cohn (1983, 1985, 1989), Handler (1988), Taussig (1987), Stocking (1987), Corrigan and Sayer (1985), Hobsbawm and Ranger (1983), Foucault (1979), and Greenblatt (1976). As Denning (1986) and Merrell (1989) note, American Studies and American ethnohistory respectively have generally lacked a comparative framework. But see, among others, Slotkin (1985), Rogin (1975, 1983), Takaki (1979), Denning (1987), and White (1983).

17. The best source for most of the narratives considered here is Vaughan and Clark's annotated edition (1981b), which contains an excellent introduction to the genre (Vaughan and Clark 1981a). All the narratives discussed here appear in facsimile in the extensive Garland series, valuable because it reprints

the entire work in which a narrative appears (Washburn 1977–80, vols. 1–6). For fuller bibliographic information, see Vail (1949) and Vaughan (1983).

18. "Wampanoag" is a general term used since the latter half of the seventeenth century to refer to a closely related group of Massachusett-speaking peoples who lived in a number of semiautonomous villages at the time of the first European explorations of New England. The earliest accounts refer to these people according to their individual towns or call them 'Pokanokets' after the largest and most powerful village. The Massachusett language was one of several languages of the eastern Algonquian family spoken in New England; Narragansett and Mohegan-Pequot were others. The Wampanoags may have numbered some 21,000 to 24,000 before being decimated in 1617–19 by an epidemic; altogether, the horticulturalists of southern New England probably numbered between 126,000 and 144,000 prior to the epidemic (Salisbury 1982a; Simmons 1986; Salwen 1978; Goddard 1978). Current knowledge of northeastern Algonquians is summarized in Trigger (1978b: 58–295); also see Salisbury's bibliography (1982b). Contemporary Wampanoags include the inhabitants of Mashpee, on Cape Cod, and Gay Head, on Martha's Vineyard, whose recent court battles for tribal recognition demonstrate, in a context quite removed from captivity, the hegemony of Anglo-American constructions of history and corporate identity (Clifford 1988b; Simmons 1986: 10–36, 257–70).

19. The epidemic has been pegged most recently as hepatitis (Spiess and Spiess 1987; cf. Cook 1973b, 1976), but also as typhus or bubonic plague (Crosby 1978). A smallpox epidemic further devastated the area in 1633. More general, but controversial, sources on postcontact epidemics are Crosby (1972), Dobyns (1983), and Thornton (1986).

20. My treatment of European abduction and enslavement of Indians draws upon Wood (1989), Kawashima (1989), Sturtevant and Quinn (1987), Axtell (1985a), Dickason (1984: 203–29), Kupperman (1984), Salisbury (1981, 1982), Trigger (1976, 1978b), Brasser (1971, 1978), Snell (1972), and Foreman (1943: xvii–33). Lauber (1913) remains an essential source. See Strong (1992) for an expanded treatment of Indian captives including Frobisher's Inuits, Tisquantum, and Pocahontas.

21. Trigger (1978a) summarizes the similarities and differences between Iroquoians and Algonquians in the Northeast. The most important members of the Iroquoian language family in the northeast were the Five Nations (Mohawks, Oneidas, Onondagas, Cayugas, Senecas) who controlled the main route westward across the Appalachians to the St. Lawrence River, and the Hurons and their Iroquoian neighbors on the Great Lakes (destroyed by the Five Nations in the 1640s and early 1650s). Together, these horticulturalists

may have numbered some 60,000, extrapolating from Trigger (1985). The Tuscaroras became the sixth nation of the Iroquois League in the 1720s. The literature on the northeastern Iroquoians is voluminous; good general accounts are found in Trigger (1978b: 296–546); see especially Fenton (1978) and Tooker (1978).

22. Significant works include Richter (1983), Abler and Logan (1988), Abler (1980), Richter and Merrell (1987), Fenton (1978, 1985), Trigger (1976, 1985), Jennings (1984), Jennings et al. (1985), Goddard (1984), Axtell (1975, 1981), Tooker (1978), Wallace (1969), Snyderman (1948), and Beauchamp ([1907] 1975).

23. Abler and Logan (1988) show that the intensity of warfare and of ritual cannibalism, in particular, also varied in prehistoric Iroquoia, increasing with the depletion of deer that followed the development of horticulture and nucleated settlements.

24. As Jean Comaroff has pointed out to me, this dichotomous characterization of captivity practices as ceremonial vs. instrumental is too sharp, and is conditioned by what Europeans perceive as instrumental (practically effective) and ceremonial (symbolically effective). Replenishing population and spiritual power had instrumental value for Iroquoians, while ransom payments of wampum had ceremonial value for Algonquians. Nevertheless, captivity practices appear to have been much more highly ritualized among Iroquoians than among Algonquians. Treatments of warfare and captivity among Algonquians or in the Northeast more generally include Salisbury (1982a, 1987), Richter (1983), Axtell (1981), Axtell and Sturtevant (1980), Vaughan and Richter (1980), Brasser (1971, 1978), Smith (1951), Knowles (1940), and Flannery (1939).

25. As Salisbury (1987) has emphasized, the subsequent commercialization of wampum, formerly a marker of spiritual and social prestige (Miller and Hammell 1986; Hammell 1987), had a profound impact upon indigenous cultures in the northeast. This would include captivity practices, an issue I am not able to explore here.

26. On the Pocahontas image, see Washburn (1988: 522–616, passim), Feest (1987a), Dearborn (1986), Kupperman (1980), Green (1975), Barnett (1975), VanDerBeets (1973), Barbour (1970), Fiedler (1969), Young (1962), Hubbell (1957), and Rourke (1942). Barbour 1970 is the best biography of Pocahontas; also see Mossiker (1976).

27. While a few Indians were enslaved in the seventeenth century for theft, the Pequot War represents New England's first entry into extensive Indian slavery. For the figure of fifteen hundred, see Cook (1973a); however, only some four hundred appear in the documents. See also Jennings

(1975, 1988), Axtell (1975, 1985a), Salisbury (1982a), Vaughan (1979), Koehler (1979), Leach (1958, 1966), Lauber (1913), Washburn (1978), and Peckham (1964).

28. Vaughan (1979) and Jennings (1975) are divergent interpretations of King Philip's War. Also see Cook (1973a), Washburn (1978), and Leach (1958). Slotkin and Folsom (1978) reprint and discuss various accounts of the war, including Mary Rowlandson's and Increase Mather's. On praying Indians in the war, see Gookin (1836) and Johnson (1977). More general sources on praying Indians include Simmons (1979), Ronda (1977), and Salisbury (1974); also see Ronda and Axtell (1978). Strong (1985, 1992) offers more extensive treatments of King Philip's War, its aftermath, and Mary Rowlandson's captivity.

29. A more spontaneous incident of torture is recorded a year after the war on the still conflict-ridden Maine frontier, where two sachems taken captive while attacking a ship were stoned to death and then torn to pieces by the women of Marblehead (Axtell 1974: 647–52; 1981: 312). Jennings (1975: 146–70) compares public brutality among Indians and Europeans; see also Axtell (1981: 16–35, 207–41), Axtell and Sturtevant (1980), and, for a powerful account of drawing and quartering in France, Foucault (1979). On Indian slavery and indenture after King Philip's War, see Koehler (1979), Sainsbury (1975), and Kawashima (1969).

30. Rowlandson ([1682] 1977) is a facsimile of the third (London) edition, complete with preface and sermon. Slotkin and Folsom (1978: 301–69) and Vaughan and Clark (1981b: 29–75) reprint, with commentary, the second (Cambridge) edition, which omits the sermon. On the popularity of captivity narratives, see Mott (1947). Quotes are taken from Vaughan and Clark (1981b), with the exception of the preface and sermon. On spiritual autobiographies, see Hambrick-Stowe (1982), Shea (1968), and Watkins (1972). On fast-day sermons and histories of the period, see Stout (1986), Slotkin and Folsom (1978), Slotkin (1973), and Orians (1970). Grumet (1980) is a largely accurate account of squaw sachems, but for more recent developments, see Strong (1985, 1992). With regard to Wetamo, see also Lurie (1985). This analysis was written before the appearance of Breitwieser (1990). Rowlandson and many scholars use "Weetamoo," but the numerous seventeenth-century variants of her name suggest that "Wetamo" is a more accurate transcription (Strong 1992).

31. Congruences between Puritan imagery of the ideal woman and the regenerate sinner are discussed in Masson (1976), Dunn (1980), Moran (1980), and Ulrich (1980, 1982).

32. In Europe, these conflicts were known as the War of the League of

Augsburg, which ended in 1697 with the Peace of Ryswick, and the War of the Spanish Succession, which ended in 1713 with the Treaty of Utrecht. Vaughan and Richter (1980) contains statistical data on captivity during these wars.

33. Orians (1970) reprints "Humiliations" with commentary. Vaughan and Clark (1981b: 147–57) includes an annotated version of the Swarton narrative.

34. The Dustan narrative is reprinted with annotations in Vaughan and Clark (1981b: 161–64). For reprints of the entire jeremiad, see Mather ([1697] 1977) and Orians (1970). For the reference to Jael, and a perceptive treatment of Dustan and other female captives, see Ulrich (1982: 167–235). Vaughan and Clark (1981a), Lowance (1980), Minter (1973), and Bercovitch (1972) discuss the Puritan use of Biblical types (such as Jael). Thoreau and Hawthorne both wrote revisions of the Dustan story; see Fiedler (1969) and Ulrich (1982).

35. Williams ([1707] 1978) reprints, in facsimile, editions published in 1707 (the first), 1758 (the third) and 1853. Williams ([1707] 1976), an annotated edition, is reprinted in Vaughan and Clark (1981b). See also Melvoin (1989), Gherman (1975), Medlicott (1965).

36. Bakhtin (1984) is an introduction to the theory of dialogism. For an application of Bakhtin to Mayan and Hispanic discourse, respectively, see Hanks (1986) and Briggs (1989).

37. Dickinson ([1699] 1961) is a scholarly version with extensive annotations; Dickinson ([1699] 1977) is a facsimile of the first edition. For analyses of European representations of cannibalism in the New World, see White (1976), Greenblatt (1976), Sturtevant (1976), Bucher (1981). Arens (1979) is disputed on ethnographic grounds by Abler (1980) among others.

38. Hanson ([1728] 1977) reprints, in facsimile, the American (1728) and English (1760) editions. The latter is reprinted and annotated in Vaughan and Clark (1981b: 227–44).

39. Gyles ([1736] 1977) is a facsimile. Vaughan and Clark (1981: 91–131) is an annotated version of the majority of the text.

40. Historical surveys of the captivity tradition include Pearce (1947, [1953] 1965), Levernier and Cohen (1977), Washburn (1983), Barnett (1975), and VanDerBeets (1971, 1972a, 1972b), all of which are reprinted in VanDerBeets (1984).

REFERENCES

Abler, Thomas S. 1980. "Iroquois Cannibalism: Fact not Fiction." *Ethnohistory* 27:309–16.

Abler, Thomas S., and Michael H. Logan. 1988. "The Florescence and Demise of Iroquoian Cannibalism: Human Sacrifice and Malinowski's Hypothesis." *Man in the Northeast* 35:1–26.

Arens, W. 1979. *The Man-Eating Myth.* New York and Oxford: Oxford University Press.

Axtell, James. 1974. "The Vengeful Women of Marblehead: Robert Roules's Desposition of 1677." *William and Mary Quarterly*, 3d ser., 31:647–52.

———. 1975. "The White Indians of Colonial America." *William and Mary Quarterly*, 3rd ser., 32:55–88. Reprinted in Axtell, *The European and the Indian; The Invasion Within.*

———. 1981. *The European and the Indian: Essays in the Ethnohistory of Colonial North America.* Oxford: Oxford University Press.

———. 1985a. *The Invasion Within: The Contest of Cultures in Colonial North America.* New York and Oxford: Oxford University Press.

———. 1985b. "The English Apostates." In Axtell, *The Invasion Within.*

———. 1988. *After Columbus: Essays in the Ethnohistory of Colonial North America.* New York and Oxford: Oxford University Press.

Axtell, James, and William C. Sturtevant. 1980. "The Unkindest Cut, or, Who Invented Scalping." *William and Mary Quarterly*, 3d ser., 37:451–72. Reprinted in Axtell, *The European and the Indian.*

Babcock, Barbara, ed. 1978. *The Reversible World.* Ithaca: Cornell University Press.

Bakhtin, Mikhail. 1984. *The Dialogical Principle.* Ed. Tzvetan Todorov. Trans. Wlad Godzich. Minneapolis: University of Minnesota Press.

Barbour, Phillip L. 1964. *The Three Worlds of Captain John Smith.* Boston: Houghton Mifflin.

———. 1970. *Pocahontas and Her World.* Boston: Houghton Mifflin.

Barbour, Phillip L., ed. 1986. *The Complete Works of Captain John Smith (1580–1631).* 3 vols. Chapel Hill: University of North Carolina Press.

Barnett, Louise K. 1975. *The Ignoble Savage: American Literary Racism, 1790–1890.* Westport, Conn.: Greenwood.

Barreiro, Jose, ed. 1988. *Indian Roots of American Democracy.* Ithaca, N.Y.: Northeast Indian Quarterly.

Basso, Keith H. 1979. *Portraits of "The Whiteman."* Cambridge: Cambridge University Press.

Beauchamp, William M. [1907] 1975. *Civil, Religious, and Mourning Councils and Ceremonies of Adoption of the New York Indians.* Rpt., Bulletin 113, New York State Museum. Albany: State Education Department, University of the State of New York.

Beauvoir, Simone de. 1953. *The Second Sex.* Ed. and trans. by H. M. Parshley. New York: Alfred A. Knopf.

Bercovitch, Sacvan. 1978. *The American Jeremiad.* Madison: University of Wisconsin Press.

Bercovitch, Sacvan, ed. 1972. *Typology and Early American Literature.* Amherst: University of Massachusetts Press.

Berkhofer, Robert F., Jr. 1978. *The White Man's Indian: Images of the American Indian from Columbus to the Present.* New York: Alfred A. Knopf.

———. 1988. "White Conceptions of Indians." In *History of Indian-White Relations*, ed. W. Washburn. Vol. 4, *Handbook of North American Indians.*

Boon, James A. 1982. *Other Tribes, Other Scribes: Symbolic Anthropology in the Comparative Study of Cultures, Histories, Religions, and Texts.* Cambridge: Cambridge University Press.

Brandon, William. 1986. *New Worlds for Old: Reports from the New World and their Effect on the Development of Social Thought in Europe, 1500–1800.* Athens and London: Ohio University Press.

Brasser, T.J.C. 1971. "The Coastal Algonkians: People of the First Frontiers." In *North American Indians in Historical Perspective*, eds. Eleanor Burke Leacock and Nancy Oestereich Lurie. New York: Random House.

———. 1978. "Early Indian-European Contacts." In *Northeast*, ed. B. Trigger. Vol. 15, *Handbook of North American Indians.*

Breitwieser, Mitchell R. 1990. *American Puritanism and the Defense of Mourning: Religion, Grief and Ethnology in Mary Rowlandson's Captivity Narrative.* Madison: University of Wisconsin Press.

Briggs, Charles L. 1988. *Competence in Performance: The Creativity of Tradition in Mexicano Verbal Art.* Philadelphia: University of Pennsylvania Press.

Bucher, Bernadette. 1981. *Icon and Conquest: A Structural Analysis of the Illustrations of de Bry's Great Voyages.* Trans. Basia Miller Gulati. Chicago and London: University of Chicago Press.

Ceci, Lynn. 1975. "Fish Fertilizer: A Native North American Practice?" *Science* 188 (April): 26–30.

———. 1990. "Squanto and the Pilgrims: On Planting Corn 'in the manner of the Indians'." In *The Invented Indian*, ed. J. Clifton.

Chiapelli, Fredi, Michael J. B. Allen, and Robert L. Benson, eds. 1976. *First Images of America*. 2 vols. Berkeley: University of California Press.

Churchill, Ward. 1988. "Sam Gill's *Mother Earth*: Colonialism, Genocide and the Expropriation of Indigenous Spiritual Tradition in Contemporary Academia." *American Indian Culture and Research Journal* 12(3): 49–67.

Clark, Michael. 1979. "The Crucified Phrase: Sign and Desire in Puritan Semiology." *Early American Literature* 13:278–93.

Clifford, James. 1988a. *The Predicament of Culture: Twentieth-Century Ethnography, Literature and Art*. Cambridge and London: Harvard University Press.

———. 1988b. "Identity in Mashpee." In Clifford, *The Predicament of Culture*.

Clifford, James, and George F. Marcus, eds. 1986. *Writing Culture: The Poetics and Politics of Ethnography*. Berkeley: University of California Press.

Clifton, James A. 1990. *The Invented Indian: Cultural Fictions and Government Policies*. New Brunswick, N.J.: Transaction Publishers.

Cohn, Bernard. 1983. "Representing Authority in Victorian India." In *The Invention of Tradition*, eds. E. Hobsbawm and T. Ranger.

———. 1985. "The Command of Language and the Language of Command." In *Subaltern Studies*, ed. Ranajit Guha. Vol. 4. Delhi: Oxford University Press.

———. 1989. "Law and the Colonial State." In *History and Power in the Study of Law*, eds. June Starr and Jane Collier, Ithaca, N.Y.: Cornell University Press.

Cook, Sherburne F. 1973a. "Interracial Warfare and Population Decline among the New England Indians." *Ethnohistory* 20:1–24.

———. 1973b. "The Significance of Disease in the Extinction of the New England Indians." *Human Biology* 45:485–508.

———. 1976. *The Indian Population of New England in the Seventeenth Century*. Vol. 12, University of California Publications in Anthropology. Berkeley: University of California Press.

Corrigan, Philip, and Derek Sayer. 1985. *The Great Arch: English State Formation as Cultural Revolution*. Oxford: Basil Blackwell.

Crosby, Alfred W. 1972. *The Columbian Exchange: Biological and Cultural Consequences of 1492*. Westport, Conn.: Greenwood Press.

———. 1978. "God . . . Would Destroy Them, and Give Their Country to Another People . . ." *American Heritage* 29(6):38–43.

Daly, Robert. 1977. "Puritan Poetics: The World, The Flesh, and God." *Early American Literature* 12:136–62.

Dearborn, Mary V. 1986. *Pocahontas's Daughters: Gender and Ethnicity in American Culture*. New York: Oxford University Press.

Denning, Michael. 1986. "The Special American Conditions: Marxism and American Studies." *American Quarterly* 38:356–80.

———. 1987. *Mechanic Accents: Dime Novels and Working-Class Culture in America*. London and New York: Verso.

Dickason, Olive Patricia. 1984. *The Myth of The Savage, and The Beginnings of French Colonialism in The Americas*. Alberta: University of Alberta Press.

Dickinson, Jonathan. [1699] 1961. *Jonathan Dickinson's Journal; or God's Protecting Providence. . . .* In *Narratives of North American Indian Captives*, eds. Evangeline Walker Andrews and Charles McLean Andrews. New Haven: Yale University Press.

———. [1699] 1977. *God's Protecting Providence Man's Surest Help and Defense . . . Evidenced in the Remarkable Deliverance of Divers Persons, from the Devouring Waves of the Sea . . . and also from the more Cruelly Devouring Jaws of the Inhumane Cannibals of Florida . . .* , ed. W. Washburn. Vol. 4.

Dobyns, Henry. 1983. *Their Number Became Thinned: Essays on Native American Population Dynamics in Eastern North America*. Knoxville: University of Tennessee Press.

Drinnon, Richard. 1980. *Facing West: The Metaphysics of Indian-hating and Empire Building*. Minneapolis: University of Minnesota Press.

Dunn, Mary Maples. 1980. "Saints and Sinners: Congregational and Quaker Women in the Early Colonial Period." In *Women in American Religion*, ed. J. James.

Elliot, Emory. 1975. *Power and the Pulpit in Puritan New England*. Princeton, N.J.: Princeton University Press.

Fabian, Johannes. 1983. *Time and the Other: How Anthropology Makes Its Object*. New York: Columbia University Press.

Fanon, Frantz. [1952] 1967. *Black Skin, White Masks*. Trans. Charles Lam Markmann. New York: Grove Press.

Feest, Christian F. 1987a. "Pride and Prejudice: The Pocahontas Myth and the Pamunkey." *European Review of Native American Studies*. 1(1):5–12. Reprinted in *The Invented Indian*, ed. J. Clifton.

Feest, Christian F., ed. 1987b. *Indians and Europe*. Aachen: Ed. Herodot, Rader-Verl.

Fenton, William N. 1978. "Northern Iroquoian Culture Patterns." In *Northeast*, ed. B. Trigger. Vol. 15, *Handbook of North American Indians*.

———. 1985. "Structure, Continuity, and Change in the Process of Iroquois Treaty Making." In *The History and Culture of Iroquois Diplomacy*, eds. Jennings et al.

Fiedler, Leslie A. 1969. *The Return of The Vanishing American*. New York: Stein and Day.

Flannery, Regina. 1939. *An Analysis of Coastal Algonquian Culture*. Catholic University of America, Anthropological Series, vol. 7.

Fogelson, Raymond D. 1985. "Interpretations of the American Indian Psyche: Some Historical Notes." In *Social Contexts of American Ethnology, 1840–1984*, ed. June Helm. *Proceedings of the American Ethnological Society–1984*. Washington, D.C.: American Anthropological Association.

Foreman, Carolyn Thomas. 1943. *Indians Abroad, 1493–1938*. Norman: University of Oklahoma Press.

Foucault, Michel. 1965. *Madness and Civilization: A History of Insanity in The Age of Reason*. New York: Random House.

———. 1979. *Discipline and Punish: The Birth of The Prison*. Trans. Alan Sheridan. New York: Random House.

Gherman, Dawn Lander. 1975. "From Parlour to Tepee: The White Squaw on the American Frontier." Ph.D. diss., University of Massachusetts.

Gill, Sam. 1987. *Mother Earth*. Chicago: University of Chicago Press.

———. 1988. "The Power Story." *American Indian Culture and Research Journal* 12(3):69–84.

———. 1990. "Mother Earth: An American Myth." In *The Invented Indian*, ed. J. Clifton.

Goddard, Ives. 1978. "Eastern Algonquian Languages." In *Northeast*, ed. B. Trigger. Vol. 15, *Handbook of North American Indians*.

———. 1984. "Agreskwe, a Northern Iroquoian Deity." In *Extending the Rafters: Interdisciplinary Approaches to Iroquoian Studies*, eds. Michael K. Foster, Jack Campisi, Marianne Mithun. Albany: State University of New York Press.

Gookin, Daniel. 1836. "Historical Account of the Doings and Sufferings of the Christian Indians in New England, in the Years 1675, 1676, 1677." *Transactions and Collections of the American Antiquarian Society [Archaeologia Americana]* 2:423–534. 1972. Reprint. New York: Arno.

Gramsci, Antonio. 1972. *Selections from the Prison Notebooks*, eds. Quintin Hoare and Geoffrey Nowell Smith. New York: International Publishers.

Green, Rayna. 1975. "The Pocahontas Perplex: The Image of Indian Women in American Culture." *Massachusetts Review* 16:698–714.

———. 1988. "The Indian in Popular American Culture." In *History of Indian-White Relations*, ed. W. Washburn. Vol. 4, *Handbook of North American Indians*.

Greenblatt, Stephen J. 1976. "Learning to Curse: Aspects of Linguistic Colonialism in the Sixteenth Century." In *First Images of America*, ed. F. Chiapelli et al.

———. 1980. *Renaissance Self-Fashioning: From More to Shakespeare*. Chicago: University of Chicago Press.

———. 1988. *Shakespearean Negotiations*. Berkeley and Los Angeles: University of California Press.

Grumet, Robert. 1980. "Sunksquaws, Shamans, and Tradeswomen: Middle Atlantic Coastal Algonkian Women During the 17th and 18th Centuries." In *Women and Colonization: Anthropological Perspectives*, eds. Mona Etienne and Eleanor Leacock. New York: Praeger Scientific.

Gyles, John. [1736] 1977. *Memoirs of Odd Adventures, Strange Deliverances, etc. in the Captivity of John Gyles, Esq.: Commander of the Garrison on St. George's River*. In *Narratives of North American Indian Captivities*, ed. W. Washburn. Vol. 6.

———. [1736] 1981. *Memoirs of Odd Adventures . . ..* In *Puritans among the Indians*, eds. A. Vaughan and E. Clark.

Hallowell, A. Irving. 1957a. "The Impact of the American Indian on American Culture." *American Anthropologist* n.s. 59:201–17.

———. 1957b. "The Backwash of the Frontier: The Impact of the Indian in American Culture." In *The Frontier in Perspective*, eds. Walker D. Wyman and Clifton B. Kroeber. Madison: University of Wisconsin Press.

Hambrick-Stowe, Charles E. 1982. *The Practice of Piety: Puritan Devotional Disciplines in Seventeenth-Century New England*. Chapel Hill: University of North Carolina Press.

Hammell, George R. 1987. "Mythical Realities and European Contact in the Northeast During the Sixteenth and Seventeenth Centuries." *Man in the Northeast* 33:63–87.

Handler, Richard. 1988. *Nationalism and the Politics of Culture in Quebec*. Madison: University of Wisconsin Press.

Hanks, William. 1986. "Authenticity and Ambivalence in the Text: A Colonial Maya Case." *American Ethnologist* 13:722–44.

Hanson, Elizabeth. [1728] 1977. *God's Mercy Surmounting Man's Cruelty, ex-*

emplified in the Captivity and Redemption of Elizabeth Hanson . . . . In Narratives of North American Indian Captivities, ed. W. Washburn. Vol. 6.

———. [1728] 1981. *God's Mercy Surmounting Man's Cruelty. In Puritans Among the Indians*, eds. A. Vaughan and E. Clark.

Hirsch, Eric Donald, Jr. 1987. *Cultural Literacy: What Every American Needs to Know.* Boston: Houghton Mifflin Co.

Hobsbawm, Eric, and Terence Ranger, eds. 1983. *The Invention of Tradition.* Cambridge: Cambridge University Press.

Honour, Hugh. 1975. *The New Golden Land: European Images of America from the Discoveries to the Present Time.* New York: Pantheon Books.

Hubbell, Jay B. 1957. "The Smith-Pocahontas Story in Literature." *Virginia Magazine of History and Biography* 65:275–300.

Humins, John H. 1987. "Squanto and Massasoit: Struggle for Power." *New England Quarterly* 60:54–70.

Jaimes, M. Annette. 1988. "On 'Mother Earth': An Interview with Russell Means." *The Bloomsbury Review* (Sept/Oct).

James, Janet Wilson, ed. 1980. *Women in American Religion.* Philadelphia: University of Pennsylvania Press.

Jennings, Francis. 1975. *The Invasion of America: Colonialism and The Cant of Conquest.* New York: W. W. Norton and Co.

———. 1984. *The Ambiguous Iroquois Empire: The Covenant Chain Confederation of Indian Tribes with English Colonies from Its Beginnings to the Lancaster Treaty of 1744.* New York and London: W. W. Norton and Co.

———. 1988. *Empire of Fortune: Crowns, Colonies and Tribes in The Seven Years War in America.* New York: W. W. Norton and Co.

Jennings, Francis, William N. Fenton, Mary A. Druke, and David R. Miller, eds. 1985. *The History and Culture of Iroquois Diplomacy: An Interdisciplinary Guide to the Treaties of The Six Nations and Their League.* Syracuse, N.Y.: Syracuse University Press.

Jewett, Robert, and John Shelton Lawrence. 1977. *The American Monomyth.* New York: Anchor Press/Doubleday.

———. 1983. "American Assassins and Mass Murderers: Saints for a Civil Religion of Death." *Mission Journal* (August):1–8.

———. 1987. "Rambo and the Myth of Redemption." Transforming Texts lecture series, Bucknell University.

Johnson, Richard R. 1977. "The Search for a Usable Indian: An Aspect of the Defense of Colonial New England." *Journal of American History* 64:623–51.

Kawashima, Yasuhide. 1969. "Legal Origins of the Indian Reservation in Colonial Massachusetts." *American Journal of Legal History* 13:42–56.

———. 1989. "Indian Servitude in the Northeast." In *History of Indian-White Relations*, ed. W. Washburn. Vol. 4, *Handbook of North American Indians*.

Knowles, Nathaniel. 1940. "The Torture of Captives by Indians of Eastern North America." *Proceedings of the American Philosophical Society* 82:151–225.

Koehler, Lyle. 1979. "Red-White Power Relations and Justice in The Courts of Seventeenth-Century New England." *American Indian Culture and Research Journal* 3:1–31.

———. 1980. *A Search for Power: The "Weaker Sex" in Seventeenth-Century New England*. Urbana: University of Illinois Press.

Kolodny, Annette. 1984. *The Land Before Her: Fantasy and Experience of the American Frontiers, 1630–1860*. Chapel Hill: University of North Carolina Press.

Kupperman, Karen Ordahl. 1980. *Settling with The Indians: The Meeting of English and Indian Cultures in America, 1580–1649*. Totowa, N.J.: Rowman & Littlefield.

———. 1984. *Roanoke: The Abandoned Colony*. Totowa, N.J.: Rowman and Allanheld.

Lauber, Almon Wheeler, 1913. "Indian Slavery in Colonial Times within The Present Limits of the United States." *Columbia University Studies in History, Economics, and Public Law* 54:253–604. 1970. Reprint. Williamstown, Mass.: Corner House.

Leach, Douglas E. 1958. *Flintlock and Tomahawk: New England in King Philip's War*. New York: Macmillan.

———. 1966. *The Northern Colonial Frontier, 1607–1763*. New York: Holt, Rinehart and Winston.

Lears, T. J. Jackson. 1985. "The Concept of Cultural Hegemony: Problems and Possibilities." *American Historical Review* 90:567–93.

Levernier, James A., and Hennig Cohen, eds. 1977. *The Indians and their Captives*. Westport, Conn.: Greenwood.

Lincoln, Charles H. 1913. *Narratives of The Indian Wars, 1675–1699*. New York: Charles Scribner's Sons. 1966. Reprint. New York: Barnes and Noble.

Lowance, Mason I., Jr. 1980. *The Language of Canaan: Metaphor and Symbol in New England from The Puritans to The Transcendentalists*. Cambridge: Harvard University Press.

Lurie, Nancy Oestreich. 1985. *North American Indian Lives*. Milwaukee: Milwaukee Public Museum.

Mannoni, O. 1964. *Prospero and Caliban: The Psychology of Colonization*. Trans. Pamela Powers. New York: Praeger.

Marcus, George, and M. Fisher. 1986. *Anthropology as Cultural Critique: An Experimental Frontier in the Human Sciences*. Chicago: University of Chicago Press.

Mariani, Giorgio. 1987. "Was Anybody More of an Indian than Karl Marx?: The 'Indiani Metropolitani' and the 1977 Movement." In *Indians and Europe*, ed. C. Feest.

Masson, Margaret W. 1976. "The Typology of The Female as a Model for The Regenerate: Puritan Preaching, 1690–1730." *Signs* 2:304–15.

Mather, Cotton. 1702. *Magnalia Christi Americana: or, The Ecclesiastical History of New-England. . . .* 7 vols. London: Thomas Parkhurst. 1977. Annotated edition, vols. 1–2, ed. Kenneth B. Murdock.

———. [1697] 1977. *Humiliations Follow'd with Deliverances . . . Accompanied and Accommodated with a Narrative, of a Notable Deliverance Lately Received by some English Captive, from the Hands of Cruel Indians . . . .* In *Narratives of North American Indian Captivities*, ed. W. Washburn. Vol. 1.

———. [1699] 1978. *Decennium Luctuosum*. In *Narratives of North American Indian Captivities*, ed. W. Washburn. Vol. 3.

Mather, Increase. [1684] 1977. *An Essay for the Recording of Illustrious Providences*. In *Narratives of North American Indian Captivities*, ed. W. Washburn. Vol. 2.

———. [1676] 1978. *A Brief History of the War with the Indians in New England*. In *So Dreadfull a Judgment*, eds. R. Slotkin and J. Folsom.

Medlicott, Alexander, Jr. 1965. "Return to The Land of Light: A Plea to an Unredeemed Captive." *New England Quarterly* 38:202–16.

Melvoin, Richard. 1989. *New England Outpost: War and Society in Colonial Deerfield*. New York: W. W. Norton and Co.

Merrell, James. 1989. "Some Thoughts on Colonial Historians and American Indians." *William and Mary Quarterly*, 3d ser., 46:94–119.

Miller, Christopher L., and George R. Hammell. 1986. "A New Perspective on Indian-White Contact: Cultural Symbols and Colonial Trade." *Journal of American History* 73:311–28.

Miller, Perry. 1953. *The New England Mind: From Colony to Province*. Cambridge: Harvard University Press.

Minter, David L. 1973. "By Dens of Lions: Notes on Stylization in Early Puritan Captivity Narratives." *American Literature* 45:335–47.

Moran, Gerald F. 1980. "'Sisters' in Christ: Women and The Church in

Seventeenth-Century New England." In *Women in American Religion*, ed. J. James.

Morgan, Edmund S. 1966. *The Puritan Family: Religion and Domestic Relations in Seventeenth-Century New England*. Revised ed. New York: Harper & Row Publishers.

Morrison, Kenneth M. 1979. "Towards a History of Intimate Encounters: Algonkian Folklore, Jesuit Missionaries, and Kiwakwe, the Cannibal Giant." *American Indian Culture and Research Journal* 3(4):51–80.

Mossiker, Frances. 1976. *Pocahontas: The Life and the Legend*. New York: Alfred A. Knopf.

Mott, Frank Luther. 1947. *Golden Multitudes: The Story of Best Sellers in The United States*. New York: Macmillan Publishing Company.

Mullaney, Stephen. 1983. "Strange Things, Gross Terms, Curious Customs: The Rehearsal of Cultures in The Late Renaissance." *Representations* 3:40–67.

Murdock, Kenneth B. 1942. "William Hubbard and The Providential Interpretation of History." *Proceedings of the American Antiquarian Society* 52:15–37.

———. 1949. *Literature and Theology in Colonial New England*. Cambridge: Harvard University Press.

———. 1955. "Clio in The Wilderness: History and Biography in Puritan New England." *New England Quarterly* 34:221–38.

Namias, June. 1989. "White Captives: Gender and Ethnicity on Successive American Frontiers, 1697–1862." Ph.D. diss., Brandeis University.

Ohnuki-Tierney, Emiko. 1987. *The Monkey as Mirror*. Princeton: Princeton University Press.

Orians, George Harrison, ed. 1970. *Days of Humiliation, Times of Affliction and Disaster: Nine Sermons for Restoring Favor with an Angry God, 1696–1762*. Gainesville, Fla.: Scholar's Facsimile and Reprints.

Pearce, Roy Harvey. 1947. "The Significances of The Captivity Narratives." *American Literature* 19:1–20.

———. [1953] 1965. *Savagism and Civilization: A Study of the Indian and the American Mind*. Revised ed. of *The Savages of America*. Baltimore and London: Johns Hopkins Press.

Peckham, Howard Henry. 1964. *The Colonial Wars, 1689–1762*. Chicago: University of Chicago Press.

Richter, Daniel K. 1983. "War and Culture: The Iroquois Experience." *William and Mary Quarterly*, 3d. ser., 40:528–59.

Richter, Daniel K., and James Merrell. 1987. *Beyond the Covenant Chain: The Iroquois and Their Neighbors in Indian North America, 1600–1800*. Syracuse: Syracuse University Press.

Rogin, Michael. 1975. *Fathers and Children: Andrew Jackson and the Subjugation of the Indians*. New York: Alfred A. Knopf.

———. 1983. *Subversive Genealogies: The Politics and Art of Herman Melville*. New York: Alfred A. Knopf.

Ronda, James P. 1977. "'We Are Well As We Are': An Indian Critique of Seventeenth-Century Christian Missions." *William and Mary Quarterly*, 3d ser., 34:66–82.

Ronda, James P., and James Axtell. 1978. *Indian Missions: A Critical Bibliography*. Bibliographical series, The Newberry Library Center for the History of the American Indian. Bloomington: Indiana University Press.

Rourke, Constance. 1942. *The Roots of American Culture and Other Essays*, ed. Van Wyck Brooks. New York: Harcourt, Brace, and World.

Rowlandson, Mary. [1682] 1913. *The Sovereignty and Goodness of God, together, with the Faithfulness of His Promises Displayed; Being a Narrative of the Captivity and Restoration of Mrs. Mary Rowlandson*. In *Narratives of The Indian Wars*, ed. C. Lincoln.

———. [1682] 1977. *The Sovereignty and Goodness of God. . . .* In *Narratives of North American Indian Captivities*, ed. W. Washburn. Vol. 1.

———. [1682] 1978. *The Sovereignty and Goodness of God. . . .* In *So Dreadfull a Judgment*, eds. R. Slotkin and J. Folsom.

———. [1682] 1981. *The Sovereignty and Goodness of God. . . .* In *Puritans among the Indians*, eds. A. Vaughan and E. Clark.

Sahlins, Marshall. 1981. *Historical Metaphors and Mythical Realities*. Ann Arbor: University of Michigan Press.

———. 1985. *Islands of History*. Chicago: University of Chicago Press.

Said, Edward W. 1978. *Orientalism*. New York: Random House.

Sainsbury, John A. 1975. "Indian Labor in Early Rhode Island." *New England Quarterly* 48:378–93.

Salisbury, Neal. 1974. "Red Puritans: The 'Praying Indians' of Massachusetts Bay and John Eliot." *William and Mary Quarterly*, 3d sers., 31:27–54.

———. 1981. "Squanto: Last of the Patuxets." In *Struggle and Survival in Colonial America*, eds. David G. Sweet and Gary B. Nash. Berkeley: University of California Press.

———. 1982a. *Manitou and Providence: Indians, Europeans, and The Making of New England, 1500–1643*. Oxford: Oxford University Press.

————. 1982b. *The Indians of New England: A Critical Bibliography*. Bibliographical series, The Newberry Library Center for the History of the American Indian. Bloomington: Indiana University Press.

————. 1987. "Social Relationships on a Moving Frontier: Natives and Settlers in Southern New England, 1638–1675." *Man in the Northeast* 33:89–99.

Salwen, Bert. 1978. "Indians of Southern New England and Long Island: Early Period." In *Northeast*, ed. B. Trigger. Vol. 15, *Handbook of North American Indians*.

Sanders, Ronald. 1978. *Lost Tribes and Promised Lands: The Origins of American Racism*. Boston: Little, Brown.

Schutz, Alfred. 1964–73. *Collected Papers*. Gen. Ed. Maurice Natanson. Vol. 1, *The Problem of Social Reality*, 4th ed., ed. Maurie Natanson. Vol. 2, *Studies in Social Theory*, ed. Arvid Brodelsen. The Hague: M. Nihoff.

Seaver, James Everett. 1824. *A Narrative of the Life of Mrs. Mary Jemison*. Canandaigua, New York.

Shea, Daniel. 1968. *Spiritual Autobiography in Early America*. Princeton: Princeton University Press.

Silverman, Kenneth. 1984. *The Life and Times of Cotton Mather*. New York: Harper & Row Publishers.

Simmons, William S. 1979. "Conversion from Indian to Puritan." *New England Quarterly* 52:197–218.

————. 1986. *Spirit of The New England Tribes: Indian History and Folklore, 1620–1984*. Hanover and London: University Press of New England.

Slotkin, Richard. 1973. *Regeneration through Violence: The Mythology of the American Frontier, 1600–1800*. Middletown, Conn.: Wesleyan University Press.

————. 1985. *The Fatal Environment: The Myth of the Frontier in the Age of Industrialization, 1800–1890*. New York: Atheneum.

————. 1987. "The Iran Arms Scandal, says a historian, shows how the power of myth can cloud a President's mind." Interview with Richard Slotkin. *People* 27:97–98 (January 19).

Slotkin, Richard, and James K. Folsom, eds. 1978. *So Dreadfull a Judgment: Puritan Responses to King Philip's War, 1676–1677*. Middletown, Conn.: Wesleyan University Press.

Smith, Marian W. 1951. "American Indian Warfare." *Transactions of the New York Academy of Science*. 2d ser., 12:348–65.

Snell, William Robert. 1972. "Indian Slavery in Colonial South Carolina, 1671–1795." Ph.D. diss., University of Alabama.

Snyderman, George S. 1948. "Behind the Tree of Peace: A Sociological Analysis of Iroquois Warfare." *Pennsylvania Archaeologist* 18(3–4):3–93.

Spiess, Arthur E., and Bruce D. Spiess. 1987. "New England Pandemic of 1616–1622: Causes and Archaeological Implication." *Man in the Northeast* 34:71–83.

Stocking, George W., Jr. 1987. *Victorian Anthropology.* New York: The Free Press.

Stout, Harry S. 1986. *The New England Soul: Preaching and Religious Culture in Colonial New England.* New York and Oxford: Oxford University Press.

Strong, Pauline Turner. 1985. "Captive Images." *Natural History* 94(12):50–57.

———. 1986. "Fathoming the Primitive: Australian Aborigines in Four Explorers' Journals, 1697–1845." *Ethnohistory* 33:175–94.

———. 1992. "Captive Selves, Captivating Others: The Practice and Representation of Captivity across the British-Amerindian Frontier, 1575–1775." Ph.D. diss., University of Chicago.

———Forthcoming. "Review of James A. Clifton, ed., *The Invented Indian.*" *American Ethnologist.*

Sturtevant, William C. 1976. "First Visual Images of Native America." In *First Images of America,* ed. F. Chiapelli, et al.

Sturtevant, William C., and David B. Quinn. 1987. "This New Prey: Eskimos in Europe in 1567, 1576, and 1577." In *Indians and Europe,* ed. C. Feest.

Takaki, Ronald. 1979. *Iron Cages: Race and Culture in Nineteenth-Century America.* Seattle: University of Washington Press.

Taussig, Michael. 1987. *Shamanism, Colonialism, and the Wild Man: A Study in Terror and Healing.* Chicago: University of Chicago Press.

Thornton, Russell. 1986. *American Indian Holocaust and Survival: A Population History Since 1492.* Norman: University of Oklahoma Press.

Todorov, Tzvetan. 1982. *The Conquest of America: The Question of the Other.* Trans. Richard Howard. New York: Harper & Row Publishers.

Tooker, Elisabeth. 1978. "The League of the Iroquois: Its History, Politics, and Ritual." In *Northeast,* ed. B. Trigger. Vol. 15, *Handbook of North American Indians.*

———. 1988. "The United States Constitution and the Iroquois League." *Ethnohistory* 35:305–36.

Trigger, Bruce G. 1976. *The Children of Aataentsic: A History of The Huron People to 1660.* 2 vols. Montreal: McGill-Queen's University Press.

———. 1978a. "Cultural Unity and Diversity." In *Northeast,* ed. B. Trigger. Vol. 15, *Handbook of North American Indians.*

————. 1985. *Native and Newcomers: Canada's "Heroic Age" Reconsidered.* Montreal: McGill-Queen's University Press.

Trigger, Bruce G., ed. 1978b. *Northeast.* Vol. 15, *Handbook of North American Indians.* Gen. Ed. William C. Sturtevant. Washington, D.C.: Smithsonian Institution Press.

Ulrich, Laurel Thatcher. 1980. "Vertuous Women Found: New England Ministerial Literature, 1668–1735." In *Women in American Religion*, ed. J. James.

————. 1982. *Good Wives: Image and Reality in the Lives of Women in Northern New England, 1650–1750.* New York: Alfred A. Knopf.

Vail, Robert William Glenroie. 1949. *The Voice of The Old Frontier.* Philadelphia: University of Pennsylvania Press.

VanDerBeets, Richard. 1971. "A Surfeit of Style: The Indian Captivity Narrative as Penny Dreadful." *Research Studies* 39:296-307.

————. 1972a. "'A Thirst for Empire': The Indian Captivity Narrative as Propaganda." *Research Studies* 40:207-15.

————. 1972b. "The Indian Captivity Narrative as Ritual." *American Literature.* 43:548-62.

————. 1984. *The Indian Captivity Narrative: An American Genre.* Lanham, Md.: University Press of America.

VanDerBeets, Richard, ed. 1973. *Held Captive by Indians: Selected Narratives, 1642–1836.* Knoxville: University of Tennessee Press.

Vaughan, Alden T. 1979. *New England Frontier: Puritans and Indians, 1620–1836.* Revised ed. New York and London: W. W. Norton Co.

————. 1982. "From White Man to Redskin: Changing Anglo-American Perceptions of the American Indian." *American Historical Review* 87:917-53.

————. 1983. *Narratives of North American Indian Captivity: A Selective Bibliography.* Garland reference library of the humanities. Vol. 370. New York and London: Garland.

Vaughan, Alden T., and Edward W. Clark. 1981a. "'Cups of Common Calamity': Puritan Captivity Narratives as Literature and History." In *Puritans among the Indians*, eds. A. Vaughan and E. Clark.

Vaughan, Alden T., and Edward W. Clark, eds. 1981b. *Puritans among the Indians: Accounts of Captivity and Redemption, 1676–1724.* Cambridge: Harvard University Press.

Vaughan, Alden T., and Daniel K. Richter. 1980. "Crossing The Cultural Divide: Indians and New Englanders, 1605–1763." *Proceedings of the American Antiquarian Society.* Vol. 90, pt. 1.

Wallace, A.F.C. 1969. *The Death and Rebirth of the Seneca.* New York: Alfred A. Knopf.

Washburn, Wilcomb. 1978. "Seventeenth-Century Indian Wars." In *Northeast,* ed. B. Trigger. Vol. 15, *Handbook of North American Indians.*

——. 1983. Introduction. In *Narratives of North American Indian Captivity: A Selective Bibliography,* ed. A. Vaughan.

Washburn, Wilcomb, ed. 1977–80. *Narratives of North American Indian Captivities.* 111 volumes. New York: Garland.

——, ed. 1988. *The History of Indian-White Relations.* Vol. 4, *Handbook of North American Indians.* Gen. Ed. William C. Sturtevant. Washington, D. C.: Smithsonian Institution Press.

Watkins, Owen C. 1972. *The Puritan Experience: Studies in Spiritual Autobiography.* London: Routledge and Paul.

Weatherford, J. McIver. 1988. *Indian Givers: How the Indians of the Americas Transformed the World.* New York: Crown Publishers.

White, Hayden. 1976. "The Noble Savage Theme as Fetish." In *First Images of America,* eds. F. Chiapelli et al.

White, Richard. 1983. *The Roots of Dependency: Subsistence, Environment, and Social Change among the Choctaws, Pawnees, and Navajos.* Lincoln: University of Nebraska Press.

Williams, John. [1707] 1976. *The Redeemed Captive,* ed. Edward W. Clark. Amherst: University of Massachusetts Press.

——. [1707] 1978. *The Redeemed Captive Returning to Zion: A Faithful History of Remarkable Occurrences, in the Captivity and Deliverance of Mr. John Williams, Minister of the Gospel, in Deerfield. . . .* In *Narratives of North American Indian Captivities,* ed. W. Washburn. Vol. 5.

Williams, Raymond. 1977. *Marxism and Literature.* Oxford and New York: Oxford University Press.

Wood, Peter H. 1989. "Indian Servitude in the Southeast." In *The History of Indian-White Relations,* ed. W. Washburn. Vol. 4, *Handbook of North American Indians.*

Young, Philip. 1962. "The Mother of Us All." *Kenyon Review* 24:391–441.

3

The Many-Headed Hydra

Sailors, Slaves, and the Atlantic Working Class in the
Eighteenth Century

Peter Linebaugh and Marcus Rediker

Introduction

Through the harsh winter of 1740–41, as food riots broke out all over
Europe, a motley crew of workers met at John Hughson's water-
side tavern in the city of New York to plan a rising for St. Patrick's
Day. The conspirators included Irish, English, Hispanic, African, and
native American men and women; they spoke Gaelic, English, Spanish, French, Dutch, Latin, Greek, and undoubtedly several African
and Indian languages. They were a mixture of mostly slaves and wage
laborers, especially soldiers, sailors, and journeymen. During their
deliberations, David Johnson, a journeyman hatter of British background, swore that "he would help to burn the town, and kill as
many white people as he could" (quoted in Horsmanden 1971: 309).
John Corry, an Irish dancing-master, promised the same, as, apparently, did John Hughson himself and many others, a large number of
African-Americans among them. And they eventually put at least part
of their plan into action, burning down Fort George, the Governor's
mansion, and the imperial armory, the symbols of Royal Majesty and
civil authority, the havens and instruments of ruling-class power in
New York. They did not succeed, as evidenced by the thirteen burned
at the stake, the twenty-one hanged, and the seventy-seven transported out of the colony as slaves or servants. The corpses of two of

the hanged dangled in an iron gibbet on the waterfront as a lesson to others. As the bodies decayed in the open air, observers noted a gruesome, yet instructive, transformation. The corpse of an Irishman turned black and his hair curly, while the corpse of Caesar, the African, bleached white. It was accounted a "wondrous phenomenon" (309; cf. Linebaugh 1983; Davis 1985).

One of the many remarkable things about this upheaval is the way in which it confounds much of contemporary historical understanding. Here we have a polyglot community of workers who by current wisdom should never have been able to conceive, much less execute, a joint rebellion. Here we have "white" Europeans pledging themselves to the destruction of "the white people" of New York, by which they obviously meant *the rich people*. Here we have, not a slave revolt or a "great Negro Plot" (as it has long been called), not a mutiny by soldiers and sailors nor a strike by wage laborers, but rather a many-sided rising by a diverse urban proletariat—red, white, and black, of many nations, races, ethnicities, and degrees of freedom (Davis 1985: 194).

The events of 1741 were part of a broader history of the Atlantic working class in the eighteenth century, a class that not only suffered the violence of the stake, the gallows, and the shackles of a ship's dark hold, but which has subsequently suffered the violence of abstraction in the writing of history. Concepts such as "nationality," "race," and "ethnicity" have obscured essential features of the history of the working class in the early modern era. Historians who consciously or unconsciously posit static and immutable differences between workers black and white, Irish and English, slave and free in the early modern era, have frequently failed to study the actual points of contact, overlap, and cooperation between their idealized types. Without such cooperation, of course, the economy of the transatlantic world could never have functioned.

Our study starts from the material organization of many thousands of workers into transatlantic circuits of commodity exchange and capital accumulation and then proceeds to look at the ways in which they translated their cooperation into anti-capitalist projects of their own, as did those who gathered and whispered 'round the fire at Hughson's tavern in New York. It is thus a study of *connections* within the working class—connections that have been denied, ignored, or simply never seen by most historians. It is also an effort to remember, literally to *re-member*, to reconnect as a way of overcoming some of the violence and the dismembering the Atlantic working class has undergone. Our effort to remember begins with a myth about dismemberment.

The Myth of the Many-Headed Hydra

The slaying of the Hydra was the second of the twelve labors of Hercules. A Greek version of the story is perhaps best known. Confronted with the monstrous, many-headed Hydra, a water snake with nine to a hundred heads, Hercules found that as soon as he cut off one head, two grew in its place. With the help of his nephew Iolaus, he learned to use a firebrand to cauterize the stump of the beast's neck. Thus they killed the Hydra. Hercules dipped his arrows in the blood of the slain beast, whose venom thus gave to his arrows their fatal power.

Allusions to the story appear often in the annals of European conquest in the seventeenth and eighteenth centuries. For instance, in 1751 Mauricius, a former governor of Surinam, returned to Holland where he wrote poetic memoirs recollecting his defeat at the hands of the Saramaka, the victorious maroons:

> There you must fight blindly an invisible enemy
> Who shoots you down like ducks in the swamps.
> Even if an army of ten thousand men were gathered, with
> The courage and strategy of Caesar and Eugene,
> They'd find their work cut out for them, destroying a Hydra's growth
> Which even Alcides would try to avoid.

> (quoted in Price 1983: 15)

Mauricius was a European conqueror writing to and for other Europeans assumed to be sympathetic with the project of conquest. They likened their labor to that of Hercules, here called Alcides. Hydra is identified with the former slaves who had freed themselves, and who

in subsequent war assured their freedom—a first permanent victory
over European masters in the New World, preceding by a generation
the victory of the Haitian people.[1]

The Hydra comparison came easily to the pens of slaveholders
worried about rebellion. Thus, in the aftermath of Bussa's Rebellion
(in Barbados in 1816), a planter wrote that Wilberforce and the African Institute "have pierced the inmost recesses of our island, inflicted
deep and deadly words in the minds of the black population, and
engendered the Hydra, Rebellion, which had well nigh deluged our
fields with blood" (quoted in Beckles 1984: 107).

However, the Hydra analogy was restricted neither to the West
Indies nor to Afro-American slaves. In 1702 when Cotton Mather
published his history of Christianity in America (*Magnalia Christi
Americana*), he entitled his second chapter on the sectarian opposition
to the New England Puritans, "Hydra Decapita." "The church of God
had not long been in this wilderness, before the dragon cast forth several floods to devour it," he wrote of the antinomian controversy of
the 1630s. The theological struggle of "works" against "grace" sub-
verted "all peaceable order." It prevented an expedition against the
Pequot Indians; it raised suspicions against the magistrates; it confused
the drawing of town lots; and it made particular appeals to women.
To Cotton Mather, therefore, the Hydra challenged legal authority,
the demarcations of private property, the subordination of women,
and the authority of ministers who refused to permit open discussions
of sermons. The antinomians of America had begun to call the King
of England "the King of Babylon." The struggle in Massachusetts
was thus a theological dress rehearsal for the English Revolution of
the 1640s.[2]

Thus in many different contexts did various ruling classes use the
ancient myth of the many-headed Hydra to understand their metropolitan and colonial problems, usually referring to the proletariat
whom European powers were either conquering or disciplining to
the life of plantation, regiment, estate, workshop, and factory. The
capitalists of London, Paris, and the Hague thus cast themselves as
Hercules. Why did they do so? One might consider the question un-
important, since this was a "classical age" in European history when

allusion to classical myth was commonplace. Yet this begs the question, for why was it a "classical age"? Part of the answer lies in a project common to Roman and European ruling classes, both of which sought by conquest and tribute to control the rest of the world.

Part of the answer lies also in the fact that the European bourgeoisie of the early modern era were only beginning to develop an understanding of their time and place in the world, and—aside from Christianity and its myths—the only tools available to them for understanding social development were those classic texts rediscovered and made available during the Renaissance, which on the one hand assisted the "scientific revolution" through the revival of Neoplatonism and other hermetic traditions, and on the other provided examples and models of social formations, or modes of production, which supported the doctrine of European progress in social development (cf. Bernal 1987).

Hercules could be seen as revolutionary. It is not just that his labors were immense, gigantic, and intercontinental; they seemed to summarize, as myths often do, an enormous transition in human history. Indeed, taking the Neolithic Revolution as the beginning of history, Hercules belonged, as the oldest of the deities in the Greek pantheon, to the dawn of the ages. Thus, by the end of the nineteenth century, the generally accepted interpretation of the myth was that it expressed the transition to agrarian civilization. A myth that summarized the Neolithic Revolution might well be used to summarize the revolutionary rise of capitalism.

By the beginning of the eighteenth century the geographic zones of this latter Herculean struggle were the four corners of the North Atlantic, or the coast of West Africa, the Caribbean islands, the North American colonies, and the maritime powers of northwestern Europe. Within these zones the experience of human labor was organized in seven basic ways. First, there were those who hunted and gathered their subsistence, like some of the Indians and European hunters of North American and the poor commoners and scavengers of countryside and city in England and Ireland. Second, the women, servants, and children whose work was consigned to domestic settings of kitchen and cabin. Third, the unwaged but "independent" farmers who themselves presented a variety of types, from the poor tenants and *klachan* farmers of Ireland, to the villagers of West Africa, to the communal cultivators among the Iroquois and the small-holders of America. Fourth, the unfree indentured servants who had been compelled to leave their vagabonding ways to be transported to the West Atlantic. Fifth, the artisans and craftworkers of town and plantation who have been so carefully studied in recent historiography. Sixth, the sailors and navvies of the mercantile powers who formed the mass of eighteenth-century wage labor. And, seventh, the unfree, unwaged slaves whose mass, cooperative labor cleared the forests, drained the swamps, built the infrastructure of roads and ports, and labored in the plantations of sugar, tobacco, coffee, and cotton. Our remarks in this paper are restricted to two zones: Europe and the North American colonies, and to two kinds of workers: wage laborers (especially sailors) and slaves (cf. Rediker 1987; Linebaugh 1991).

We will look at four moments in the history of the many-headed Hydra in the eighteenth century: 1747 when in the Knowles Riot in Boston, sailors and slaves fought the King's press gangs and in so doing created one of the central ideas of the Age of Revolution; 1768 when in the London port strike, sailors, Irish coalheavers, and others pioneered one of the central ideas and activities of the modern working-class movement, the strike; 1776 when in the American Revolution, sailors and slaves helped to instigate and then to win the world's first colonial war for liberation; and 1780 when in the Gordon Riots, the polyglot working class of London liberated the prisons amid the greatest municipal insurrection of the eighteenth century. All of these moments were in crucial ways the work of "a motley crew"—a multiracial, multiethnic, transatlantic working class, whose presence, much less agency, is rarely, if ever, acknowledged in the historiographies of these crucial events.

1747: Seamen, Slaves, and the Origins of Revolutionary Ideology

Free wage laborers, mostly seamen and others who congregated in urban areas, and unfree unwaged laborers, slaves who lived in city and countryside, were two of the rowdiest heads of the hydra in Britain's North American colonies. Their numerous revolts were not only connected in important ways, they were, taken together, much more crucial to the genesis, process, and outcome of the American Revolution than is generally appreciated.

Jesse Lemisch made it clear years ago that seamen were one of the prime movers in the American Revolution. They played a major part in a great many of the patriot victories between 1765 and 1776. Seamen led a series of militant riots against impressment between 1741 and 1776, and indeed their agency was acknowledged by both Tom Paine (in *Common Sense*) and Tom Jefferson (in the Declaration of Independence), both of whom listed impressment as a major grievance and spur to colonial liberation (Lemisch 1968: 371–407).

But what has been less fully appreciated is how the sailor's involvement in revolutionary politics was part of a broader, international cycle of rebellion that spanned the better part of the eighteenth century. For merchant seamen entered the revolutionary era with a powerful tradition of militancy well in place. They had already learned to use portside riots, mutiny, piracy, work stoppage, and desertion to assert their own ends over and against those mandated from above by merchants, captains, and colonial and royal officials. They would soon learn new tactics.

After the declaration of war against Spain in 1739, struggles against impressment took on a new intensity as seamen fought pitched battles against press gangs all around the Atlantic. Seamen rioted in Boston twice in 1741, once when a mob beat a Suffolk County Sheriff and a Justice of the Peace for their assistance to the press gang of H.M.S. *Portland* and again when 300 seamen armed with axes, clubs, and cutlasses attacked the commanding officer of the *Astrea*. They rose twice more in 1745, first roughing up another Suffolk County sheriff and the commander of H.M.S. *Shirley*, then, seven months later, engaging Captain Forest and H.M.S. *Wager* in action that resulted in two seamen being hacked to death by the press gang's cutlasses. Seamen also animated crowds that attacked the Royal Navy and its minions in Antigua, St. Kitts, Barbados, and Jamaica throughout the 1740s.[3]

The most important early development in the seaman's cycle of

rebellion took place in Boston in 1747, when Commander Charles
Knowles of *H.M.S. Lark* commenced a hot press in Boston. A mob,
initially consisting of 300 seamen but ballooning to "several thousand
people," quickly seized some officers of the *Lark* as hostages, beat a
deputy sheriff and slapped him into the town's stocks, surrounded
and attacked the Provincial Council Chamber, and posted squads at
all piers to keep naval officers from escaping back to their ship (Lax
and Pencak 1976: 188–92). The mob was led by laborers and seamen, black and white, armed with "clubs, swords, and cutlasses"; the
"lower class," observed Thomas Hutchinson, "were beyond measure
enraged" (Hutchinson 1936: 330). The sailors originally assembled for
self-defense, but there was a positive element to their protest as well.
As Knowles remarked:

> The Act [of 1746] against pressing in the Sugar Islands, filled the
> Minds of the Common People ashore as well as Sailors in all the
> Northern Colonies (but more especially in New England) with not
> only a hatred for the King's Service but [also] a Spirit of Rebellion
> *each Claiming a Right* to the same Indulgence as the Sugar Colonies
> and declaring they will maintain themselves in it. (quoted in Lax and
> Pencak 1976: 182; emphasis added)

Maintain themselves in it they did: sailors defended their "liberty"
and justified their resistance in terms of "right."[4]

This was the essential idea embodied in the seamen's practical
activity, in their resistance to unjust authority. Sam Adams, who
watched as the maritime working class defended itself, began to trans-
late its "Spirit of Rebellion" into political discourse. According to
historians John Lax and William Pencak, Adams used the Knowles
Riot to formulate a new ideology of resistance, in which the "natural
rights of man" were used for the first time to justify mob activity.
Adams saw that the mob "embodied the fundamental rights of man
against which government itself could be judged." But the self-activity
of some common tars, "zealous abetters of liberty," came first (Lax
and Pencak 1976: 205, 214). Their militant resistance produced a major
breakthrough in libertarian thought that would ultimately lead to
revolution.[5]

This was only the beginning, for both the rebellion of seamen and for the articulation of a revolutionary ideology in the Atlantic world. In the aftermath of the 1740s, Jack Tar proceeded to take part in almost every port-city riot in England and America for the remainder of the century. Whether in Newport, Boston, New York, Philadelphia, Charleston, London, Liverpool, Bristol, or in the Caribbean, tars took to the streets in rowdy and rebellious protest on a variety of issues, seizing in practice what would later be established as "right" by law (Rediker 1987: 205–53).

The years leading up to the Knowles Riot were ones in which the winds of rebellion also slashed through many of the slave societies of the New World. The struggles included the First Maroon War of Jamaica (1730–40), slave rebellions on St. John in the Danish Virgin Islands and in Dutch Guyana (1733), a plot in the Bahama Islands (1734), a slave conspiracy in Antigua (1735–36), a rebellion in Guadeloupe (1736–38), the Stono Rebellion (1739), the St. Patrick's Day rising in New York (1741), and a series of disturbances in Jamaica (early 1740s). The connections among these events are not always easy to discover, but the life of a slave named Will, who took part in the rebellion of St. John, then the conspiracy of Antigua, and finally the plot of New York, suggests something important about the movement and exchange of subversive experience among slaves. Another Antigua conspirator, banished from his own island, turned up as a leader of a plot on the Danish Island of St. Croix in 1759.[6]

The movement toward rebellion among African-Americans accelerated after 1765, as demonstrated in some important recent work by Peter Wood, who has argued that "black freedom struggles on the eve of white independence" intensified as slaves seized the new opportunities offered by splits between imperial and colonial ruling classes (1986: 166). Running away increased at a rate that alarmed slaveholders everywhere, and by the mid–1770s, a rash of slave plots and revolts sent the fears of masters soaring. Slaves organized risings in 1772 in Perth Amboy, New Jersey; in 1774 in St. Andrews Parish, South Carolina, and in a joint African-Irish effort in Boston; and in 1775 in Ulster County, New York; Dorchester County, Maryland; Norfolk, Virginia; and the Tar River region of North Carolina. In the last of these, a slave named Merrick plotted with a white seafarer to get the arms that would make the intended revolt possible.[7]

Such conspiracy and exchange was facilitated by the strategic position that many urban slaves or free blacks occupied in the social division of labor in the port towns, as day laborers, dockworkers, seamen, and river pilots. Northern ports, with their promise of anonymity and an impersonal wage in the maritime sector, served as a magnet to runaway slaves and free blacks throughout the colonial period and well into the nineteenth and even twentieth centuries. Many found work as laborers and seamen. Slaves also were employed in the maritime sector, some with ship masters as owners, others hired out for a given time. By the middle of the eighteenth century, slaves dominated Charleston's maritime and riverine traffic, in which some 20 percent of the city's adult male slaves labored. The freedom of Charleston's "Boat negroes" had long upset Charleston's rulers, at no time more than when they involved themselves in subversive activities, as alleged against Thomas Jeremiah, a river pilot, in 1775. Jeremiah was accused of stockpiling guns as he awaited the imperial war that would "help the poor Negroes" (quoted in Wood 1978: 284). Jeffrey J. Crow has noted that black pilots were "a rebellious lot, particularly resistant to white control" (1980: 85).[8]

Peter Wood concludes that between 1765 and 1776 North American slaves generated a "wave of struggle" that became "a major factor in the turmoil leading up to the Revolution." "It touched upon every major slave colony, and it was closely related to—even influential upon—the political unrest gripping many white subjects in these years" (1986: 168). Wood's treatment of this cycle of rebellion as "a significant chapter in the story of worker and artisan political unrest" invites us to link it to the revolutionary struggles of other workers (181).[9]

1776: The Mob and the "Many-Headed Power" in America

Revolutionary crowds, rowdy gatherings of thousands of men and women, began in 1765 to create an imperial crisis of unprecedented dimensions. Mobs were crucial to the effective protests against the Stamp Act, the Townshend Revenue Act, the increased power of the British customs service, the Quartering Act, the Tea Act, the Intolerable Acts, and therefore in the revolutionary rupture itself. All of this we can now appreciate because of important recent scholarship.[10]

What has not been appreciated is that most of these mobs were interracial in character, and that these potent if temporary unions of free waged and unfree unwaged laborers were instrumental in winning many of the victories of the revolutionary movement. The Sons of Neptune (themselves both black and white), other free blacks, and slaves were probably most united and most effective in their battles against impressment. The crucial Knowles Riot of 1747, which witnessed the birth of the revolution's language of liberation, was led by "armed Seamen, Servants, Negroes, and others" (Hutchinson 1936: II, 332). Later, as the revolutionary movement began in 1765, some five hundred "seamen, boys, and Negroes" rioted against impressment in Newport, Rhode Island, and in 1767 a mob of armed whites and blacks attacked Captain Jeremiah Morgan in a press riot in Norfolk (Lemisch 1968: 386). Lemisch noted that after 1763, "Armed mobs of whites and Negroes repeatedly manhandled captains, officers, and crews, threatened their lives, and held them hostage for the men they pressed" (1968: 391).[11]

Workers white and black also participated in the popular upsurges against the Stamp Act, whose successful repeal was perhaps the key moment in the development of a revolutionary movement. In 1765 "disorderly negroes, and more disorderly sailors" rioted against the Stamp Act in Charleston (Maier 1970b: 176). A few months later, Charleston slaves (some of whom may have taken part in the earlier action with seamen) assembled and cried for "liberty," which moved city elders to keep the city under armed guard for ten days to two weeks. One protest led to another in which the slogan took on a different, more radical meaning.[12]

Seamen, again assisted by African-Americans, also led the militant opposition to the renewed power of the British customs service in the late 1760s and early 1770s. As Alfred F. Young has shown, seamen even drew upon the custom of the sea to forge a new weapon in the arsenal of revolutionary justice, the tarring and feathering that intimidated a great many British officials in the colonies (1984: 193–4). We can hear the clunk of the brush in the tar bucket behind Thomas Gage's observation in 1769 that "the Officers of the Crown grow more timid, and more fearfull of doing their Duty every Day" (quoted in Schlesinger 1955: 246).[13]

Seamen also led both the Golden Hill and Nassau Street Riots of New York and the King Street Riot, better remembered as the Boston Massacre. In both instances, sailors and other workers resented the ways in which British soldiers labored for less than customary wages along the waterfront; in New York they also resented the soldiers' efforts to destroy their 58-foot liberty pole, which, not surprisingly, resembled nothing so much as a ship's mast. Rioting and street fighting ensued. Thomas Hutchinson and John Adams, among others, believed that the actions in New York led directly to the "Fatal Fifth of March" in Boston. Adams, who defended Captain Preston and his soldiers in trial, called the mob that assembled on King Street nothing but "a motley rabble of saucy boys [i.e., apprentices], negroes and molattoes, Irish teagues, and out landish Jack Tarrs" (1965: III, 266). Seamen also took part in the Tea Party, provoking Britain to a show of naked force in the Intolerable Acts, and an eventual confrontation that proved irreconcilable. During the revolution itself, tars took part in mobs that harassed Tories and rendered their efforts less effective.[14]

Occasionally we get a glimpse of radical ideas and practices in transit, how the oppositional ideas of "these most dangerous people" actually spread from one port to another during the imperial crisis. Governor William Bull of South Carolina, facing Stamp Act protests in Charleston, found that the "minds of Men here were so universally poisoned with the Principles which were imbibed and propagated from Boston and Rhode Island." Soon, "after their example the People of this Town resolved to seize and destroy the Stamp Papers." In explaining this development, Bull noted that "at this time of Year, Vessels very frequently arrive" from Boston and Newport, where seamen and slaves had helped to protest the Stamp Act, just as they would do in Charleston (quoted in Bridenbaugh 1955: 313–14; see also 114–15). "Principles" as well as commodities were transported on those ships![15]

Those whom Adams called "saucy boys, negroes and molattoes, Irish teagues, and out landish Jack Tarrs" made up a huge portion of the urban population that was linked by tenacious cultural ties. A subculture of "apprentices, servants, slaves, and perhaps some journeymen, laborers, and sailors," revolved around common work experiences and a common cultural life of revels, masques, fairs, May-day celebrations, street parties, taverns, and "disorderly houses" (E. Foner 1976: 48). "Apprentices, servants, and even negroes" drank together in Hell Town in Philadelphia, just as "seamen and Negroes" caroused "at unseasonable hours" in Charleston, and workers black and white congregated at Hughson's tavern in New York (Salinger 1987: 102; Morgan 1984: 219). Magistrate Daniel Horsmanden suggested that such taverns provided

> opportunities for the most loose, debased, and abandoned wretches amongst us to cabal and confederate together and ripen themselves into these schools of mischief, for the execution of the most daring and detestable enterprizes. I fear there are yet many of these houses amongst us, and they are the bane and pest of the city. It was such that gave the opportunity of breeding this most horrid and execrable conspiracy. (quoted in Davis 1985: 248)

Grogshops, tippling houses, and dancing cellars existed in every Atlantic port, much to the despair of colonial ruling classes, who sought to criminalize and otherwise discourage contact between the free and unfree workers who used such settings to hatch conspiracies and even form a "maritime underground railroad" through which many escaped to freedom (Hall 1985: 491–92). There was, therefore, a history of interracial cooperation that underlay the joint protests of sailors and slaves against impressment and other measures during the revolutionary era.[16]

Seamen and slaves thus expressed a militant mood summed up by Peter Timothy when he spoke of Charleston, South Carolina, in the summer of 1775: "In regard to War & Peace, I can only tell you that the Plebeians are still for War—but the noblesse [are] perfectly pacific" (quoted in Maier 1970b: 181). Seamen in particular and wage workers in general were foremost among the most radical parts of the colonial population, who pushed the revolutionary vanguard to more extreme positions and eventually to independence itself. Contrary to the recent argument of scholars who claim that sailors, laborers, slaves, and other poor workingmen were in no position to "shape the revolutionary process" (Wellenreuther 1983: 442), it is clear that these groups provided much of the spark, volatility, momentum, and the "sustained militance" for the attack on British policy after 1765 (Countryman 1981: 37, 45). In the process they provided an image of interracial cooperation that should cause us to wonder whether racism was as monolithic in white society as is often assumed.

Paul Revere's famous but falsified account of the Boston Massacre quickly tried to make the "motley rabble" respectable by leaving black faces out of the crowd and putting into it entirely too many fancy waistcoats. It is not, therefore, surprising that well-to-do colonists often fearfully called the mob a "Hydra," a "many-headed monster," a "reptile," and more sympathetically, a "many-headed power," using the same mythic terms that other parts of the Atlantic bourgeoisie had long used to describe and interpret their struggle against a diverse Atlantic working class.[17]

Such fears are understandable, for the politicized mob was one of the three most important "mass organizations" (along with the militia and the army) in the revolutionary movement, and it was probably the hardest of these to control. Moreover, it was in most instances relatively democratic—not only could anyone join, but workingmen could even rise to positions of momentary or long-term leadership. Given these facts, and the way in which such mobs were absolutely crucial to the making of the revolution, their subsequent suppression by former revolutionaries can be seen as part of an American Thermidor, their condemnation by big landowners, merchants, and even artisans as part of a literal "enclosure movement" designed to move politics from "out-of-doors" to legislative chambers. When Sam Adams, who helped to draw up Massachusetts's Riot Act of 1786, ceased to believe that the mob "embodied the fundamental rights of man against which government itself could be judged," he cut himself off from an important source of democratic creativity and expression, the force that years ago had given him the best idea of his life (Lax and Pencak 1976: 214).[18]

Of the five workingmen killed in the Boston Massacre in 1770, John Adams said: "the blood of the martyrs, right or wrong, proved to be the seed of the congregation" (quoted in Schlesinger 1955: 250). Adams thus made clear the working-class origins of the revolution and the new nation, for the blood of the martyrs, as everyone knew, was the blood of a journeyman, an apprentice, and three wage laborers; a ropewalker and two seamen, one of whom was a half-black, half-Indian runaway slave who lived in the Bahama Islands. His name was Crispus Attucks. Of this martyr John Adams had said earlier, his "very looks would be enough to terrify any person," or at least any person like Adams himself (Adams 1965: III, 269). He might well have said the same about the "motley rabble" Attucks had led into battle, thereby speaking the fearful mind of the moderate leadership of the revolutionary movement. It would not be long before workingmen and women all over America would be marching against the British under flags that featured a serpent and the motto, "Don't Tread on Me" (Kaplan and Kaplan 1989: 68–69; Richardson 1982).

1768: From Ireland to London, Where the Serpent Learns to Strike

Patrick Carr, another Boston worker who was to be a martyr of the coming revolution, represented that part of the Atlantic working class that hailed from Ireland. Carr, like many others, left Ireland in the 1760s well experienced in the ways of mobs and their confrontations with British military power. Many of his compatriots went to London, where they helped to make the London port strike of 1768 (Zobel 1970: 192, 199).

Indeed, the strike in London cannot be understood apart from Ireland, where the hangman's noose and the woodsman's axe had centuries before been the principal tools of the English Ascendancy. Following the Williamite confiscations of the 1690s, the forests, and the human culture dependent upon them, were largely destroyed; the agrarian policy subsequently introduced into Ireland promoted pasturage for the export of cattle rather than an arable farming that could feed the population. As a result, a large population, having neither forests nor lands to subsist upon, either left the land altogether or submitted to a standard of subsistence so utterly mean that it beggared the powers of description of independent observers and caused even the rulers to wonder at how an oppressed population could tolerate such conditions. The Irish language was "banished from the castle of the chieftain to the cottage of the vassal," from whence in hard times it migrated to the boozing kens of London and the low tippling houses of American and Caribbean ports. The "hidden Ireland"—its conspiratorial tradition and willingness to act outside the law—was carried along in the diaspora within people like Patrick Carr.[19]

The "Whiteboy Outrages," the name given to the largest and longest of agrarian rebellions in Ireland (1761–65, with sporadic outbursts through 1788), was a major part of the subversive experience of the mobile Irish. These protests took place in a period of increased expropriation and accumulation, intensified by the demands of two world wars. With the outbreak of cattle disease, the murrain, in continental Europe, and the passage in 1759 of the Cattle Exportation Act, the value of Irish land increased greatly. The poorest of the cottiers who had a potato patch or a cow kept on the common land suddenly found that even these were to be denied as landlords, their agents, and bailiffs evicted them in search of new grazing lands, taking over whole baronies and erecting walls, hedges, and fences to keep their herds in and the former tenants out. Against this, the Irish cottier and laborer reacted with what Lecky called "an insurrection of despair" (1893: II, 226).[20]

In October 1761 nocturnal bands of two hundred to four hundred people, dressed in flowing white frocks and white cockades, threw down fences enclosing lands in Tipperary. The movement quickly expanded to new areas in Cork, Kilkenny, Limerick, and Waterford, and to actions designed to redress other grievances, such as the manifold tithes (of potatoes, agistment, turf, or furze) imposed by an alien religious establishment. Sounding horns, carrying torches, and riding commandeered horses, the Whiteboys opened jails, rescued prisoners, attacked garrisons, stole arms, released apprentices, maimed cattle, ploughed wasteland, prevented export of provisions, burned houses, reduced prices, and everywhere tore down walls, fences, hedges, and ditches. These rebels were originally known as, and often called, "the Levellers."

The overall strength of the Whiteboys remains unknown, although it was reported that 14,000 insurgents lived in Tipperary in 1763. Their largest gatherings, five hundred to seven hundred strong, took place in 1762 in Cork and Waterford. Using military techniques, the poorest cottiers and laborers (many of them spalpeens, or migratory laborers) formed themselves into an autonomous organization quite separate from the middle and upper classes. Indeed, the proletarian experience of the hundreds of thousands of Irishmen who had soldiered in the French army since 1691 lay behind the Whiteboy movement.[21]

Of necessity much of their movement was anonymous and mysterious. It was conducted "under the sanction of being fairies," it was said in 1762, and led by mythological figures such as "Queen Sieve" who wrote,

> We, levellers and avengers for the wrongs done to the poor, have unanimously assembled to raze walls and ditches that have been made to inclose the commons. Gentlemen now of late have learned to grind the face of the poor so that it is impossible for them to live. They cannot even keep a pig or a hen at their doors. We warn them not to raise again either walls or ditches in the place of those we destroy, nor even to inquire about the destroyers of them. If they do, their cattle shall be houghed and their sheep laid open in the fields (Lecky 1893: II, 41).

Whiteboy captains who would carry out these threats called themselves "Slasher," "Lightfoot," "Fearnot," and "Madcap Setfire."[22]

Theirs was a movement inspired by strong notions of justice. The High Sheriff of Waterford, for instance, could find no person willing to whip a convicted Whiteboy, although he offered twenty guineas and though a large body of troops was present for the occasion. When English law was enforced, as in the hanging of Father Sheehy in 1766, the people undermined its effect. The earth over his grave was treated as holy ground; a "Sheehy Jury" became proverbial for partiality. Four years later his executioner was stoned to death, and ten years later his prosecutor killed, by people who refused to forget.[23]

The Whiteboy movement attacked tithes and alarmed many Protestants, but it ought not be interpreted as a sectarian phenomenon, since both Catholics and Protestants were present among both the Whiteboys and their victims, and since wealthy Catholics and Protestants cooperated to stop the risings.[24] And although it began in rural settings against enclosures, the movement ought not be interpreted exclusively as "agrarian unrest." Just as the creation of a landless proletariat is a necessary corollary to the expropriation of land, so the forms and experience of that struggle will move with the wandering, roving proletariat thus created. An historian of the transported convicts to Australia wrote, "The Whiteboy Associations were, in a sense, a vast trades union." Whiteboy sabotage, according to Constantia Maxwell, was taken up by Dublin journeymen. The Friendly Society of Philadelphia's ship carpenters, its historian avers, was also associated with the Whiteboys. Therefore, when in the late 1760s the terms of exchange between England and Ireland included one-and-a-half-million pounds in remittances to absentee landlords, three million pounds worth of exports, and thousands of hungry laboring people, we need to add to such material commerce a cultural exchange that is broader than coleric playwrights and sad balladeers, and which includes the rebellious organizations of "hidden Ireland," because these surfaced in London in 1768 with great effect. (Maxwell 1936: 270; Shaw 1966: 173; Hutson 1971; Prior 1769).[25]

Proletarian labors in London were characterized by high turnover, by absence of guild fellowships, by ethnic heterogeneity, and by working conditions that were seasonal, dangerous, and subject to harsh discipline. The productive power of such social labor arose from the assembly of many people in one place at one time. Harvesting and road-making, canal-digging and soldiering required such labor, as did the loading, sailing, and unloading of ships. The Irish concentrated in the mass labor of coalheaving, a hot, filthy, back-breaking line of work, but crucial to the energizing of England's greatest city. Individually weak and pitiful, such wage laborers had power and posed danger as a collective mass (Ashton and Sykes 1964). "A body of men working in concert has hands and eyes both before and behind, and is, to a certain degree, omnipresent," wrote Karl Marx (1938: 315).

In the 1760s it took more money to eat, and the hungry people of London began to act directly against price increases. River workers led the groups who stole fresh vegetables, forced vendors to sell their wares at popular prices, and intimidated merchants into both closing down their shops/exchanges and burying their plate. On 11 May a group of sailors assembled at the Stock Exchange "and would not suffer any Person except their own Body to enter it" (*Public Advertizer*, 14 May 1768). These actions were not peaceful; murder was a frequent occurrence during the spring and summer. Thomas Davis, for instance, said he "did not care who they killed, rather than his family should starve" (*Westminster Journal*, 14 May 1768). When a "Gentleman" asked a young man whether it was foolish for people to risk their lives, he was answered: "Master, Provisions are high and Trade is dead, that we are half starving and it is as well to die at once, as die by Inches" (*Berrow's Worcester Journal*, 19 May 1768).[26]

Otherwise, the hungry took indirect actions to increase their wages. The sailors petitioned and marched upon Parliament to increase their wage payments. The shoemakers met often in mass meeting in Moorfields as part of their attempts to get greater wages. The bargemen struck for more money. The sawyers were threatened by the recent introduction of a steam-powered engine installed in Limehouse. They destroyed it. A thousand glass grinders petitioned for higher wages; thousands of London tailors did the same. Leaders were sent to prison, like the three tailors sent to Bridewell "for irritating their Bretheren to Insurrection, abusing their Masters, and refusing to work at the stated prices" (CLRO, SP, Bundle 1768).

In many ways, the riots of the spring and early summer of 1768 appear to be classic instances of the eighteenth-century plebeian mob in action: the forms (petitioning, marching, illuminations, smashing of windows), the heterogeneity of the "trades" (tailors, shoemakers, carpenters), and generally the subordination of its demands and actions to the middle-class reform movement led by John Wilkes. Yet the activities of that year need to be seen not only as the licensed outrages of the plebeian mob, but as something new, unlicensed, insurrectionary, and proletarian. "The Extremities to which the Cry of Liberty is carried, seem to threaten the Destruction of all Civil Society," as one newspaper put it (*Public Advertizer*, 21 July 1768). Wilkes and his men could not control the protests of 1768, as demonstrated when some sailors chanted, "No Wilkes, No King."[27] Nor did artisans lead these events. The river workers led them, closing river shipping for a time and almost causing a general strike. In July "A Spectator" observed the pattern of recent months: "Thus Sailors, Taylors, Coopers, Lightermen, Watermen, &c. follow one another, the adventurous Coalheavers leading the Van" (*Berrow's Worcester Journal*, 12 May 1768).

The leaders of the coalheavers, many knew, were "of the Gang of White Boys in Ireland, driven out from thence for the most Enormous Crimes, as they have bragg'd and given it out themselves," to quote the Solicitor-General of England (TSP 11/442/1408). The involvement of Whiteboys among the coalheavers was reported by several newspapers and assumed by Samuel Foote, who wrote *The Tailors; A Tragedy for Warm Weather* (1778) about the strikes of '68–'69. Horace Walpole, the Earl of Orford, noted that the coalheavers "are all Irish Whiteboys"; his certainty of this fact allowed him to use the terms coalheavers and Whiteboys interchangeably (Walpole 1973: XXXV, 324; see also XXIII, 33). Thus the Hydra-head slain by the noose and the axe in Ireland reappeared with force in London as insurgent Irish wage labor. It may have been little enough solace to John Brennan's wife, who had carried the severed Whiteboy's head through the streets and shops of Kilkenny "collecting money from the populace" after his execution (Donnelly 1978–9: 50). But the inescapable truth remained, as recognized by the Chief Baron of Ireland's Exchequer: in Ireland, "England has sown her laws like dragon's teeth, and they have sprung up, armed men" (quoted in Reid 1977: 142).[28]

The working men and women of riverside London came out of 1768 armed in a new way. The sailors, who collectively decided to "strike" the sails of their vessels and thereby halt the commerce and international accumulation of capital in the empire's leading city, had in conjunction with Irish coalheavers and others made a major addition to the political language and activity of the working-class movement: the strike.[29]

1780: Insurrectionary London

As several heads of the Hydra fought for "independence" beneath the symbol of the serpent in America, several others—"*a motley crew, and of every color*"—struck against British power in the Gordon Riots, the most serious municipal insurrection of the eighteenth century (*The Proceedings . . . of the Old Bailey*, 28 June 1780). The riots of 6 June 1780 were named after Lord George Gordon, a Scottish peer who led the Protestant Association, a mass organization dedicated to the repeal of an Act passed two years earlier for the "Relief of Roman Catholics." Parliament and the Bank of England were attacked; aristocrats found their houses demolished and their persons besieged. London parks became military encampments; strategic points were defended by artillery; the municipal bourgeoisie armed itself. Between four and five hundred people were killed. To the London working class, 6 June 1780 was a glorious day because the prisoners of Newgate were liberated.[30]

Exact estimates of the number of prisoners freed on the nights of 6 and 7 June 1780 must vary because of the disorders of the night and because of the many different prisons, jails, and other places of confinement that were opened. More than twenty crimping houses (where impressed sailors were confined prior to embarkation) and spunging houses (where debtors were held at the pleasure of their creditors) were forcibly opened in Southwark. The prisoners of Newgate, the largest and most terrible dungeon, were liberated amid such fire and destruction that one spectator felt "as if not only the whole metropolis was burning, but all nations yielding to the final consummation of all things" (*The Morning Post*, 9 June 1780).

The prisoners delivered from Newgate were of several ethnicities—English, Irish, African-American, but also Italian, German, and Jewish. Of those liberated whose original cases can be found, five had been charged with crimes against the person (a rapist, a bigamist, an anonymous letter writer, and two murderers), and two were charged with perjury. The overwhelming majority were imprisoned for crimes against property: two counterfeiters, six burglars, ten highway robbers, and fifty larcenists escaped—most were propertyless. Several inside Newgate had American connections; they, like others both inside and outside the prison walls, had been affected by the revolutionary war under way for independence and the pursuit of happiness. Continuing the struggles sailors had waged over the previous forty years against impressment, the rioters fought for freedom against confinement. They did so in a "Republican Phrenzy" and a "levelling spirit" (*The London Chronicle*, 6–8 June 1780).[31]

In fact, sailors themselves were prominent among the rioters, as indicated by the frequent mention of cutlasses and marlin spikes as principal weapons in the armory of the crowd. It had been a terrible year for sailors—the winter was cold, the war had been a fatigue, the press-gangs marauded the streets. The incidence of mutiny in the Royal Navy had begun to increase soon after the American Revolution broke out (Gilbert 1987: 111–21). A seaman by the name of Richard Hyde was tried for the liberation or "delivery" of the Newgate prisoners. One of the Newgate turnkeys insisted that Hyde had insulted him, calling him "one of Akerman's Thieves," and threatened him by saying he would "cut his Throat and kill his Master" (*Proceedings of the Old Bailey*, 28 June 1780). Other sailors broke into prison-keeper Akerman's house, where they obtained the keys to the jail's main gate.

Two other deliverers of Newgate, "not having the Fear of God before their Eyes but being moved and seduced by the Instigation of the Devil," to use the language of the indictments against them, were named John Glover and Benjamin Bowsey. They were African-Americans and former slaves. Their activities at Newgate were decisive, and for that reason their importance to the subsequent history of Atlantic working people can be likened to the more well known leaders of the Afro-London population, Ottobah Cugoano and Olaudah Equiano, whose fame partly arises because they were writers. Glover and Bowsey were activists.[32]

John Glover lived in Westminster where he was reputed to be a quiet, sober, and honest man. He worked as a servant to one Philips, Esq., who was evidently an attorney, for during the afternoon of 6 June he sent Glover to his chambers in Lincoln's Inn to fetch some papers. The streets were full of people and news: the day before the mobbing of the Lords had taken place, petitioners were returning from Parliament, the ballad singers were exhausting their talents, the clerks and law men of the Inns of Court had begun to arm themselves to do duty against the mob. Ignatius Sancho, a well-to-do African grocer, wrote from Westminster that evening observing "at least a hundred thousand poor, miserable, ragged rabble . . . besides half as many women and children, all parading the streets—the bridge—the Park—ready for any and every mischief" (Sancho 1782: 40). The day was a moment of truth when none could avoid taking sides. Glover did not gather the law papers, but instead joined one of the columns forming toward Newgate whose approach filled him with determination, for on Snow Hill he was seen striking the cobblestones with a gun barrel and shouting, "Now Newgate!" He was one of the first persons who showed his face at the "chequers of the gate," whose keeper was addressed by him as follows: "Damn you, Open the Gate or we will Burn you down and have Everybody out," a threat he made good, for he was later observed "to be the most active Person Particularly in piling up combustible matters against the Door and putting fire thereto" (Sancho 1782: 40).

The London black community (10,000–20,000 people) was active during the week of 6 June. Later, Ottobah Cuguoano spoke from, of, and for this community when he said, "The voice of our complaint implies a vengeance" (1787: 106). Such were the voices of 6 June. While Glover and others were busy at Newgate, Charlotte Gardiner, "a negro," marched with a mob ("among whom were two men with bells, and another with frying pan and tongs") to the house of Mr. Levarty, a publican, in St. Katherine's Lane, near Tower Hill. Charlotte Gardiner was a leader of this march, shouting encouragements ("Huzza, well done, my boys—knock it down, down with it") and directions ("Bring more wood to the fire"), as well as taking two brass candle sticks from the dining room (*The London Chronicle*, 4–8 July 1780). She did not even attempt to defend herself at the Old Bailey, and on 4 July she was found guilty and sentenced to die. The following Tuesday she was hanged.[33]

John Glover was identified well enough at the Old Bailey for purpose of hanging. But for historical purposes, his identification, like that of the nameless millions of the African diaspora, is much more difficult. Yet there is evidence to suggest that he took his name from an early member of the Committee of Correspondence of Marblehead, Massachusetts, a General John Glover who raised an American military regiment in 1775 among the multiethnic mariners and fishermen of this important Atlantic port. The John Glover who helped to deliver Newgate was probably a captured prisoner from General Glover's regiment.[34]

The problem of identification arises again when we consider a second African-American, Benjamin Bowsey, a man who came as close as any to being the leader of the 6 June delivery. His voice was apparently exciting, encouraging, and capable of arousing indignation. He was among the group of thirty who first approached the prison, marching three abreast, armed with spokes, crows, and paving mattocks. Later, he was indicted on three bills, one for riot; one for pulling down Akerman's house; and one for breaking, entering, and stealing. Bowsey had been in England for six years and had probably been a slave in Virginia.

Men like Glover and Bowsey and women like Gardiner arrived in growing numbers in London, where they found work as fiddlers, lovemakers, cooks, boxers, writers, and especially domestic servants, day laborers, and seamen. The overall coherence (learned on plantation and shipboard) of the African population posed a police problem in London where it was expressed in clubs for dance, music, eating, and drinking, or in knots of American runaways and London servants. John Fielding, the Chairman of the Westminster Quarter Sessions whose office was attacked during the riots, was some years earlier already alarmed at the growing immigration of this population. The plantocrats, he said,

> bring them to England as cheap servants having no right to wages; they no sooner arrive here than they put themselves on a footing with other servants, become intoxicated with liberty, grow refractory, and either by persuasion of others or from their own inclinations, begin to expect wages according to their own opinion of their merits; and as there are already a great number of black men and women who made themselves troublesome and dangerous to the families who have brought them over as to get themselves dis-

charged, these enter into societies and make it their business to corrupt and dissatisfy the mind of every black servant that comes to England. (Fielding 1768: 144–5)

The Afro-London community by the 1770s had begun to fight for the freedom of a proletarian—mobility and money.[35] They continued the fight in attacking Newgate, one of the chief symbols of state power and repression, amid a war across the Atlantic that continued a discussion of popular rights inaugurated generations earlier by the Levellers and other radicals of the English Revolution.

Conclusion

By looking at the revolts of the many-headed Hydra—laborers black and white, Irish and English, free and enslaved, waged and unwaged —we can begin to see how the events of 1747, 1768, 1776, and 1780 were part of a broad cycle of rebellion in the eighteenth-century Atlantic world, in which continuities and connections informed a huge number and variety of popular struggles. A central theme in this cycle was the many-sided struggle against confinement—on ships, in workshops, in prisons, or even in empires—and the simultaneous search for autonomy. The circulation of working-class experience, especially certain forms of struggle, emerges as another theme, linking urban mobs, slave revolts, shipboard mutinies, agrarian risings, strikes, and prison riots, and the many different kinds of workers who made them—sailors, slaves, spalpeens, coalheavers, dockworkers, and others, many of whom occupied positions of strategic importance in the international division of labor. That much of this working-class experience circulated *to the eastward*, from American slave plantations, Irish commons, and Atlantic vessels, back to the streets of the metropolis, London, cannot be overemphasized. This interchange within a predominantly urban, portside proletariat took place over, around, beneath, and frequently against the artisans and craftsmen who are generally credited with creating the early working-class movement.

What consciousness pertained to this motley proletariat? We do not have a complete or definite answer to this question, although it is important that some points be raised despite the fact that we have in this segment of our longer study concerned ourselves only with slaves and maritime wage workers. First, we need to emphasize that consciousness arose from experience. The struggle against confinement led to a consciousness of freedom, which was in turn transformed into the revolutionary discussion of human rights. The experience of cooperation on plantation, ship, and waterfront led to a consciousness of interdependence and produced perforce new means of communication in language, music, and sign. Second, the various workers we have considered here brought with them the traditions of their own histories, which were preserved and amplified within the Atlantic world of the eighteenth century. Thus, pan-Africanism originated in Africa— not on the slavers—and became a potent Atlantic force by the 1780s. The antinomian and antiauthoritarian traditions of self-government, a heritage of the English Revolution of the 1640s, was preserved and expanded in North America. Finally, a third point arises from our investigation. At its most dynamic the eighteenth-century proletariat was often ahead of any fixed consciousness. The changes of geography, language, climate, and relations of family and production were so volatile and sudden that consciousness had to be characterized by a celerity of thought that may be difficult to comprehend by those whose experience has been steadier.

We hope our conclusions will be of interest to all those who think that a working class did not exist in the eighteenth century (before the rise of the factory system), and to all those whose conceptions of nation, race, and ethnicity have obscured both a field of force in which all history unfolds and a popular world of vital cooperation and accomplishment. The many heads of the transatlantic hydra may be likened to a popular drink of the eighteenth century called "All Nations," a compound of all the different spirits sold in a dram shop, collected in a single vessel into which the dregs and drainings of all the bottles and pots had been emptied (Grose 1785). We shall have to study all nations to understand the beast who has called forth such great violence, physical and conceptual, down through the ages.

NOTES

1. This paper, which represents work-in-progress, is a continuation of themes we first struck in Rediker (1988) and Linebaugh (1988). Our work has received much encouragement from Christopher Hill, and we particularly appreciate Hill (1975).

2. For quotations, see Mather (1702: ch. 2).

3. See Nash (1979: 221–22); Lax and Pencak (1976: 166–67); Clark (1931: 217); Bridenbaugh (1955: 115); Pares (1937: 48–49).

4. On the relationship between "liberty" and "right," see Lemisch (1968: 400).

5. The interpretation offered here, stressing the ways in which the seamen's actions generated revolutionary ideology, is exactly the opposite of that proposed by Bernard Bailyn, who sees the ideas of revolutionary movement as giving meaning to the seamen's "diffuse and indeliberate anti-authoritarianism" (1965: 583).

6. See Gaspar (1985: 37, 210); Craton (1982: 335–39); Wood (1974); Davis (1985: 158).

7. See Wood (1978: 276); Wood (1986: 170, 172–75); Crow (1980: 85–86); Aptheker (1943: 87, 200–202).

8. See Nash (1988: 72); Quarles (1961: 84); Lemisch (1968: 375). For the percentages of black workers in the maritime sector in the early nineteenth century, see White (1988: 453–54); Dye (1976: 358). On South Carolina, see Morgan (1984: 200); Wood (1978: 276).

9. Wood argues that the cycle entered a new phase—to last until 1783—when Lord Dunmore made his famous proclamation of 15 November 1775 that offered freedom to any slave who would fight in the king's army (1986: 177).

10. It is important to note that early American mobs acted within relatively undeveloped civil societies that lacked police forces and usually lacked standing armies; local militias could not easily be mobilized against them because militiamen were often part of the crowds. Urban mobs thus created enormous disequilibrium because there were so few other institutions or corporate groups to counterbalance them and guarantee social stability. Local authorities were too close to the action at hand, imperial authorities too far away. Crowds were, therefore, extremely powerful. They often succeeded in achieving their aims and usually managed to protect their own, which meant that individual members of the crowd were rarely arrested and prosecuted. Crowd activity itself was thus infrequently criminalized (even when it was condemned), a singular fact that makes it difficult for the historian to establish

the precise social composition of early American crowds, as, for example, George Rudé has done for crowds in England and France in the eighteenth century (1962). But such difficulties do not make it impossible to understand the role of sailors and slaves, for the power of the crowd insured that it would be the object of extensive commentary, if not the kind of direct legal analysis that would have come in the wake of repression.

11. See also Bridenbaugh (1955: 309). For specific accounts of the riots, see *Newport Mercury* 16 July 1974 and 10 June 1765; *New York Gazette, Weekly Post-Boy*, 12 July 1764 and 18 July 1765; *Weyman's New York Gazette*, 18 July 1765.

12. Schlesinger (1955: 244); Bridenbaugh (1955: 313–14); Morgan (1984: 233); Wood (1978: 277).

13. See Rosswurm (1987: 32–33); Hoerder (1977: 241).

14. See Boyer (1973: 289–308); Zobel (1970); Hoerder (1977); Rosswurm (1987: 46–48).

15. E. Foner (1976: 54), Lemisch (1968: 391), Nash (1988: 38–39) and P. Foner (1975: 37–38) are among the few historians who have noted the presence of African-Americans in revolutionary crowds. Others have not, perhaps because they distrusted some of these descriptions of "boys, sailors, and negroes" in colonial crowds, seeing them as self-serving efforts to protect well-to-do citizens who participated in mobs or as means to criticize mob activity by blaming it on the poorer parts of urban society. This seems to be the position of Dirk Hoerder, who admits that seamen and boys were common members of Boston crowds but argues that the presence of African-Americans was "negligible" (1977: 374). Sometimes the descriptions of crowds cannot be taken at face value, as when the Boston town meeting sought in 1747 to lay all blame upon "Foreign seamen, Servants, Negroes, and other Persons of Mean and Vile Condition" for the Knowles Riot, when in fact these groups could not have made up the "several thousand" who took part in the protest—even if these "Persons of Mean and Vile Condition" did in fact lead the riot, especially in its early stages (Resolution of the Boston Town Meeting in *Boston News-Letter*, 17 December 1747). Something similar was going on in John Adams's famous characterization of the mob involved in the Boston Massacre in 1770 quoted above. Other sources, written with less tendentious purposes, make it clear that such descriptions of various colonial crowds contained a strong element of truth.

16. Nash, Smith and Hoerder (1983: 418, 435) note that social structure varied by city as they delineate common occupational patterns. See also Nash (1988: 260, 320–21); Salinger (1987: 101–2, epilogue); Rosswurm (1987: 37);

Morgan (1984: 206–7, 219); Davis (1985: 81, 194); Linebaugh (1983); Gaspar (1985: 138, 204); Rediker (1987: ch. 1).

17. See Linebaugh (1983); Godard quoted in Steffen (1984: 73); Gouverneur Morris to Mr. Penn, 20 May 1774, in Force (1837: I, 343); Governor William Bull of South Carolina quoted in Maier (1970b: 185); Franklin (1961: III, 106). For a copy and discussion of Revere's engraving of the Boston Massacre, see Brigham (1969: 41–57).

18. Maier (1970b: 181, 186, 188); Maier (1970a: 33–35); Hoerder (1977: 378–88). Gordon Wood notes that "once-fervent Whig leaders began to sound like the Tories of 1775" when confronted by the mobs, popular committees, and "People Out-of Doors" in the 1780s (1969: 326).

19. This section depends on chapter nine of Linebaugh (1991), "If You Plead for Your Life, Plead in Irish," and is also indebted to Corkery (1925), which describes what we think is unique, viz., aristocratic verse forms applied to a proletarian experience whose consequent feeling—nostalgia—has been so successfully exploited by bourgeois nationalism on both sides of the water. Lecky (1893) is the best traditional account, but it should be checked against modern scholarship summarized in Miller (1985).

20. Musgrave writes that the Whiteboy movement began around 1759 (1802: I, 36–54), but most modern historians agree that the Whiteboys first appeared in 1761. Although their movement waned by 1765, their name lived on to describe a variety of agrarian movements throughout the 1780s and well into the nineteenth century. The best modern studies are Wall (1973: 13–25) and especially Donnelly (1978–79: 21–54). Lecky's pages on the Whiteboys are especially valuable because they preceded the destruction of the Castle archives in 1916 (1893: II, ch. 3); see also Miller (1985: 61–67). Beames (1983) provides a useful study of the Whiteboy movements of the nineteenth century. Elsewhere we will discuss the Irish-African connection as it appeared in the seventeenth-century Caribbean (forthcoming). That experience only grew with the momentous migrations of the eighteenth century, and it spread to as yet unstudied areas in Ireland and in West Africa. We think that it was a major development as the two societies had much in common—a pastoral economy, the relative absence of a commercial sector, the predominance of large kinship groupings as the social basis of production, the absence of individualism, and the emphasis upon collective mores, identities, music, and culture. These commonalities represented a basis for exchange when these two peoples found themselves occupying the most cooperative forms of eighteenth-century work—gang labor.

21. See Donnelly (1978–79: 26, 24, 34–35, 37–38, 39, 41–43); Beames

(1983: 33–34); "A Succinct Account of a Set of Miscreants in the Counties of Waterford, Cork, Limerick and Tipperary, called Bougheleen Bawins [i.e., White Boys]," *The Gentleman's Magazine*, 32: 182–3, in which is noted the capture of a man who "has been some time in the *French* service." Many thousands of Irishmen served in French armies in the century after 1691; see Linebaugh (1991: ch. 11).

22. See Moody et al. (1982); Froude (1874: II, 25); Wall (1973: 16); Donnelly (1978–79: 28).

23. See Lecky (1893: 2, 41–45); Wall (1973: 19, 20). It is worth noting that Sheehy was the only priest known to have been involved with the Whiteboys. The overwhelming majority of priests were strongly opposed, which, according to Maurine Wall, helps to explain the increasing popular intimidation of priests in the 1770s.

24. See Wall (1973: 18); Connolly (1987: 43). Richard Aston, chief justice of the Court of Common Pleas in Ireland, noted that "papist and protestant were promiscuously concerned" in the Whiteboy movement (quoted in Donnelly 1978–79: 46).

25. The drought of 1765 and ensuing starvation in Ireland forced many to migrate to London and America (Donnelly 1978–79: 52–53).

26. Ashton (1959: 181); Beveridge et al. (1939: 292).

27. Quotation in "Memorials of a Dialogue betwixt several Seamen a certain Victualler & a S——l Master in the Late Riot," SB, vol. XCXXX.

28. See also *The Westminster Journal*, 16 July 1768; *Berrow's Worcester Journal*, 23 June 1768, 14 July 1768; TSP 11/818/2696.

29. It may be true, as John Rule has recently pointed out, that the verb "to strike" was already in circulation among the working class of London by 1765 (1989: 103). This would not alter the accepted etymology of the term, its origins of among the labors of seamen, nor would it lessen the importance of the events of 1768, which represented the greatest strike then known in Britain. See the *Oxford English Dictionary*, s.v. "strike."

30. Castro (1926) and Hibbert (1958) are two good introductions. They may be supplemented by the materials in Stevenson (1979), Hayter (1978), and Rudé (1973: 268–92). The story as presented here draws upon the fuller treatment and the sources presented in Linebaugh (1991: ch. 10).

31. CLRO, SP, "London Prisoners," 1780; *The Proceedings . . . of the Old Bailey*, 8 December 1779 and 14 April 1779.

32. CLRO, IB; CLRO, GB; CLRO, SP, June 1780. See also Cugoano ([1787] 1971) and Equiano ([1789] 1971). It should be noted that Glover, Bowsey, and Hyde (the sailor) represented half of those tried, presumed by the state to have been the ringleaders, for the attack on Newgate.

33. Discussions of the size of the London black population may be found in Fryer (1984), Walvin (1971), Shyllon (1974), and Shyllon (1977).

34. In "A list of Massachusetts Soldiers and Sailors in the War of the Revolution" several "John" or "Jonathan" Glovers are listed as deserting or captured before 1780, and some are described as of dark complexion. For a fuller discussion of Glover's identity, and of Bowsey's, discussed below, see Linebaugh (1991: ch. 10).

35. See Lorimer (1981) cited in Fryer (1984: 203, 541).

References

Adams, John. 1965. *Legal Papers of John Adams.* Vol. 3. Eds. L. Kinvin Wroth and Hiller B. Zobel. Cambridge, Mass.: Belknap Press.

Aptheker, Herbert. 1943. *American Negro Slave Revolts.* New York: Columbia University Press.

Ashton, Thomas Southcliffe. 1959. *Economic Fluctuations in England, 1700–1800.* Oxford: Clarendon Press.

Ashton, Thomas Southcliffe and Joseph Sykes. 1964. *The Coal Industry in the Eighteenth Century.* 2d ed. Manchester: Manchester University Press.

Bailyn, Bernard. 1965. *Pamphlets of the American Revolution.* Cambridge, Mass.: Belknap Press.

Beames, M. R. 1983. *Peasants and Power: Whiteboy Movements and their Control in Pre-Famine Ireland.* New York: St. Martin's Press.

Beckles, Hilary. 1984. *Black Rebellion in Barbadoes: The Struggle Against Slavery, 1627–1838.* Bridgetown, Barbados: Antilles Publications.

Bernal, Martin. 1987. *Black Athena: The Afroasiatic Roots of Classical Civilization.* Vol. 1. *The Fabrication of Ancient Greece 1785–1985.* New Brunswick, N.J.: Rutgers University Press.

Beveridge, William, et al. 1939. *Prices and Wages in England from the Twelfth to the Nineteenth Century.* Vol. 1. *Price Tables: Mercantile Era.* London: Frank Cass.

Boyer, Lee R. 1973. "Lobster Backs, Liberty Boys, and Laborers in the Streets: New York's Golden Hill and Nassau Street Riots." *New York Historical Society Quarterly* 57:289–308.

Bridenbaugh, Carl. 1955. *Cities in Revolt: Urban Life in America, 1743–1776*. New York: Capricorn Books.

Brigham, Clarence S. 1969. *Paul Revere's Engravings*. New York: Atheneum.

Castro, J. Paul de. 1926. *The Gordon Riots*. London: H. Milford, Oxford University Press.

Clark, Dora Mae. 1931. "The Impressment of Seamen in the American Colonies." In *Essays in Colonial History Presented to Charles McLean Andrews by His Students*. New Haven: Yale University Press.

Connolly, James. 1987. *Labour in Irish History*. London: Bookmarks.

CLRO. See under Archival Sources.

Corkery, Daniel. 1925. *The Hidden Ireland: A Study of Gaelic Munster in the 18th Century*. Dublin: M. H. Gill and Son, Ltd.

Countryman, Edward. 1981. *A People in Revolution: The American Revolution and Political Society in New York, 1760–1790*. Baltimore: Johns Hopkins University Press.

Craton, Michael. 1982. *Testing the Chains: Resistance to Slavery in the British West Indies*. Ithaca: Cornell University Press.

Crow, Jeffrey J. 1980. "Slave Rebelliousness and Social Conflict in North Carolina, 1775 to 1802." *William and Mary Quarterly*, 3d ser., 37:79–102.

Cugoano, Ottobah. [1787] 1971. "Thoughts and Sentiments on the Evil and Wicked Traffic of the Slavery and Commerce of the Human Species." In *Three Black Writers in Eighteenth-Century England*, eds. Francis D. Adams and Barry Sanders. Belmont, California: Wadsworth Publishing Co.

Davis, T. J. 1985. *Rumor of Revolt: The "Great Negro Plot" in Colonial New York*. New York: Free Press.

Donnelly, James S., Jr. 1978–79. "The Whiteboy Movement, 1761–1765." *Irish Historical Studies* 21:21–54.

Dye, Ira. 1976. "Early American Merchant Seafarers." *Proceedings of the American Philosophical Society* 120:358.

Equiano, Olaudah. [1789] 1971. "The Interesting Narrative of the Life of Olaudah Equiano, or Gustavus Vassa, the African, Written by Himself." In *Three Black Writers in Eighteenth-Century England*, eds. Francis D. Adams and Barry Sanders. Belmont, California: Wadsworth Publishing Co.

Fielding, John. 1768. *Extracts from the Criminal Law*. London.

Foner, Eric. 1976. *Tom Paine and Revolutionary America*. New York: Oxford University Press.

Foner, Philip S. 1975. *Blacks in the American Revolution*. Westport, Conn.: Greenwood Press.

Force, Peter, ed. [1837] 1963. *Tracts and Other Papers Relating Principally to the Origin, Settlement, and Progress of the Colonies in North America. . . .* 4 vols. Gloucester, Mass.: Peter Smith.

Franklin, Benjamin. 1961. *The Papers of Benjamin Franklin.* Vol. III. Ed. Leonard W. Labaree. New Haven: Yale University Press.

Froude, James Anthony. 1874. *The English in Ireland in the 18th Century.* New York: Longmans, Green and Co.

Fryer, Peter. 1984. *Staying Power: The History of Black People in Britain.* London: Pluto Press.

Gaspar, David Barry. 1985. *Bondmen and Rebels: A Study of Master-Slave Relations in Antigua, with Implications for Colonial British America.* Baltimore: Johns Hopkins University Press.

Gilbert, Arthur N. 1987. "The Nature of Mutiny in the British Navy in the Eighteenth Century." In *Naval History: The Sixth Symposium of the U.S. Naval Academy,* ed. David M. Masterson. Wilmington, Del.: Scholarly Resources, Inc.

Grose, Francis. 1785. *A Classical Dictionary of the Vulgar Tongue.* London: S. Hooper.

Hall, N. A. T. 1985. "Maritime Maroons: Grand Marronage from the Danish West Indies." *William and Mary Quarterly,* 3d ser., 42: 476–98.

Hayter, Tony. 1978. *The Army and the Crowd in Mid-Georgian London.* London: Macmillan.

Hibbert, Christopher. 1958. *King Mob: The Story of Lord George Gordon and the Riots of 1780.* London and New York: Longmans, Green.

Hill, Christopher. 1975. "The Many-Headed Monster." In *Change and Continuity in 17th-Century England.* Cambridge, Mass.: Harvard University Press.

Hoerder, Dirk. 1977. *Crowd Action in Revolutionary Massachusetts, 1765–1780.* New York: Academic Press.

Horsmanden, Daniel. 1971. *The New York Conspiracy,* ed. Thomas Davis. Boston: Beacon Press.

Hutchinson, Thomas. 1936. *The History of the Colony and Province of Massachusetts Bay,* ed. Lawrence S. Mayo. Cambridge, Mass.: Harvard University Press.

Hutson, James H. 1971. "An Investigation of the Inarticulate: Philadelphia's White Oaks." *William and Mary Quarterly,* 3d ser., 18:3–25.

Kaplan, Sidney, and Emma Nogrady Kaplan. 1989. *The Black Presence in the*

Era of the American Revolution. Revised ed. Amherst: University of Massachusetts Press.

Lax, John and William Pencak. 1976. "The Knowles Riot and the Crisis of the 1740s in Massachusetts." *Perspectives in American History* 19:163–214.

Lecky, W.E.H. 1893. *History of Ireland in the Eighteenth Century.* London: Longmans, Green.

Lemisch, Jesse. 1968. "Jack Tar in the Streets: Merchant Seamen in the Politics of Revolutionary America." *William and Mary Quarterly*, 3d ser., 25:371–407.

Linebaugh, Peter. 1983. "A Letter to Boston's 'Radical Americans' from a 'Loose and Disorderly' New Yorker, Autumn 1770." *Midnight Notes* 4:17–26.

———. 1988. "All the Atlantic Mountains Shook." In *Reviving the English Revolution: Reflections and Elaborations on the Work of Christopher Hill*, eds. Geoff Eley and William Hunt. London: Verso.

———. 1991. *The London Hanged: Crime and Civil Society in the Eighteenth Century.* London: Allen Lane.

Linebaugh, Peter and Marcus Rediker. Forthcoming. *The Many-Headed Hydra: The Atlantic Working Class in the Seventeenth and Eighteenth Centuries.*

Lorimer, Douglas A. 1981. "Black Slaves and English Liberty: A Re-examination of Racial Slavery in England." Paper presented to the International Conference on the History of Blacks in Britain, London.

Maier, Pauline. 1970a. "Popular Uprising and Civil Authority in Eighteenth-Century America." *William and Mary Quarterly*, 3d ser., 27:33–35.

———. 1970b. "The Charleston Mob and the Evolution of Popular Politics in Revolutionary South Carolina, 1765–1784." *Perspectives in American History*, 4:173–96.

Marx, Karl. 1938. *Capital: A Critical Analysis of Capitalist Production.* Trans. Dona Torr. London: George Allen and Unwin, Ltd.

Mather, Cotton. 1702. *Magnalia Christi Americana: or, The ecclesiastical history of New-England. . . .* 7 vols. London: Thomas Parkhurst.

Maxwell, Constantia. 1936. *Dublin under the Georges, 1714–1830.* London: G. G. Harrap.

Miller, Kirby A. 1985. *Emigrants and Exiles: Ireland and the Irish Exodus to North America.* New York: Oxford University Press.

Moody, T. W., et al. 1982. *A New History of Ireland.* Vol. 3. *A Chronology of Irish History to 1976.* Oxford: Clarendon Press and New York: Oxford University Press.

Morgan, Philip D. 1984. "Black Life in Eighteenth-Century Charleston." *Perspectives in American History*, new ser., 1: 187–232.

Musgrave, Richard. 1802. *Memoirs of the Different Rebellions in Ireland*. Vol. 1. 3d ed. Dublin: Printed by R. Marchbank and sold by J. Archer.

Nash, Gary B. 1979. *The Urban Crucible: Social Change, Political Consciousness, and the Origins of the American Revolution*. Cambridge, Mass.: Harvard University Press.

———. 1988. *Forging Freedom: The Formation of Philadelphia's Black Community, 1730–1840*. Cambridge, Mass.: Harvard University Press.

Nash, Gary B., Billy G. Smith, and Dirk Hoerder. 1983. "Laboring Americans and the American Revolution." *Labor History* 24:414–39.

Pares, Richard. 1937. "The Manning of the Navy in the West Indies, 1702–1763." *Royal Historical Society Transactions* 20:31–60.

Price, Richard., ed. 1983. *To Slay the Hydra: Dutch Colonial Perspectives on the Saramaka Wars*. Ann Arbor: Karoma.

Prior, Thomas. 1769. *A List of Absentees in Ireland*. 2d ed. Dublin: Printed for R. Gunne.

The Proceedings . . . of the Old Bailey. 1714–1800.

Quarles, Benjamin. 1961. *The Negro in the American Revolution*. Chapel Hill: University of North Carolina Press.

Rediker, Marcus. 1987. *Between the Devil and the Deep Blue Sea: Merchant Seamen, Pirates, and the Anglo-American Maritime World, 1700–1750*. Cambridge: Cambridge University Press.

———. 1988. "Good Hands, Stout Heart, and Fast Feet: The History and Culture of Working People in Early America." In *Reviving the English Revolution: Reflections and Elaborations on the Work of Christopher Hill*. eds. Geoff Eley and William Hunt. London: Verso.

Reid, John P. 1977. *In a Defiant Stance: The Conditions of Law in Massachusetts Bay, the Irish Comparison, and the Coming of the American Revolution*. University Park: Pennsylvania State University Press.

Richardson, Edward H. 1982. *Standards and Colors of the American Revolution*. Philadelphia: University of Pennsylvania Press.

Rosswurm, Steven. 1987. *Arms, Country, and Class: The Philadelphia Militia and the "Lower Sort" during the American Revolution*. New Brunswick: Rutgers University Press.

Rudé, George. 1962. *Wilkes and Liberty: A Social Study of 1763–1774*. Oxford: Clarendon Press.

————. 1973. *Paris and London in the Eighteenth Century*. New York: Viking Press.

Rule, John. 1989. "Review of *Between the Devil and the Deep Blue Sea*, by M. Rediker." *Bulletin for the Society for the Study of Labour History* 54:103.

Salinger, Sharon V. 1987. *"To Serve Well and Faithfully": Labor and Indentured Servitude in Pennsylvania, 1682–1800*. Cambridge: Cambridge University Press.

Sancho, Ignatius. [1782] 1971. "Letters." In *Three Black Writers in Eighteenth-Century England*, eds. Francis D. Adams and Barry Sanders. Belmont, California: Wadsworth Publishing Co.

SB. See under Archival Sources.

Schlesinger, Arthur Meier. 1955. "Political Mobs and the American Revolution." *Proceedings of the American Philosophical Society* 99:244–50.

Shaw, Allan George Lewers. 1966. *Convicts and Colonies: A Study of Penal Transportation from Great Britain to Australia and Other Parts of the British Empire*. Victoria: Melbourne University Press.

Shyllon, F. O. 1974. *Black Slaves in Britain*. London: Published for the Institute of Race Relations by Oxford University Press.

————. 1977. *Black People in Britain*. London: Published for the Institute of Race Relations by Oxford University Press.

Steffen, Charles G. 1984. *The Mechanics of Baltimore: Workers and Politics in the Age of Revolution, 1763–1812*. Urbana: University of Illinois Press.

Stevenson, John. 1979. *Popular Disturbance in England, 1700–1870*. London: Longman.

Thompson, E. P. 1963. *The Making of the English Working Class*. New York: Vintage.

TSP. See under Archival Sources.

Wall, Maurine. 1973. "The Whiteboys." In *Secret Societies in Ireland*, ed. Desmond T. Williams. Dublin: Gill and MacMillan.

Walpole, Horace. 1973. *Horace Walpole's Correspondence*, eds. W. S. Lewis et al. New Haven: Yale University Press.

Walvin, James. 1971. *The Black Presence: A Documentary History of the Negro in England, 1555–1860*. New York: Schocken Books.

Wellenreuther, Hermann. 1983. "Labor in the Era of the American Revolution: An Exchange." *Labor History* 24:536–600.

White, Shane. 1988. "'We Dwell in Safety and Pursue Our Honest Callings': Free Blacks in New York City, 1783–1810." *Journal of American History* 75:445–70.

Williams, Desmond T., ed. 1973. *Secret Societies in Ireland*. Dublin: Gill and Macmillan.

Wood, Gordon. 1969. *The Creation of the American Republic, 1776–1787*. Chapel Hill: University of North Carolina Press.

Wood, Peter H. 1974. *Black Majority: Negroes in Colonial South Carolina from 1670 through the Stono Rebellion*. New York: W. W. Norton Company.

————. 1978. "'Taking Care of Business' in Revolutionary South Carolina: Republicanism and the Slave Society." In *The Southern Experience in the American Revolution*, eds. Jeffrey J. Crow and Larry E. Tise. Chapel Hill: University of North Carolina Press.

————. 1986. "'The Dream Deferred': Black Freedom Struggles on the Eve of White Independence." In *In Resistance: Studies in African, Caribbean, and Afro-American History*, ed. Gary Y. Okihiro. Amherst: University of Massachusetts Press.

Young, Alfred. 1984. "English Plebian Culture and Eighteenth-Century American Radicalism." In *The Origins of Anglo-American Radicalism*, eds. Margaret Jacob and James Jacob. London: George Allen & Unwin.

Zobel, Hiller B. 1970. *The Boston Massacre*. New York: W. W. Norton Company.

ARCHIVAL SOURCES

CLRO, GB   Corporation of London Record Office, Gaol Book.
CLRO, IB   Corporation of London Record Office, Indictment Bills.
CLRO, SP   Corporation of London Record Office, Sessions Papers.
SB   Shelbourne Papers, William Clements Library, University of Michigan.
TSP   Treasury Solicitor Papers, Public Record Office, London.

4

British Reaction to the Amritsar Massacre, 1919–1920

Derek Sayer

> You think Jallianwala proves that the British are lying, talking freedom but acting tyrannically and dealing destruction? Again you are wrong. Jallianwala could never have happened if the British who talk freedom were not sincere. It happened because they are sincere.
>
> —Paul Scott (*The Day of the Scorpion*)

> "We're not out here for the purpose of behaving pleasantly!"
> "What do you mean?"
> "What I say. We're out here to do justice and keep the peace. Them's my sentiments. India isn't a drawing-room."
> "Your sentiments are those of a god," she said quietly.
>
> —E. M. Forster (*A Passage to India*)

On the afternoon of 13 April 1919, Brigadier General Reginald Dyer led fifty riflemen of the 1/9th Gurkhas, 54th Sikhs and 59th Sikhs[1] through the streets of Amritsar to the Jallianwala Bagh, where a meeting was being held in defiance of his proclamation banning such gatherings. The Bagh was a piece of waste ground, some two hundred yards long, wholly enclosed by the backs of houses and low boundary walls. It had three or four narrow entrances, the main one only broad enough for two people to walk abreast. This proved too small to permit passage of the two armored cars, with mounted machine guns, which Dyer had brought with him. Shortly after five, he led his troops up the narrow alley. The crowd in the Bagh was later estimated at upward of twenty thousand people. Among them were many villagers from the surrounding countryside, in Amritsar for the *Baisakhi* holiday and the cattle market held on that day.

Within thirty seconds of his arrival Dyer ordered his men to open fire. No warning, or demand that the crowd disperse, was given. The firing continued for ten minutes; in all 1650 rounds were spent. Dyer ordered fire to be focused where the crowd was thickest, including the exits. He gave the order to cease fire only when his ammunition was virtually exhausted. According to official figures, 379 people were killed and more than twelve hundred wounded; Indian estimates are much higher. Dyer later acknowledged that had he been able to use his machine guns he probably would have, with inevitably larger casualties. He made no provision for the wounded; it was, he said, "not my job" (Hunter 1920: 1120). Such was "Amritsar," the single event which by common consent did most to undo British rule in India.

I

Winston Churchill, the Secretary of State for War at the time, called it "an episode . . . without precedent or parallel in the modern history of the British Empire . . . an extraordinary event, a monstrous event, an event which stands in singular and sinister isolation." Herbert Asquith claimed "there has never been such an incident in the whole annals of Anglo-Indian history nor, I believe, in the history of our Empire from its very inception down to the present day . . . It is one of the worst outrages in the whole of our history" (Hansard 1920: cxxxi, cols. 1725, 1736). In some ways they were undoubtedly right. The British had put down armed uprisings in India and elsewhere in the past with exemplary brutality.[2] But no previous use of military force, in the United Kingdom or colonies, against an unarmed and peaceable crowd had resulted in a remotely comparable loss of life. Peterloo left eleven dead, and perhaps five hundred wounded (Thompson 1968: 754). There is no evidence that the Amritsar massacre was an act of deliberate policy, comparable to Nazi reprisals at

Lidice and elsewhere. It appears, on the face of it, a tragic aberration in British imperial history, and Dyer's individual responsibility alone.

Perceptions of Amritsar's singularity have dominated the English historiography. One sign of this is just how little has been written, outside India, on what A.J.P. Taylor has called "the decisive moment when Indians were alienated from British rule" (quoted in Fein 1977: xii). This stems, I believe, from more than embarrassment in the face of one of the less glorious chapters in British history. The construction of the Amritsar massacre from the start as "singular and sinister" marginalizes it. There has been no felt need to agonize over Amritsar as in any sense a national shame, because it is aberrant, in a category by itself, not part of the national history at all. Those few English works that do exist on the topic have for the most part accepted this frame of reference. They assume, and then seek to explain, the exceptionality of Dyer's action. Furneaux suggests that Dyer's judgment was impaired by the arteriosclerosis from which he suffered. He and others have also made much of the discrepancies in Dyer's testimony at various times, arguing that it was only his subsequent hailing as the "Saviour of the Punjab" which led him to explain his action as stemming from anything other than fear of being overwhelmed by the crowd (1963: 174ff).[3] If this is true, it is itself revealing. To defend Dyer on the grounds that he was "trailing his coat" before Anglo-Indian[4] opinion begs the question of the character of that opinion itself.

But by no means all have agreed in seeing Dyer's action as "singular." Indian voices are significantly different. Gandhi wrote, "We do not want to punish Dyer. We have no desire for revenge. We want to change the system that produced Dyer" (cited in Datta 1969: frontispiece). Raja Ram claims—in my view, without supporting evidence—that the massacre "was not the result of a decision taken by an individual (General Dyer) on the spur of the moment, but of a premeditated plan, carefully designed in advance, and executed on the appointed day, by the British bureaucracy" (1969: vii). V. N. Datta insists that it was not an isolated phenomenon but "an expression of a confrontation between ruler and ruled" (1969: ix). Helen Fein, an American sociologist, likewise concludes that Jallianwala was "a prototypical instance of a repressive collective punishment practiced by the British in black and Asian colonies" (1977: xii–xiii).

Similar points were made by contemporaries. Ben Spoor M.P., speaking for the Labour Party during the 1920 Commons debate on the Dyer case, contended that "Amritsar was not an isolated event any more than General Dyer was an isolated officer" (Hansard 1920: cxxxi, col. 1739). Three weeks before, at the Labour Party Annual Conference, Ramsay MacDonald had warned that Dyer must not be allowed to be made the scapegoat for the broader failings of civil government in India (*Times* 25 June 1920). This denial of Amritsar's singularity was not confined to the critics of British imperialism in India or Britain. Many others, on the opposite side of the fence from Gandhi or MacDonald, did not see Dyer's action as "singular" (or, in their case, as "monstrous") either. At the time, the British government's disavowal of Dyer was deplored by the bulk of Anglo-Indian opinion, sections of the press in both India and Britain, a very substantial minority in the House of Commons, a majority in the Lords, and (eventually) the Court of King's Bench—not to mention the many who gave in their droves to Dyer's defense fund. For them too, the massacre was no aberration. It was exactly what Dyer said it was: "my duty—my horrible, dirty duty" (quoted in *Daily Mail*, 4 May 1920). My contention here will be that these contemporaries were correct. Although Amritsar was in some quite obvious ways singular, its explanation lies rather in the ways it was not.

In the British responses to Jallianwala Bagh in 1919–20, we can see different constructions of events in the making. I shall say little more in this paper about the Labour Party view, save to register its existence. It needs to be placed on record that some British men and women did see Jallianwala in terms of the pathology of a system, not an individual. These included Anglo-Indians like Benjamin Guy Horniman, the editor of the *Bombay Chronicle*, who was deported to Britain for his criticisms of the handling of the Punjab disturbances. No attempt is offered here to assess how representative such sentiments were. My concern is rather with the responses of those we can loosely call the governing classes, both in India and "at home." One response, which started with the findings of the Hunter Committee set up to investigate the disorders, was to become the authorized version. This was the view of the British government, somewhat reluctantly acquiesced in by the Government of India, and of the more liberal press. It was intimately bound up with changes in forms of colonial rule, symbolized by the Montagu-Chelmsford reform scheme of 1919, which provided for limited Indian participation in some areas of government on the road to eventual Dominion status.[5] It is this official version which has set the terms for much of the historiography. The other view I will look at here is the version espoused by Dyer's many supporters. It was anchored in the social rituals and practices of rule of the post-Mutiny era in India.[6] It was also, and not incidentally, linked with struggles going on at the time in Ireland; Sir Edward Carson was one of Dyer's most passionate advocates. If not the majority view at the time, it undoubtedly commanded very wide assent. It also, I shall argue, makes sense—of a sort—of the massacre. Antecedent events alone do not; what is critical is the meanings that were put on them.

II

Disaffection was widespread in India in 1919.[7] The war had led to much hardship, and the Montagu-Chelmsford reforms were widely seen as poor recompense. Annie Besant spoke for many when she called them "unworthy of Britain to offer or India to accept" (quoted in Datta 1969: 28); they were rejected by both Congress and the Muslim League. The Rowlatt Bills—the immediate target of Indian protests early in 1919—added insult to injury. The first bill passed into law on 21 March as the Anarchical and Revolutionary Crimes Act. It provided for the trial of political offenses by three High Court Judges, with no jury or right of appeal. Trials could take place in camera, and hear evidence which would not be admissible under the Indian Evidence Act. The Executive was empowered to arrest, search without warrant, and confine suspects without trial for renewable periods of up to a year. The second Rowlatt Bill, eventually dropped, would also have made possession of seditious publications an imprisonable offense. Indian politicians fought a fierce campaign against Rowlatt, and demonstrations took place across India. Gandhi's *Satyagraha* movement was launched in Bombay. There was rioting in Ahmedabad, Delhi, and several districts of the Punjab.

Sir Michael O'Dwyer, the lieutenant governor of the Punjab from 1913 to 1919, had a name for "tough" rule. His allegedly coercive recruiting practices during the war (the Punjab, with a thirteenth of India's population, supplied some sixty percent of the troops recruited there) added specific local grievances to those general throughout India.[8] O'Dwyer's Anglo-Irish background—he was one of fourteen children of a middling landlord—is not irrelevant to his perceptions of what his job demanded of him. "He knew from boyhood," says Philip Mason, "what conspiracy and outrage mean to peaceful folk" (Woodruff 1954: 238). General Dyer also had early formative experiences in Ireland, having been educated at Middleton College, County Cork. O'Dwyer was, according to the *Dictionary of National Biography*, "a warm sympathizer with the rural classes," but firmly believed in "the necessity of British control of India for that country's welfare."[9] He opposed the Montagu-Chelmsford reforms. During the war he had ruthlessly crushed dissent—most notably the Ghadr movement, launched by Sikhs in North America—muzzled the Indian press, and excluded Indian activists from entering the Punjab. Controls on the press were stepped up early in 1919.

There had been several protest meetings in Amritsar itself over Rowlatt, leading to a *hartal*,[10] or general strike, on 30 March. The Punjab government prohibited two of the organizers of the protests, Drs. Satyapal and Kitchlew, from speaking in public, communicating with the press, or leaving Amritsar. A second *hartal* was set for 6 April. At a meeting of 50,000 people two demands were made: the repeal of Rowlatt, and the rescinding of the orders against Kitchlew and Satyapal. The *hartal* passed off without violence. Nonetheless, Miles Irving, the deputy commissioner, requested an increase in military forces to defend the Civil Lines, the area outside Amritsar proper where the Europeans lived.

April ninth was a day of Hindu religious festival, *Ram Naumi*. Remarkable scenes of "fraternization" between Hindus and Moslems, including the public sharing of water vessels, were witnessed by Miles Irving—uneasily. The Hunter Report later commented that "in Amritsar as elsewhere efforts towards 'unity' had been made largely indeed frankly in a political interest," such cooperation of "the warring creeds" testifying to the influence of Kitchlew and other leaders (Hunter 1920: 20).[11] That evening orders were received by Irving from O'Dwyer for the arrest, deportation from Amritsar, and detention of Kitchlew and Satyapal. It was decided to invite the two men to Irving's bungalow at 10 A.M. the next day and spirit them out of Amritsar. Pickets were to be posted to defend the Civil Lines, and plans were laid for evacuation of European women and children to the Gobindgarh fort.

On 10 April, the news of the deportation of Satyapal and Kitchlew spread swiftly, and crowds—who by then knew also of Gandhi's arrest the previous evening—collected rapidly. They moved through the center of the city, heading for the Civil Lines where they intended to protest the arrests at Irving's bungalow. At this stage there was no violence, and Europeans encountered by the crowd were not molested. Nor was any property attacked. But at two of the bridges separating the city from the Civil Lines there was bloodshed. In both cases it would seem that the crowds pushed forward, resorted eventually to stoning the troops, and were fired upon. Prominent local lawyers tried to intercede; one of them, Maqbool Mahmood, claimed that "if the authorities had a little more patience we would have succeeded in taking the crowd back" (quoted in Datta 1969: 76).[12] The firing—official figures give twelve dead and twenty to thirty wounded—changed the temper of the crowd.

By the end of the day many buildings had been looted and burned down, and five Europeans beaten to death. One such assault, the attack on the manager of the City Mission School, Miss Sherwood— who was left for dead, but given first aid by Hindu shopkeepers—was particularly to incense Dyer, who arrived in Amritsar late the next evening to take effective control of the city from the civil authorities. The rest of the European women and children were safely ensconced in the fort by 4 P.M. on 10 April. The railroad lines had been damaged, and telegraph and telephone wires cut. Word came in, magnified by rumor, of riot, murder, and arson elsewhere in the Punjab.

III

Grave as the situation in Amritsar undoubtedly was on Dyer's arrival, it does not fully account for what happened at Jallianwala two days later. For by 13 April, the beleaguered garrison had been amply reinforced, and no further violence had broken out; indeed "ringleaders" were being arrested on the twelfth. Dyer's shooting was not necessitated, in any military sense, by the situation within Amritsar. To comprehend the massacre we need to look beyond the events I have outlined.

It is revealing, however, of both the moral relations involved and the way these continue to haunt the historiography, that a simple narrative of the events which culminated in the rioting of 10 April *has* frequently served as justification for the massacre, beginning with an article "By an Englishwoman" in *Blackwood's Magazine* in April 1920. This is an eyewitness account of the riots of 10 April and the crowded, insanitary, and servantless conditions suffered by the European women and children "who had never known a day's real hardship before" in the fort during the next few days. It concluded that "General Dyer's action alone saved them" (Anonymous 1920: 444, 446). The author felt no need to explain how or why this was so; she simply took it to be self-evident. In a much later book, Alfred Draper achieves much the same effect by his liberal use of purple prose: the "mobs" were "frenzied" and "half-crazed," their cries "like the howling of wolves" (1981: 64ff).[13] Knowingly or otherwise he echoes Dyer's contemporary supporters. "A Planter" wrote in 1920 to the Calcutta *Statesman*, berating twenty-five missionaries who had had the temerity to criticize Dyer's "Prussianism": "I wonder if they will think of the man whom they have helped to malign if ever they have the experience of being chased by a maddened mob of coolies who are out for their blood" (*Statesman*, 20 July 1920). Draper's mob also bayed for "white blood" (1981: 71).

What is conveyed through the silences in the anonymous Englishwoman's account and the imagery of Draper's narrative, is that—contrary to Lord Birkenhead's argument in the debate on Dyer in the Lords—conduct was called for in Amritsar which would never be thinkable "in Glasgow or Belfast or Winnipeg" (Hansard 1920: xli, col. 279).[14] That it was British actions, from the flagrant disregard of "due process" in Rowlatt, to the arrest and deportation of Kitchlew and Satyapal, and the initial British firing at the bridges, which provoked Indian retaliation, or that far more Indians (who remain nameless) than Europeans were killed or wounded on 10 April, let alone on 13 April, is lost sight of. India is represented as a different moral universe; violence by British and Indians is not equivalent. Helen Fein has made this point in her study. It is an important one. The *otherness* of India—an otherness which was nurtured in the social distancing fundamental to British life in and rule of India—was fundamental to the legitimation of the actions of Dyer and others, enabling their transmutation from what would otherwise be seen as crimes into moral acts. Fein's conclusion that colonial rulers exclude the ruled from their own domain of moral obligation is, however, an oversimplification (1977).[15]

It is certainly true that different moral standards were applied to British and Indian actions. But this does not mean that the British recognized no obligations toward Indians. On the contrary, Dyer's actions were defended by contemporaries just because he *had* acted morally—dutifully—according to the canons of mutual obligation between rulers and ruled, as they were defined by the former. This is, in many ways, what is most revealing in British responses to Jallianwala, for it testifies to what is always a key dimension of rule. Legitimation is as centrally a matter of authorizing the actions of rulers as of securing the compliance of the ruled; it is better analyzed as an essential, animating component of power than as its mere *post festum* rationalization. Morality, in the context of governance, colonial or otherwise, is far more than ideology (Corrigan and Sayer 1985). British India rested as firmly on a set of moral relations as it did on bayonets or bullets. Underpinning these is a positive constitution of Indians as particular sorts of subjects, in a way which Draper's book echoes sixty years later.[16] It was this which permitted a coherent moral defense of Dyer's action, and goes far toward explaining it.

IV

Certain other British actions during that spring in the Punjab provide us with one point of entry into this (intensely) moral universe. On 15 April martial law was imposed on Amritsar and four other districts of the Punjab. At O'Dwyer's behest it was backdated to 30 March, in order "to deal appropriately with the local leaders whose speeches during the preceding fortnight did so much to inflame classes who have joined the disturbances" (telegram from chief secretary of Punjab government to secretary of Government of India, quoted in Draper 1981: 125). This meant that Kitchlew and Satyapal, despite being in custody on the tenth, could still be tried under martial law regulations, which created summary courts under one or more military officers, and set up four martial law commissions for more serious cases. The latter sat in camera, were not obliged to record evidence, and permitted only limited cross-examination. Choice of counsel was in any case severely restricted since outside lawyers were banned from the Punjab. Of the 852 accused, 581 were convicted; 108 were sentenced to death, and 264 (including Kitchlew and Satyapal, convicted on the testimony of an "official approver")[17] to transportation for life. There was no appeal. After much protest about procedure, protest largely vindicated by a later judicial review, martial law commission sentences were commuted by royal proclamation in December 1919. But by then eighteen men had been publicly hanged.

In the summary courts, flogging was the normal punishment. In around half the cases it was done publicly. There are reports from Lahore of European spectators enthusiastically urging the wielders of the cane to strike harder. A wedding party was flogged for being an illegal gathering, and a group of men were whipped before an audience of prostitutes for visiting a brothel during curfew. There are numerous accounts by Indian witnesses of attempts to coerce them, both physically and otherwise, into giving false evidence.[18]

Collective punishments were widely imposed. In Amritsar, water and electricity supplies were shut off. Vehicles, including bicycles, were commandeered; so were fans, for the relief of soldiers. The issue of third- and intermediate-class rail tickets was withdrawn, effectively closing the railroads to the Indians. A strict curfew remained in force. In Lahore, students were expelled from colleges, not on the basis of proven participation in the disturbances, but by quota. Students were also forced to march up to seventeen miles a day in the sun. In Chuhar Kara, peasants were forbidden to harvest their crops. There were cases of attempted aerial bombing, in one instance of a girls' school, in another of a mosque.

But what most distinguishes many of the martial law orders was their ritualistically humiliating character. Thus, Captain Doveton in Kasur, the man who devised the whipping in front of the prostitutes, numbered among his "fancy punishments" making people skip, recite poems, and touch the ground with their noses. It is also alleged that he had people whitewashed. In Malawakal and Sheikupura all males were made to do the work of sweepers—untouchables. In Amritsar, Dyer had all the lawyers in the city act as "special constables." Their "policing duties" included menial work and the witnessing of floggings. Salaaming, saluting, and descending orders were widely promulgated. The text of one such order runs as follows:

> Whereas it has come to my notice that certain inhabitants of the Gujranwala District are habitually exhibiting a lack of respect for gazetted or commissioned European Civil and Military Officers of His Majesty's Service, thereby failing to maintain the dignity of that Government: I hereby order that the inhabitants of the Gujranwala District shall accord to all such officers, whenever met, the salutation usually accorded to Indian gentlemen of high social position in accordance with the customs of India. That is to say, persons riding on animals or on or in wheeled conveyances will alight, persons carrying opened and raised umbrellas shall lower them, and all persons shall salute or "salaam" with the hand. (Hunter 1920: 1087–88)

Questioned by the Hunter Committee on this order, Lieutenant Colonel O'Brien, district commissioner at Gujranwala, commented, "The tendency of the present day is to abolish respectfulness. The Indian father will tell you that sons are not respectful even to their parents" (Hunter 1920: 1127). One man, at Wazirabad, is alleged to have been made to lick an officer's boots for failing to salute. The most notorious order of this kind, however, was Dyer's.

On 19 April he visited the badly wounded Miss Sherwood, and "searched his brain for a suitable punishment." He closed the street where she had been assaulted, erected a whipping triangle at one end, posted pickets, and ordered that any person wishing to pass through the street (including its residents) had to do so on all fours. In practice people had to squirm through the filth of the lane on their bellies, prodded along by the boots and bayonets of the soldiers. Prisoners were deliberately routed through the "Crawling Lane." Dyer later explained:

> It is a complete misunderstanding to suppose that I meant this order to be an insulting mark of race inferiority. The order meant that the street should be regarded as holy ground, and that, to mark this fact, no one was to traverse it except in a manner in which a place of special sanctity might naturally in the East be traversed. My object was not merely to impress the inhabitants, but to appeal to their moral sense in a way which I knew they would understand. (Statement to Army Council 1920: 693)

Within the "Crawling Lane," at the same time, a sacred building (to Hindus) was defiled, and "the wells . . . were polluted by the soldiers easing themselves near them." (Fein 1977: 42). Six youths were arrested on suspicion of involvement in the assault on Miss Sherwood. Dyer, dispensing with the niceties of a trial, had them flogged there. Even O'Dwyer found Dyer's crawling order unacceptable, rescinding it on 25 April.

There is a systematic pattern to these events. Martial law, declared after the major disturbances had been put down, served to facilitate punishment rather than to control disorder. There was scant regard for the hallowed principles of British justice. The hasty passage by the Indian government of an Act of Indemnity in October 1919 which sought "to protect from legal proceedings *bona fide* action taken with a reasonable belief that it was necessary to suppress disorder" conveyed essentially the same message. Individual guilt was neither here nor there, on either side. Many martial law punishments were openly, and onerously, collective, and collectively—that is to say, racially—degrading. They underlined the social distance between rulers and ruled. Dyer's crawling order epitomizes the symbolism: including the elevation of that which was the ultimate taboo for the Indian male, white womanhood, to sacredness. It is worth underlining the recurrence of the theme of "violation" (Miss Sherwood was not raped) in contemporary images of these events.[19] The sacred, as Emile Durkheim observed, is that which is "*set apart*, that which is *separated*"; "any mixture, or even contact, *profanes* it." The sacred and the profane are "heterogeneous and incommensurable" (Durkheim 1974: 70). What was being restored in the Punjab was a properly hierarchized and duly sanctified moral order.

V

Immediately after the massacre, Dyer had sought and got approval for his actions from his commanding officer, General Beynon, and O'Dwyer. He was widely lauded as "the saviour of the Punjab." He claimed (as did others, then and later) that he enjoyed the support of loyal Indians:

> the leading men from the district came forward to me and offered me 10,000 Sikhs to fight for the Raj, and invited me to command them. I and my Brigade Officer received the unusual honour of being made Sikhs, and I was acclaimed on various occasions by native gatherings as the officer who had saved the situation. (Statement to Army Council 1920: 697)

The manager of the Golden Temple, where Dyer was allegedly made an honorary Sikh, Arur Singh, was a government appointee, and martial law was in force. Both the temple authorities and the Sikh League issued a prompt denunciation of British use of the temple for political purposes. But the story was to be made much of at home, where it was taken as confirmation of the gratitude of the loyal native. The symbolism of this incident is as instructive as that of the "Crawling Lane."

On 8 May Dyer left Amritsar to fight on the Afghan border. In August he filed his official report to the General Staff, 16th Indian Division, on his actions in Amritsar.[20] Confident then that he enjoyed the full support of his superiors, Dyer was far less guarded than in some of his later statements. He considered it his "bounden duty" to fire on the crowd. He believed in the use of minimum force, but "at Amritsar the case was different." The meeting was held in defiance of his proclamation banning all gatherings, and must have received ample warning of his coming. The villagers there, he understood— without giving any evidence for this belief—had been enticed to the meeting by a promise that their taxes and land revenues would be re- duced "as the British 'Raj' was at an end. Evidently those who came believing the British 'Raj' was at an end were themselves not very innocent." He did not suggest that fear of attack by the mob led him to fire. He did make it quite clear that he "had ample time to con- sider the nature of the painful duty I might be faced with," and "had considered the matter from every point of view." He was, in short, resolved on firing before he reached the Bagh.

On arriving there, "there was no reason to further parley with the mob; evidently they were there to defy the arm of the law." Notice how a peaceful crowd has already become a "mob." Dyer then states, succinctly, exactly why he acted as he did:

> The responsibility was very great. If I fired I must fire with good effect, a small amount of firing would be a criminal act of folly. I had the choice of carrying out a very distasteful and horrible duty or of neglecting to do my duty, of suppressing disorder or of be- coming responsible for all future bloodshed . . . What faced me was what on the morrow would be the Danda Fauj (Rebel Army). I fired and continued to fire until the crowd dispersed and I consider this the least amount of firing which would produce the necessary moral and widespread effect it was my duty to produce, if I was to justify my action. If more troops had been at hand the casualties would have been greater in proportion. It was no longer a question of merely dispersing the crowd, but one of producing a sufficient moral effect, from a military point of view, not only on those who were present but more specially throughout the Punjab. There could be no question of undue severity. (Hunter 1920: 1136)

It is an astoundingly frank passage. The actual behavior of the crowd was irrelevant. The point, rather, was that "every man who escaped from the Jallianwala Bagh was a messenger to tell that law and order had been restored in Amritsar." The massacre was an exercise in moral education. Dyer's message, I might add, was pertinent to all those parts of the globe (some one-quarter of its land surface at the time) where the maps were colored with the red of the British Empire. Certainly it was heard as such, whether by Sir Edward Carson or, as we will see, British workers fearful of "Dyerism" at home.

Dyer's report was filed on 25 August. In October he was given permanent command of a brigade, and in January temporary command of a division. His actions in Amritsar were vigorously defended both in the debate on the Indemnity Bill in the Imperial Legislative Council,[21] and in the Punjab government's own statement on the disturbances.[22] But events were beginning to move against him.

Edwin Montagu, secretary of state for India, under pressure in the Commons and from Indian nationalists, had promised in May 1919 to set up an inquiry into the disturbances. Many British in India, including the commander in chief of the Army, General Sir Charles Monro; the home member of the government of India, Sir William Vincent; and Sir Harcourt Butler, governor of the United Provinces, opposed an inquiry of any sort. They felt it would drag the military into disrepute, provide a platform for Indian militants, and inflame "racial feelings." There was much dispute between Montagu and the Government of India over the appropriate form and terms of reference of the inquiry. Eventually Montagu telegrammed Chelmsford on 18 July announcing that a committee would be appointed by the government of India, with a chairman chosen by the secretary of state. The inquiry would consider not only the causes of the disorders but also "the measures taken to cope with them." Lord Hunter's Committee began its hearings on 29 October.

In his testimony,[23] Dyer substantially reiterated what he said in his earlier report, including that "my mind was made up as I came along in my motor car." When asked whether he had feared attack he answered "No . . . I had made up my mind that I would do all men to death if they were going to continue the meeting." He also confirmed that he would probably have used his machine guns had he been able to. Questioned on whether his aim had been to produce a "moral effect" throughout the Punjab rather than just dispersing the crowd,

Dyer stated, "these were rebels and I must not treat them with gloves on. They had come out to fight if they defied me, and I was going to give them a lesson [. . .] I was going to punish them. My idea from the military point of view was to make a wide impression. Yes, throughout the Punjab. I wanted to reduce their *morale*; the *morale* of the rebels" (113). Asked whether such use of terror might not in fact discredit the Raj, he replied, "It was a merciful though horrible act and they ought to be thankful to me for doing it. I thought it would be doing a jolly lot of good and they would realize that they were not to be wicked." The childishness of the language here threads Dyer's testimony and speaks volumes about his perceptions of Indians and the role of the British in relation to them. Asked later what he meant by saying that his action had a "salutory effect," Dyer responded: "I want to punish the naughty boy; it would be difficult to say what would be the effect of punishment on a boy who is not naughty."

Another strand in Dyer's testimony is equally revealing. Admitting that the crowd began to disperse immediately after he began firing, and probably could well have been dispersed without any firing at all, he explained why he continued firing nonetheless:

> I could disperse them for some time, then they would all come back
> and laugh at me and I considered I would be making myself a fool.

He felt no need to elaborate. The importance of maintaining face in India was something he clearly took to be self-evident. Fear of being laughed at may seem a bizarre (not to say an obscene) justification for a massacre, and ample confirmation, if any be needed, of Dyer's pathology. But in this, as in much else, he was merely articulating the consciousness of a caste. "For a century," a former cabinet minister had written in 1892, "the Englishman has behaved in India as a demi-god . . . Any weakening of this confidence in the minds of the English or of the Indians would be dangerous" (Sir Charles Wentworth Dilke, quoted in Kiernan 1972: 57). Unbridgeable distance was materialized in every detail of Anglo-Indian social life, from the prohibitions on miscegenation to the architecture of the Civil Lines. Such distancing sustained the fictional construction of Indians which provided the Raj with its moral underpinnings, if at the cost of fueling a chronic fear of what lay (in the title of Kipling's chilling story) "beyond the pale." Representations of power are always integral to its exercise, and they were especially so in post-Mutiny India. The handful of British were acutely aware of their vulnerability; they were few and depended for military security on a largely Indian army. They sought, magically, to wield power through its symbols, adapting caste (the Indian Civil Service called themselves the "heaven-born"), appropriating the *Durbar*. Dyer was simply voicing the commonplace.

VI

The Hunter Committee report—or more accurately reports, for the Committee split on racial lines—were submitted to the government of India on 8 March 1920 (Hunter 1920). The majority censured Dyer for firing without giving the assembly a chance to disperse, and for continuing to fire after it had already started to do so. His justification in terms of the "moral effect" his action would produce elsewhere was "a mistaken conception of his duty" (Hunter 1920: 1034). There was no firm evidence of a conspiracy to overthrow British power, or basis for the belief that Dyer had "saved the situation in the Punjab and averted a rebellion on a scale similar to the Mutiny" (1035). His crawling order was "injudicious" and objectionable because it "punished innocent as well as guilty," an "act of humiliation" causing "bitterness and racial ill-feeling" (1087). Other actions taken under martial law were criticized, and irregularities admitted in the procedures of the summary courts. But such abuses were not seen as systematic, and O'Dwyer and the Punjab government escaped criticism.

The minority report, signed by the three Indian members of the committee, was considerably more hostile. Dyer was further rebuked for inadequately publicizing his proclamation prior to the meeting at the Bagh. His firing was condemned as an act of "frightfulness" comparable to German atrocities in France and Belgium, something "inhuman and un-British"—an interesting choice of words. He was criticized for making no provision for the wounded. Martial law orders "were designed and were used for punitive purposes." The humiliating features of these orders, their intention of "teaching the Indian population a lesson," are stressed and amply documented (Hunter 1920: 1112, 1115, 1122). The minority were considerably more scathing over the action of the police, military, and courts under martial law, and question the necessity for its imposition in the first place. They were also far more critical of O'Dwyer, concluding that his "point of view was and still is the same as that of General Dyer" (1118)—not unreasonably, as O'Dwyer's vigorous advocacy of Dyer's cause was subsequently to show.

The viceroy's executive council accepted the majority's conclusions regarding Dyer. There was near-unanimity that he should be retired from the army, but without being cashiered or otherwise prosecuted. This, in Monro's words, would "arouse the sentiments of the services" (quoted in Datta 1969: 134). On 3 May the Government of India wrote to Edwin Montagu. Dyer's action at the Jallianwala Bagh "exceeded the requirements of the case and showed a misconception of his duty." Dyer however "acted honestly," and "in the result his action checked the spread of the disturbances." It was "with pain" that the government was requesting the commander in chief to take appropriate action. This exonerating language may have genuinely reflected the government of India's view, or been a sop to Anglo-Indian public opinion; in any event, it is indicative of what the latter was. Despite "irregularities" and "injudicious and irresponsible acts" in the administration of martial law, no other officers named in Hunter (1920) merited censure. As for O'Dwyer, his "decision and vigour . . . [were] largely responsible for quelling a dangerous rising which might have had widespread and disastrous effects on the rest of India" (*Correspondence* 1920: 649–76).

The secretary of state's response, though polite, was much less equivocal. Montagu condemned Dyer's firing in much stronger terms and described the "crawling order" as offending "against every canon of civilised government." He also took issue with the Hunter Majority over martial law abuses, detecting

> a spirit which prompted—not generally, but unfortunately not uncommonly—the enforcement of punishments and orders calculated, if not intended, to humiliate Indians as a race, to cause unwarranted inconvenience amounting on occasions to injustice, and to flout stan-

dards of propriety and humanity, which the inhabitants, not only
of India in particular, but of the civilised world in general, have a
right to demand of those set in authority over them. (*Correspondence*
1920: 674)

The officers involved should be censured. Montagu also pointed out
"the extreme divergence between sentences required by the charges as
presented to [martial law] courts and by the dictates of justice as they
presented themselves to the reviewing authorities" in the later judicial
review, and criticized O'Dwyer for his part in this, and for his overly
hasty support of Dyer's action at Amritsar. Diplomatic as Montagu's
language unfailingly is, it cannot hide the deep rifts between London
and Simla. In private correspondence, Montagu went to the heart of
the matter: "I feel that [O'Dwyer] represents a regime that is doomed"
(letter to Chelmsford quoted in Draper 1981: 212).

VII

Dyer landed at Southampton on 3 May. He was interviewed on arrival
by the *Daily Mail*. "The General, burnt brick-red by thirty-five years
of service in India . . . with greying hair and kindly blue eyes," derided
the Hunter Committee and complained that he had been sentenced
without trial (4 May 1920). Shortly after, he applied to the India Office
for leave to state his case to the Army Council. Montagu, meantime,
had asked for legal advice on whether or not further action could be
taken against Dyer.[24] The burden of Sir Edward des Chamier's note
was that Dyer could indeed be tried for culpable homicide under the
Indian Penal Code, but that any jury in either India or England would
likely acquit him. Montagu's cabinet committee decided to do all it
could to forestall any private prosecution being brought.

Amongst Dyer's supporters were military members of the Army
Council. Sir Henry Wilson, chief of the imperial general staff, insisted, against cabinet pressure, upon Dyer being given the opportunity to submit a statement in his defense. He wrote in his diary, after
a particularly stormy meeting with Churchill, "The Frocks [politi-
cians] have got India (as they have Ireland) into a filthy mess. On
that the soldiers are called in to act. This is disapproved of by all the

disloyal elements and the soldier is thrown to the winds" (quoted in Draper 1981: 222).[25] (Wilson was assassinated in 1922 by Sinn Fein, against whom, as the *Dictionary of National Biography* puts it, "he never ceased to advocate a system of drastic coercion.") Speculation was rife in the press that the Army Council would repudiate the findings of the Hunter Committee; indeed the *Guardian* reported this as fact (7 July). The *Times* cautioned: "it has been accepted in this country since the day when Charles I lost his head [that] the civil power should be supreme over the military power. Are the relative positions of the Army Council and the Cabinet at this juncture a violation of this principle?" (26 June). The ritual invocation—which is to say, the reconstruction—of British "tradition" was to be a dominant motif of these debates, on both sides. Even the Indian minority on Lord Hunter's committee chose to condemn Dyer in terms of his "un-British" behavior. In the event, the Army Council endorsed Dyer's removal from his command, but did not feel any further action was called for.

O'Dwyer, meantime, published a statement in the *Times* on 9 June which branded Hunter's composition as "defective" and charged its minority as "not impartial." He also implied that Montagu had misled parliament and public, providing evidence of this in a further letter to the *Times* of 2 July. Montagu had claimed, in the Commons on 16 December 1919, to have first known the details of the Amritsar massacre from press reports the same month. O'Dwyer said he had personally told Montagu on 30 June of that year of Dyer's having fired without warning, the number of rounds fired, the extent of casualties, and the "crawling order." The *Times* of 14 June reported "extraordinary interest throughout India" in O'Dwyer's statement, and "intense bitterness of British feeling in India against the Secretary of State." The Anglo-Indian press had condemned Montagu's "mendacity and equivocations." The council of the European Association of India cabled: "General body of Europeans in India strongly uphold Dyer and condemn actions of Government of India and Secretary of State" (Letter to *Times* from G. Morgan, 10 June). Montagu was repeatedly harassed in the Commons (Hansard 1920: cxxx, cols. 2149–54 and cxxxi, cols. 452–54, 1411–21).[26]

Correspondents to the press pointed to Indian support for Dyer's action (some citing the Sikh investiture),[27] participation of villagers who were not "innocent and ignorant" in the riots and looting,[28] and the reality of conspiracy in India.[29] Although some letters were critical, most supported Dyer.[30] One man who had served under him offered a testimonial.[31] Carlyon Bellairs M.P. captured the tone of much of this correspondence:

> The [Dyer] controversy may, indeed, be a turning point in our Im-
> perial history. British rule has been respected because it has been
> wisely strong without being cruel, and because the word of the
> Englishman was his bond . . . under democracy there has been a
> progressive decline in both these directions . . . Chatham gave his
> men a free hand. He certainly censured for sins of omission, but one
> would be surprised to come upon any episode in his career where
> he excitedly censured the too thorough execution of any task [. . .]
> In the wake of every great achievement, as in Dyer's case, there is
> dust and dirt . . . When a handful of whites are faced by hundreds
> of thousands of fanatical natives, one cannot apply one's John Stuart
> Mill. (*Times* 8 July)

The Oxford Union, in a debate on 10 June, upheld the government stance on Dyer, but very narrowly. The majority was 130 to 121.

There was one sharply different response, which I have touched on already. The Labour Party Conference at Scarborough unanimously passed a resolution on 24 June which denounced the "cruel and bar-barous actions" of British officers in the Punjab, and called for their trial, the recall of O'Dwyer and Chelmsford, and the repeal of repres-sive legislation. Delegates "rose in their places as a tribute to 'India's martyred dead'" (*Times*, report 25 June). This undoubtedly reflects a wider working-class identification with the victims of Jallianwala, and fear that their strikes might meet with the same treatment. Per-ceptions of popular struggles as Bolshevik-inspired conspiracies were not confined to the Punjab, nor to Sir Michael O'Dwyer. This was 1920, and the papers were full of Bolshevik atrocities. The *Manchester Guardian*, sensitive to these fears, editorialized against "our well-to-do Prussians" and the Labour resolution, which it saw as extremist.[32] The point, of course, was to individualize the massacre as Dyer's purely personal misjudgment, a process now well under way.

VIII

Dyer's case was debated in the Commons on 8 July.[33] The *Times*' plea that there were more important issues facing India—"We do not welcome the prospect of an Amritsar day in the House of Commons" (3 June)—fell on deaf ears. Most British papers gave it lead editorials, the *Times* opining that Dyer's "crawling order" was a "lamentable betrayal of the British tradition of equanimity and restraint," while his censure alone had "served to restore the reputation of British justice in the eyes of India." "Events such as those at Amritsar . . . obscure our national purpose and betray the ideals which inspire it." The *Guardian* and *Pall Mall Gazette* argued similarly. Both Dyer and O'Dwyer, as well as a number of Indian princes, were in the gallery. The benches were more crowded than for a year, except—a sign of the times— for some debates on Russia. The atmosphere was "electric" (*Times*, 8 July). The *Pall Mall Gazette*'s "Clubman" reported "I have seldom seen feeling run so high" (9 July).[34]

Montagu opened for the government. He asked members: "Are you going to keep your hold upon India by terrorism, racial humiliation and subordination, and frightfulness, or are you going to rest it upon the good will, and the growing good will, of the people of your Indian Empire? I believe that to be the whole question at issue" (Hansard 1920: cxxxi, col. 1708). Sir Edward Carson, the next to speak, shifted the ground—dramatically. On how India should be governed, he concurred with Montagu. He was being less than ingenuous here: Carson's advocacy of Dyer was not unrelated to considerations of methods of government for Ireland. And indeed, almost all the anti-government votes at the close of the debate were cast by coalition Unionists, and Ulster members were disproportionately represented. In one way, crystal clear at the time, the whole Dyer controversy was a thinly coded discussion of Ireland, then in open revolt. And of more. The *Guardian* next day observed that "General Dyer's more thorough supporters by no means intend to stop at India . . . After India, Ireland. After Ireland, British workmen on strike" (Editorial, 9 July).[35]

But the issue before the House, Carson continued, was not the governance of India. It was whether Dyer had been fairly treated; and manifestly he had not:

> You talk of the great principles of liberty which you have laid down. General Dyer has a right to be brought within those principles of liberty. He has no right to be broken on the *ipse dixit* of any Commission or Committee, however great, unless he has been fairly tried—and he has not been tried.

Carson concluded, to "loud and prolonged cheers": "to break a man under the circumstances of this case is un-English" (Hansard 1920: cxxxi, cols. 1712, 1719).

Churchill and Asquith replied: they have been quoted above (p. 143). Churchill too played on the theme of national character: "such ideas ['frightfulness'] are absolutely foreign to the British way of doing things," and Dyer's censure was needed to make this "absolutely clear" (Hansard 1920: cxxxi, cols. 1729, 1730). Ben Spoor put the Labour view. Sir William Joynson-Hicks quoted a letter from Miss Sherwood and pointed out the overwhelming support Dyer had among the British community in India. He also claimed (instancing Dyer's claim of being made an "honorary Sikh") that "General Dyer was and is today beloved of the Sikh nation." Brigadier General Surtees bluntly opined that if a plebiscite were held in India on who should rule, it would go against Britain; and drew the moral "if we do not hold India by moral suasion, then we must hold it by force." Surtees, like Dyer and O'Brien, was sensitive to issues of face. White rule would be overwhelmed throughout the empire, he asserted, "but for one thing. That one thing is British prestige. Once you destroy that British prestige, then the Empire will collapse like a house of cards." Colonel Wedgewood was as zealous in his concern for British prestige, but drew different conclusions:

> The principal charge I make against Dyer is not that he shot down Indians, but that he placed on English history the gravest blot since

in days gone by we burned Joan of Arc . . . The safety of women
and children, even, is of no importance compared with the honour
of England.

His priorities are instructive. Bonar Law, in closing for the government, reiterated that Dyer's "moral effect" argument was "a principle
opposed to the whole British Empire." [36] When the vote was taken the
government won by 230 to 129. There were many abstentions on the
government side. Had not almost all of the 66 Labour and Independent Liberal members voted with the government, Carson's motion
would have passed.

The Commons vote was welcomed by the *Guardian* ("No British
tribunal, however constituted, could fail to condemn the action taken
at Amritsar" [9 July])—the Lords were shortly to prove this benign
self-image quite wrong—and the *Observer* ("There is no question of
moral turpitude. General Dyer was not the conscious and bloodthirsty
author of a massacre . . . [But] his judgement was lamentably, fatally
and tragically at fault" [11 July]). In acrimonious correspondence to
the press, Sydenham deplored the decision of the Army Council,
which would "disastrously affect the interests of all loyal Indians,"
who could hardly now be counted upon to "stand by the handful of
English men and women in India" if their own government did not
(*Times*, 13 July).[37] Ronald McNeill M.P. (whose assessment of the relative import of Indian lives and British prestige also bears remarking)
vilified Montagu: to proclaim "to the world without a scrap of justification that a large section, or any section, of the House of Commons
favours terrorism, frightfulness and racial humiliation for India" was
"a more mischievous error of judgement than General Dyer's" (*Times*,
16 July).

The Lords debated the issue two weeks later (Hansard 1920: xli,
cols. 221–308, 311–78). The *Guardian* said it was impossible to justify a
debate at all: the affair was best decently buried (Editorial, 20 July).[38]
But it was by all accounts a glittering occasion. "There was a really
brilliant scene in the House of Lords last night . . . Not since before the war," wrote "Clubman," "has there been such a gathering
of peeresses, and the Stranger's Gallery was crowded with distin-

guished Anglo-Indians and Indians. The Indians, many of them, wore
gorgeous turbans, and the ladies wonderful robes of silk" (*Pall Mall
Gazette*, 20 July). The recently invested Duke of York (the future
George VI) chose this occasion to attend his first Lords debate (*Pall
Mall Gazette*, 21 July). Among the sixteen speakers were five former
governors of Indian provinces, one former viceroy, and three former
secretaries of state for India. Only six of them supported Viscount
Finlay's motion that "this House deplores the conduct of the case of
General Dyer as unjust to that officer and as establishing a prece-
dent dangerous to the preservation of order in the face of rebellion."
Nevertheless the motion passed, by a majority of 129 to 86. Dyer
was present at the debate, and "pleased with the division . . . many
peers greeted him afterwards in the lobby" (*Pall Mall Gazette*, 21 July).
The *Times* profoundly regretted the decision (Editorial, 21 July).[39] The
Guardian commented:

> A vote in favour—even indirectly—of "Prussianism" in India by
> a House representing especially the old British "governing classes"
> must not merely do harm in India . . . It must also do harm at home,
> where the minds of a dangerously large number of workmen are
> already possessed with the explosive idea that the "capitalist" classes
> are working themselves up to an attempt to reestablish their de-
> clining power with machine-guns. (Editorial, "An Unwise Vote,"
> 21 July)

The Dyer lobby's "obduracy in a course inspired by contempt for
subject races and by fear of popular movements," it added, by now
inevitably, "is too Bourbon or Hohenzollern to be quite English."

Lord Sumner's passionate speech in Dyer's defense merits quotation at length. It too sounds a very English refrain:

> If General Dyer had been tried—tried in any form that you like,
> such as enables a man to have it called a trial—he would have been
> entitled to have a definite charge formulated against him in writing
> before the Inquiry began, so far as it related to him; he would have
> been entitled to know what the charge was; he would have been
> entitled to know who was to be called against him; he would have
> been entitled to cross-examine those persons and to call witnesses
> to answer them; he would have been entitled to be represented; he

would have been entitled to be present at every stage of the hearing, and he would have been entitled if he chose, to offer himself as a witness, with the protection of advisers if he gave evidence, not in the capacity of a person charged, but in the capacity of a person who, as an Officer of the Government, was bound to give an account of his doings. He would have been entitled to be warned that there were certain questions that he need not answer . . . He was heard without any of these protections (Hansard 1920: xli, col. 334).

We are a long way from the Rowlatt Acts, martial law commissions, and summary justice of the "Crawling Lane" and Jallianwala Bagh.

IX

In the run-up to the Commons debate, the *Morning Post* was daily editorializing that it was Montagu, not Dyer, who should be on trial.[40] Dyer's action was necessary to protect "the honour of European women." The vile attack on Miss Sherwood was recalled. Immediately after the Commons defeated the censure on Montagu, the *Post* launched an "Appeal to Patriots" for funds for Dyer. It was meant to assure him that the British people "dissociated themselves from the mean and cowardly conduct of the politicians and the time-servers" who had so cravenly deserted him. "While General Dyer saved India, the politicians are saving themselves at his expense. It is a burning reproach to the British nation that such a thing could be possible."

The announcement of the fund drive (10 July 1920) was accompanied by an editorial headed "These be thy Gods, O Israel," and two days later, under the headline "The cause of world unrest (the Jews)," the *Post* began a two-week serialization of the (fraudulent) *Protocols of the Learned Elders of Zion*. Montagu was Jewish. The *Times* too, notwithstanding its anti-Dyer stance, had drawn attention to this in its coverage of the Commons debate: "Mr Montagu, patriotic and sincere English Liberal as he is, is also a Jew, and in excitement has the mental idiom of the East." His speech had been insensitive to "our inductive English method of political argument"[41] (by contrast, the *Guardian* of 9 July described it as "plain speaking . . . obviously embarrassing to the soldier's apologists"). T. J. Bennett M.P. complained to the *Times* that the atmosphere in the Commons debate had been "not free . . . from the racial prejudice which worked mischief in France during the Dreyfus controversy" (Letter to *Times*, 12 July). There can be little doubt he was right.

The response to the appeal was staggering. Within twenty-four hours £1,500 had been raised; by 16 July, £10,000; and when the fund was eventually closed, £26,317 4s. and 10d., a vast sum of money. The contributors were very varied. There were many aristocrats, including the Countess of Bathurst, the Duke of Westminster, the Earl of Harewood, and the Duke and Duchess of Somerset. Rudyard Kipling sent £10 (with the laconic and, I believe, thoroughly accurate observation: "He did his duty, as he saw it"). O'Dwyer subscribed. Despite the Indian Government's prohibition of contributions from its officers and servants (many regimental messes and civil servants made them pseudonymously), large amounts were raised in India, amounting to one-third of the total collected. Money was donated by jute and railway workers, schoolchildren, Anglo-European associations and clubs, and forwarded through the Anglo-Indian newspapers. In Bengal, 6,250 British women petitioned the Prime Minister protesting Dyer's treatment. A committee of 13 women set out to present "the Saviour of the Punjab with a sword of honour and a purse," expressing their "indignation at the dangers of pandering to a small band of disloyal agitators whose noisy mouthings the deluded British public are mistaking for the voice of the loyal millions of India." Many smaller donations, from evidently poorer people, often with army connections, flooded in: "poor and proud," "a widow's mite," "a patriotic Englishwoman and one of the new poor," "a mite for the gallant soldier," "daily breader." Most individual contributions from India were of less than ten rupees. The voice of those who "knew India," and whose resentment at "the man on the ground" not being trusted to use his own judgment is palpable, is well represented: "Another disgusted sahib," "one of the many wives who have to spend most of their time in India," "eight years in the East," "a daughter and sister of officers who have served in India." And the *Post*'s anti-Semitism struck a responsive chord: one contributor signed himself "a believer in the Jewish peril," another "Pogrom." I do not believe such support can be dismissed merely as the voice of a small reactionary fringe. "The condemnation of a loyal Soldier by the 'Gallipoli Gambler'" aroused deep and widespread outrage, an outrage at least as great as the Amritsar slaughter itself.

X

Why should this be so? Or, to put the question more sharply, how could the perpetrator of the Jallianwala Bagh massacre come to be so widely perceived as its principal victim?

Dyer's support appears to have come largely from upper- and middle-class groups, or those with direct connections with India or the army. His advocates formed a well-organized and extremely favorably located claque. However, the claim that Dyer was a victim of shoddy political expediency was plausible. Montagu's evasiveness on when he first learned the details of the massacre, Churchill's leaning on the Army Council, and the semipublic chasm between the home and Indian governments—extensively debated in the press[42]—all conspired to confirm this. So did the delay of almost a year between the massacre and Dyer's censure, during which time he was twice in effect promoted. From the point of view of the British government, the findings of the Hunter Committee were evidently convenient. Dyer alone could shoulder the blame for martial law excesses, and Jallianwala, meantime, furnished a fine occasion for enunciating a self-congratulatory conception of "Britishness" as something quite different from "Dyerism," and much better suited to the new era of the reforms which bore Montagu's name. "Frightfulness," said Churchill, with more pomposity than historical accuracy, "is not a remedy known to the British pharmacopoeia"—it was the kind of thing, he added, that the Bolsheviks went in for (Hansard 1920: cxxxi, col. 1728).

But it was all somewhat transparent, and Dyer's supporters were in their own way both more honest and every bit as moral. Bellairs, for one, in the letter I have already quoted, was not ashamed to claim an historical precedent for Jallianwala Bagh in Governor Eyre's bloody suppression of the Jamaica rebellion of 1865 (*Times*, 8 July

1920).[43] Dyer's expectation of support for his actions by the authorities was not unreasonable, given the way India had been administered since the Mutiny. Indeed he had originally been supported by both Beynon and O'Dwyer. Nor was that action itself quite so foreign to the British imperial mores of the period as was claimed. The clearest indication of this is not simply the impressive extent of Dyer's following, but its lack of apology or embarrassment in elevating "preventive massacre" to the high moral status of Duty. It is the sheer rectitude of the Dyer lobby that is so striking—the more so given the undeniable sense in which Jallianwala was self-evidently singular. Such confidence strongly suggests that Dyer's defense was rooted in widely held norms. The question, then, is what kind of ethos could have allowed, indeed obligated, the actions he took.

I mentioned Helen Fein's conclusion that India's British rulers excluded Indians from their universe of moral obligation and sought to qualify this. To be sure, double standards were grotesquely evident. As T. J. Bennett observed at the time, those who bewailed Dyer's lack of a fair hearing did not extend their respect for due process to "the six lawyers of Gujranwala who were led in handcuffs through the streets of that town, kept in gaol for six weeks, and then released uncharged and untried" (Letter to *Times*, 12 July 1920). But this is not the whole story. Comprehension of the massacre, I believe, lies in what it leaves out.

Men like Dyer and O'Dwyer had a clear conception of their duty toward Indians, and of Indians' obligations toward the Raj, and this conception—though clearly, by 1919, one no longer shared by the London government—was by no means confined to them alone. Central to it was maintenance of order, and the supreme value placed on order was in turn predicated on their construction of Indians as unfit to govern themselves. The Mutiny, which loomed large in their imagination, was a recurrent symbol of what could happen when order broke down; a symbol, too, of Indian untrustworthiness and British vulnerability in the face of Bellairs's "hundreds of thousands of fanatical natives." The maintenance of order was justified by Anglo-Indians as being in the interests of their Indian subjects, and it was the Indians whom they would be failing if they "shirked" this duty, however unpleasant. In the Lords debate Lord Sumner argued that "It was in mercy to them ['the Indian population themselves'], in order that they might not die, that it became the duty of General Dyer to use force and put to death those who were challenging the authority of the Government, who were rebels, only not in arms" (Hansard 1920: xli, col. 338). The Marquess of Salisbury extended the argument to the point where massacre became a beneficent form of moral pedagogy: "The people of India are entering upon a great experiment; and surely the lesson which, above all others, you must teach them is that there is nothing in self-government which authorises disorder" (Hansard 1920: xli, col. 375).

Central to this ethos was a definite construction of the Indian as subject, and extreme social distancing was an essential mechanism for sustaining such fictions. This was, needless to say, an enduringly racist construction, but of a specific sort; and its particularity needs to be acknowledged if the events of 1919 in the Punjab are to be comprehended. In much Anglo-Indian mythology, the "authentic" India was the India of the villager and the loyal sepoy; "simple manly fellows, far more congenial to it than the Bombay *bania* or shopkeeper-moneylender, or the voluble Bengali *babu* or clerk, or the Madrasi lawyer, heir of a long line of Brahminical logic-choppers" (Kiernan 1972: 55–56). There is a powerful romance here too, well capable of sustaining affection, respect, and even love for India and Indians thus imagined on the part of its "Platonic Guardians." Kipling evokes it, above all in *Kim*. Philip Mason recalls:

> the tolerant and bantering but none the less real affection of master and officer on one side, the soldier's or villager's trust, the confidence he mingled with a shrewd perception of character like that with which small boys nickname a schoolmaster. Those feelings were real; servant and master, officer and soldier, risked and sometimes laid down their lives for each other. (Woodruff 1954: vol. 2, 17)[44]

But, he continues, "the relationship was not one of equality; there could be no familiarity and no unguarded speech." His reference to "small boys" is telling. So is his comment on Sir Michael O'Dwyer's formative experiences as a settlement officer in the Western Punjab:

"in camp [such an officer] comes to think of the peasants as his children, and the more masculine his character the harder he finds it to believe that anyone else can look after them. And there could be few characters more masculine than O'Dwyer's" (237).

Among Anglo-Indians, the dominant conception of imperial purpose throughout this period, molded by the experience of the Mutiny, and haunted by the specter of its recurrence, was a paternalistic one. Indeed it was abidingly patriarchal: the obverse of O'Dwyer's masculine power is Miss Sherwood, the female embodiment of violability. Within this vision and in sharp contrast to the "improving" ethos so widespread earlier in the century,[45] the educated Indian was an anomaly, a transgressor of social boundaries, an offense (and a danger) to the moral classifications on which the Raj reposed. The simple villager would be easily led astray by such men, who if not agents must be dupes of the Kaiser or the Bolsheviks whom O'Dwyer saw lurking everywhere. This is a cast of mind within which political activity could only be comprehended in terms of conspiracy, ordinary Indians having been defined as incapable of political rationality. What was expected of them was obedience, loyalty, and gratitude of the kind symbolized in investing Dyer as an "honorary Sikh." They had a right to fatherly care—and this entailed, when necessary, fatherly chastisement.

What stand out most for me in the testimony surrounding the 1919 Punjab disorders are the recurrent vocabularies of the schoolroom. Doveton employed punishments redolent of the public schools in which his kind were raised. Dyer spoke of "teaching a lesson" to "naughty boys"; and his frequent references to his "horrible duty" recall nothing so much as the schoolmaster's "this will hurt me as much as it hurts you." Salisbury took the argument to its grotesque extreme. I do not doubt either that the situation was perceived as dangerous to whites, with the experience of the Mutiny very much in mind, or that there were other, time-honored racial myths at work, as in the persistent references to "violation" of white women. But what makes most sense of the Amritsar massacre—what allowed it to happen and muted the horror that undoubtedly would have been aroused had it happened in Glasgow, Belfast, or Winnipeg—is the rendering of Indians as children: children who once abandoned to their own devices would revert to savagery, like the boys in Golding's *Lord of the Flies*. Kipling, in his "White Man's Burden," speaks of colonial charges as "new-caught, sullen peoples, half-devil and half-child," which captures it exactly. Anglo-Indian fondness for the "martial races" of India is not unconnected with this imagery. For military relations involve abjuring of adult responsibility: soldiers are always "boys."

It was the place Indians occupied *within* their rulers' moral universe, not their exclusion from it, which explains why, in the situation which prevailed at Amritsar—a "rebellion," as it was necessarily defined by the same set of conceptions—they could be slaughtered for moral effect, like the cattle to whom O'Dwyer once compared them, grazing, as he put it, in the shadow of the British oak (quoted in Draper 1981: 33). It is this which makes Jallianwala anything but "singular," for what authorized it were the norms of "British India" during this period. It is also this which makes it most enduringly sinister. For if it is thought that the moral consciousness I have tried to reconstruct here is impoverished—that to equate massacre with a jolly good caning betrays a lack of proportion—then the appropriate answer is an old one. One thing Chatham did say, contrary to Bellairs, was that "unlimited power is apt to corrupt the minds of those who possess it" (*History, Debates and Proceedings of both Houses of Parliament of Great Britain 1743–1774* 1792: vol. 5, 141).

XI

General Dyer died on 23 July 1927. Obituaries were sympathetic, and he was given a military funeral; wreaths and flowers were laid at the Cenotaph in Whitehall. Sir Michael O'Dwyer fought and won a libel action in the Court of King's Bench in 1922. Mr. Justice McCardie advised the jury that in his view "General Dyer, in the grave and exceptional circumstances, acted rightly, and [. . .] was wrongly punished by the Secretary of State for India" (quoted in Draper 1981: 260). The jury agreed, by a majority of eleven to one (the dissenter was Harold Laski). On 13 March 1940, O'Dwyer was shot by a Sikh who was at Jallianwala on the day of the massacre. Udham Singh was tried, and hanged; his statement to the jury was suppressed under the Emergency Powers (Defence) Act of 1939. The avenger of Amritsar has not been entirely forgotten, however. In 1987, in the London Borough of Hounslow, a motion to name a street after Udham Singh caused resignations within the Labour Party on the grounds that he was, "in the final analysis, a murderer" (*Sunday Times*, 10 April 1988).

It is not altogether inappropriate to give the last word to an Irishman. Bernard Shaw once remarked that "There is nothing so bad or good that you will not find an Englishman doing it; but you will never find an Englishman in the wrong . . . His watchword is always Duty; and he never forgets that the nation which lets its duty get on the opposite side of its interest is lost" (1948: 1, 743).[46] Moral rhetorics were ubiquitous in the Dyer affair. It would be the gravest of errors to conclude from this that they were a mere gloss, irrelevant to practical questions of governance, on either side.

Notes

I am indebted to John Comaroff, Philip Corrigan, John Gartrell, Victor Kiernan, Philip Lawson, P. A. Saram, Teodor Shanin, and Hugh Wilson for comments on earlier drafts of this paper. I owe E. P. Thompson particular thanks both for comments and for making available unpublished work of his own. A slightly different version of this paper was published in *Past and Present* 131 (1991).

1. Born at Murree, a small hill station in the Punjab, in 1864, Dyer was educated at Bishop Cotton School, Simla; Middleton College, County Cork; and the Royal Military College, Simla. He was commissioned in the Queens Royal Regiment in 1885, tranferring to the Indian Army in 1888, where he served with distinction. During World War I, he commanded British operations in Southeast Persia, receiving a C.B. The *Dictionary of National Biography* describes him as a simple and courageous soldier—an image touted by his supporters in 1919–20 (see, for example, the letter to *Times* of 1 June 1920, on the relief of Thal, by one of his men). This paper is indebted to a number of studies of the Amritsar massacre, although my argument differs from

theirs: Datta (1969); Draper (1981); Fein (1977); Furneaux (1963); Ram (1969); Swinson (1964).

2. During the Indian Mutiny reprisals had been savage, while in 1872 local officials at Maler Kotla in the Punjab had sixty-five Kuka rebels blown from the mouths of cannon (without prior trial). This action was approved by the Punjab Government but reproved by the Government of India, who removed its perpetrator from office (with a pension). In Jamaica, in 1865, Governor John Eyre had four hundred (arbitrarily selected) blacks killed, six hundred flogged, and one thousand huts burned by way of reprisal for rebellion: he was removed from office and prosecuted by John Stuart Mill. In the United Kingdom, we might recall the four hundred or so killed in the suppression of the Gordon Riots.

3. Furneaux cites Captain Briggs, who was with Dyer at Jallianwala, and Miles Irving, the district commissioner, on Dyer's behavior immediately afterwards, in support of this view. It was Edward Thompson (1930) who publicized Irving's testimony, pp. 102, 104. He did not do so with the intention of exonerating Dyer; as he said in a speech at "Amritsar Day" (London, Conway Hall, 13 April 1945) Dyer's action "was indefensible," and much of what was said in his defense in subsequent debates "if I were an Indian, I should find it almost impossible to forgive"; "To Indians of every race and religion, Amritsar was a flashlight. It revealed what their rulers thought of them . . ." I owe this information to E. P. Thompson.

4. "Trailing his coat" was Miles Irving's description (see Thompson 1930: 104). Throughout this paper the term "Anglo-Indian" is used to refer to British in India, as distinct from in Britain.

5. Montagu's moral and personal commitment to his reforms was undoubted. He was appointed secretary of state for India in June 1917; from November 1917 to May 1918 he toured India, consulting and cajoling. His personal diary of this tour was published posthumously by his wife (1930); in it he remarks—referring to his Jewishness—that "there might be some truth in the allegation that I am an Oriental. Certainly that social relationship which English people find so difficult comes quite easily to me." The aim of the reforms, as defined by him in the House of Commons on 20 August 1917, was "the gradual development of self-governing institutions with a view to the progressive realisation of responsible government as an integral part of the British Empire" (Hansard 1917, xcvii, col. 1695).

6. There is no space here to do more than allude to this, but I want to underline the historical specificity of the set of moral attitudes I trace here. "Colonial" attitudes changed over time (and not always to the more liberal),

in part in response to the struggles of the colonized, as after the Mutiny. A good brief discussion is contained in Kiernan (1972). Fiction is a good source for Anglo-Indian attitudes during this period, notably that of Kipling, especially his early stories ([1888] 1989a, [1889] 1989b). E. M. Forster's *Passage to India* ([1924] 1985) is also seminal.

7. Datta (1969: introduction, chap. 1) is excellent on the wartime and immediate postwar background. Fein (1977: chap. 3) discusses the period 1858–1919.

8. The majority report of the Hunter Committee denied that recruitment was a factor in the 1919 Punjab disturbances (Hunter 1920: 1066); Datta (1969: 9–20) makes a convincing and well-documented case to the contrary.

9. See O'Dwyer (1925) for his views.

10. A *hartal* is a cessation of ordinary activity, in effect a general strike. It has religious connotations. Murli Dhar explained in *The Tribune* of 13 April 1919: "What is Hartal? . . . when the dead body of the Rowlatt Acts is still in our midst, we have suspended all business and must remove the corpse from the house before the people can break their fast and resume business."

11. Note how communal antipathy is taken as normal here, while its absence is disturbing and artificial. Such conceptions served as justifications for British rule. It is open to question how much the sort of conceptions evidenced here were actively constitutive of the communal violence they portray as endemically native. Social identities are not just given, they are made, in part through the forms in which power is exercised.

12. Mahmood was afterwards put under pressure to give false evidence; see Fein (1977: 38).

13. I do not suggest Draper is being deliberately racist; the point is the clichéd "appropriateness" of such narrative devices. The chapter is entitled, "Murder, Looting and Arson", not, for instance, "Duplicity, Repression and Resistance" as it might be from a different viewpoint.

14. The Winnipeg reference is to the General Strike of May–June 1919.

15. It is Fein's major explanatory hypothesis, building on Emile Durkheim.

16. On the sense in which I am using "positivity" here, see any of Michel Foucault's later writings, but particularly (1982); for the construction of knowledge in/of India, see Cohn (1988).

17. Hans Raj, who may have been an *agent provocateur*. See Draper (1981: 58–62, 79–80, 86–87, 128–36).

18. Evidence of martial law abuses, judicial and otherwise, cited here is taken mainly from Hunter (1920). The fullest source is Indian National

Congress (1920). Congress boycotted the Hunter Committee and established its own inquiry into the disorders, denounced as biased by Anglo-Indians because Gandhi was one of its members. See also Fein (1977: 35–47).

19. Apart from instances cited in my text, see *Times* report, 1 June 1920, on "incitements to the mob at Lyallpur to outrage Englishwomen." The two novels from which I have taken the quotes which open this paper both have rapes as their centerpiece: in *The Jewel in the Crown* (vol. 1 of *The Raj Quartet*), though the heroine is raped, the man punished for doing it was not the rapist but her (Indian) lover (Scott 1966); in *A Passage to India* Forster ([1924] 1978) leaves it open whether a rape occurred at all. Both heroines are naive English outsiders to the Raj and its codes.

20. Passages quoted from Dyer's report are taken from Draper (1981: 154–56); and Hunter (1920: 116).

21. See for example the speech by the adjutant general of India, Sir Henry Havelock Hudson, appended by Dyer to his Statement to the Army Council (1920). See also Draper (1981: 158–61).

22. *Reports on the Punjab Disturbances, April 1919* (1920). See especially pp. 938–39, on what were seen as the beneficial results of Dyer's action.

23. Dyer's testimony is reproduced in *Evidence Taken Before the Disorders Inquiry Committee* (1920: vol. 3, 114–39). The quotes in this and the following paragraph are from pages 117, 123, 126, and 131. He disputed parts of the record, including the assertion that he "would do all men to death"— but committee members recall being struck by the oddity of the phrase as he uttered it. Substantial extracts are given in Hunter (1920), especially the Minority Report, Datta (1969), and Draper (1981). Two more volumes were withheld from publication by Montagu at Chelmsford's request: these contained evidence given in camera by O'Dwyer and by the Governments of the Punjab and of India, among others.

24. Draper gives a detailed account of this incident, based on cabinet papers closed until 1971 (1981: 217–19).

25. In linking India and Ireland (as well as in his pronounced anti-Bolshevism) Wilson was representative of many of Dyer's prominent supporters. There is, of course, an older and deeper intertwining of various "Indians" and Ireland in English discourses; see J. Muldoon (1975).

26. Montagu's claims in *Hansard* (1920: cxxx, cols. 2149–54) flatly contradict those of O'Dwyer in his letter of 2 July, so one of them was lying. Montagu was criticized for the release of Mohammed Bashir, sentenced to death by a martial law commission for his alleged part in the Amritsar riots, then released after the later judicial review. See also Gwynne's speech in the

Dyer debate of 8 July and the exchange of 14 July, when Montagu was accused of pressuring the Indian Government to change its line on Dyer (Hansard: 1920, cxxxi, cols. 1793–1804, 2347–51).

27. Lord Sydenham and Constance Tuting, both in *Times*, 1 June; see also the later letters of Sydenham and Lord Lamington, 13 and 23 July respectively.

28. S. R. Purnell, *Times*, 4 June.

29. Sydenham in *Times*, 5 July; see also letter from "Freelance," 8 June, defending Dyer's "moral effect" argument.

30. Exceptions, apart from those otherwise cited here, were J. D. Rees M.P., *Times*, 10 July; K. S. Gupta, *Times*, 26 July; J. Callan and others, *Manchester Guardian*, 6 July. On 14 July the Calcutta *Statesman* published a letter from twenty-five missionaries attacking the "Prussianism" of Dyer's action—it unleashed a flood of invective.

31. *Times*, 1 June.

32. See editorials of 8 and 19 July.

33. See Hansard (1920: cxxxi, cols. 1705–1820). All quotations from speeches in the debate in the following pages are from this source. All of the books on the massacre cited above give fairly full coverage. The *Times* of 9 July devoted almost two full pages to the debate, giving the speeches verbatim, as well as printing Dyer's lengthy statement to the Army Council in full.

34. The *Times* likewise reported that "the most remarkable aspect of the debate was the bitter feeling shown towards Mr Montagu . . . No attack of such concentrated violence on an individual Minister has been made since . . . coalition government began" (9 July).

35. The *Guardian* characterized the vote as a "Unionist revolt"; it also expressed concern about how "every Indian demagogue of the future" might use Jallianwala.

36. For above quotes, see Hansard (1920: cxxxi, cols. 1762, 1777, 1775, 1788, 1811).

37. *Times*, 13 July. Sydenham drew the Irish parallel—"The decision of the Army Council will carry not peace but the sword to an India dominated, like Ireland, by intimidation."

38. The *Times* in its report (20th) of the first day of the debate (19th) likewise opined: "the material is wearing thin." Five days earlier its "Political Notes" had reported that the government was 'straining every nerve to secure a favourable outcome" in the debate.

39. The Editorial concluded: "many Englishmen in the East [. . .] are out of touch with the newer conditions of imperial rule." Exactly!

40. For fuller details of the *Morning Post* campaign, see Draper (1981: 236–38), Fein (1977: 169–171)—excellent on the anti-Semitism—or Furneaux (1963: 153, 156, 160, 162–63). Quotations from the *Morning Post* below are taken from these sources.

41. Report of the debate in *Times*, 9 July—there is more of the same. Churchill's was by contrast "a brilliant speech."

42. See the correspondence around O'Dwyer's statements in the *Times*: letters from Holford Knight, 10 June; G. Morgan (President of the European Association of India), 17 June; H. Beechey, 30 June; G. Morgan, 2 July; H. Beechey, 5 July; M. W. Fenton, 8 July. Only Beechey supported Montagu, denouncing the "hoodwinking of the Secretary of State" by the Governments of the Punjab and India as "an official crime of the first magnitude." Holford Knight was no Dyer supporter; he had lobbied for an early inquiry on behalf of the Indian National Congress. See also the Commons exchanges cited above, n. 26.

43. Brigadier General Surtees drew the same parallel in the Commons debate on Dyer (Hansard 1920: cxxxi, col. 1776).

44. The (apt) description "Platonic Guardians" is his—he was himself a twenty-year veteran of the Indian Civil Service, albeit at a later date, and well placed to comment on its self-conceptions.

45. I am thinking of the views of, e.g., C. E. Trevelyan or Lord Macaulay. See Kiernan (1972).

46. I owe this reference to my colleague P. A. Saram.

REFERENCES

Anonymous. 1920. "Amritsar. By an Englishwoman." *Blackwood's Magazine*. Vol. CCVII, No. MCCLIV.

Cohn, Bernard. 1988. *An Anthropologist Among the Historians and Other Essays*. New Dehli and New York: Oxford University Press.

Correspondence 1920. *Correspondence between the Government of India and the Secretary of State for India on the Report of Lord Hunter's Committee*. Parliamentary Papers, Cmd. 705, xxxiv, pp. 649–76. London: H.M.S.O. (Published as addendum to Hunter 1920.)

Corrigan, Philip, and Derek Sayer. 1985. *The Great Arch: English State For-*

mation as Cultural Revolution. Oxford and New York: Blackwell. 1991. Revised ed. Oxford and Cambridge, Mass.: Blackwell.

Datta, Vishwa Nath. 1969. *Jallianwala Bagh.* Ludhiana: Kurukshetra [Kurukshetra University Books and Stationery Shop for] Book Depot.

Draper, Alfred. 1981. *Amritsar: The Massacre that Ended the Raj.* London: Cassell.

Durkheim, E. 1974. *Sociology and Philosophy.* New York: Free Press.

Evidence Taken Before the Disorders Inquiry Committee. 1920. 5 vols. Calcutta.

Fein, H. 1977. *Imperial Crime and Punishment: The Massacre at Jallianwala Bagh and British Judgement, 1919–1920.* Honolulu: University Press of Hawaii.

Foucault, Michel. 1982. "The Subject and Power." *Critical Inquiry* 8.

Forster, E. M. [1924] 1985. *A Passage to India.* London: E. Arnold.

Furneaux, Rupert. 1963. *Massacre at Amritsar.* London: G. Allen & Unwin.

Hansard. 1917, 1919 and 1920. *Parliamentary Debates* (Lords and Commons). 5th series. London: H.M.S.O.

Hunter. 1920. *Report of the Committee Appointed by the Government of India to Investigate the Disturbances in the Punjab, etc.* Parliamentary Papers, Cmd 681, xiv, pp. 1001–1192. London: H.M.S.O.

History, Debates and Proceedings of both Houses of Parliament of Great Britain 1743–1774, 1792. Vol. V. London.

Indian National Congress. 1920. *Report of the Commissioners Appointed by the Punjab Sub-Committee of the Indian National Congress.* 2 vols. Bombay.

Kiernan, V. G. 1972. *The Lords of Human Kind.* London: Penguin.

Kipling, Rudyard. [1888] 1989a. *Plain Tales from the Hills.* London and New York: Penguin.

——— . [1889] 1989b. *Wee Willie Winkie.* London and New York: Penguin.

Montagu, Edwin Samuel. 1930. *An Indian Diary.* London: Heinemann.

Muldoon, J. 1975. "Indian as Irishman." *Essex Historical Institutes* III.

O'Dwyer, Sir Michael. 1925. *India as I Knew It: 1885–1925.* London.

Ram, R. 1969. *The Jallianwala Bagh Massacre: A Premeditated Plan.* Chandigarh: Punjab University, Publication Bureau.

Reports on the Punjab Disturbances, April 1919. 1920. Parliamentary Papers, Cmd. 534, xiv, pp. 931–1000. London: H.M.S.O.

Scott, Paul. 1976. *The Day of the Scorpion.* In *The Raj Quartet.* London: Heinemann.

——— . 1966. *The Jewel in the Crown.* New York: Morrow.

Shaw, George Bernard. 1948. *The Man of Destiny*. In *Selected Plays*. Vol. 1. New York.

Statement to Army Council. 1920. *Disturbances in the Punjab. Statement by Brig. General R. E. H. Dyer, C. B.* Parliamentary Papers, Cmd. 771, xxxiv, pp. 677–704. London: H.M.S.O.

Swinson, A. 1964. *Six Minutes to Sunset*. London: P. Davies.

Thompson, Edward. 1930. *A Letter from India*. London.

Thompson, E. P. 1968. *The Making of the English Working Class*. London and New York: Penguin.

Woodruff, P. [pseud. Philip Mason]. 1954. *The Guardians*. Vol. 2. *The Men Who Ruled India*. New York: St. Martin's Press.

5
Tales of the City
Between *Algérie Française* and *Algérie Algérienne*

David Prochaska

Albert Camus is probably the single best known *pied noir*, or French settler, of colonial Algeria. And one of the most puzzling, too. Author of *L'Etranger*, a novel more important in the postwar history of literature and philosophy than in the history of imperialism and colonialism, even though the main event is Meursault's murder of—significantly—a nameless Algerian. Author of *La Peste*, a fable about totalitarianism in Europe but set in the Algerian port of Oran, a city in which the Europeans appear but the Algerians tend to disappear. A man of the Left, a former Communist and *résistant*, Camus broke with the French Left generally and with Jean-Paul Sartre particularly over the Algerian war, choosing his mother— *Algérie française*—over justice—*Algérie algérienne* (McCarthy 1982; Lottman 1980; O'Brien 1970; Guerin 1986).

Camus was born in 1913 in Mondovi, now called Dréan, which is located some twenty kilometers outside Bône, now called Annaba. At the time, Mondovi was one of the chief wine producing centers in the Bône plain. One of the largest and richest estates, known as Guébar, belonged to Jérome Bertagna, who died in Mondovi in 1903, ten years before Camus was born there. Bertagna's position as the single most powerful person in the Bône region at the time of his death was reflected in the grandeur of his estate. Guébar encompassed 7,500 acres; the three-story chateau he had erected at the end of a long, tree-lined drive looked not unlike the stately chateaux of the wine barons of southwestern France. Today in France, Jérome

Bertagna's descendants reside in Nice, Cannes, and Paris, where they live off the inheritance from the family's Algerian fortune. Yet today in Algeria it is not easy to find Bertagna's former estate. The farm has been nationalized, most of the vines uprooted, the brand name of the wine changed, and when you ask Algerians directions, no one seems to recognize the name. But then there it is: set back from the highway, the chateau itself in ruins, the roof caved in, the stone walls collapsing, it is now uninhabited, but on the grounds a number of Algerian families have thrown up *gourbi*-s, thatched huts.

Just down the road a piece from Dréan lies the *qubba*, or tomb, of Sidi Denden. The *qubba* itself, a white plastered dome, sits on a low promontory which juts out over the surrounding plain of Annaba, visible from the highway long before you reach the cutoff. *Qubba*-s dot the Annaba plain today like the now vanished jujube trees (*al-'Anab*), which give Annaba its name, used to. Yet every Algerian you ask has heard of Sidi Denden, and most can provide surprisingly precise directions, from the scruffy taxi driver in town to the bemused guys lounging at another *qubba* outside town. It is unclear when either the shrine or cult of Sidi Denden was founded, but the tomb was there certainly before the French invaded in 1830.

At the time of the 1876 census, Sadek Denden was seven years old and lived in the older, Muslim section of Bône with his parents and five brothers and sisters (APCA, Liste nominative, 1876: 285). Perhaps Sadek Denden was a descendant of the original Sidi Denden, perhaps not.[1] The former, a secularized, Francophone Algerian, who looked more to France than to Islam, issued from the latter, a family of traditional Muslim religious adepts: that would make for a nice historical irony. Whether descended from Sidi Denden or not, Sadek Denden is the best-known member of the so-called *Jeune Algérien* movement, the young Algerians, to have come out of Bône at the turn of the twentieth century. Together with his *confrère*, Khélil Kaid Layoun, Denden edited newspapers, drafted petitions, and staged mass meetings during the same time Bertagna reigned as mayor of Bône. While Denden moved on to Algiers and colony-wide *Jeune Algérien* activities, Khélil Kaid Layoun remained in Bône to lead the movement there.

Sadek Denden may have died penniless and Jérome Bertagna wealthy, but Bertagna's familial descendants were later run out of Algeria by the nationalist descendants of Sadek Denden and Khélil Kaid Layoun. Therefore, we have on the one hand, Jérome Bertagna, who did so much to make Algeria French, and on the other hand, Sadek Denden and Khélil Kaid Layoun, who did so much to unmake *Algérie française*. The three men are linked so tightly geographically yet separated by so much in every other way that it is no wonder Albert Camus was so *complexé*.[2]

Throughout the historiographical literature, the struggle for hegemony in colonial Algeria is depicted primarily as a two-way battle waged between the French on one side, and the Algerians on the other. That the European settlers—the French, Spanish, Italians, Maltese, and other Europeans who became known collectively as the *pieds noirs*—comprised a third significant force has been recognized yet never systematically analyzed (Nora 1961; Prochaska 1990: 1–28). Yet Algeria was a settler colony; alongside the Algerians and temporary migrants from France (colonial administrators, military personnel), the permanent European settlers constituted a third major element in the colonial equation.

Louis Althusser, Jacques Derrida, Albert Memmi, and Claudia Cardinale—all are *pieds noirs*.

Moreover, the relations between these three social groupings shifted over time. Typically in settler colonies—examples include Kenya, Rhodesia/Zimbabwe, and South Africa, as well as Algeria—conflicts arise between the settlers and administration during the period of colonization. But it is usually only during the period of decolonization that a full-blown nationalist movement forms, and the indigenous people develop into a third force capable of driving a wedge between the settlers and the colonial power (Denoon 1983; McMichael 1984; Mosley 1983). This three-sided conflict also accounts in large part for why decolonization is often more violent in settler colonies.

The historical roles played by the three protagonists in colonial Algeria passed through three distinct stages. During the period of direct colonial rule between 1830 and 1870, the French army established and staffed the basic bureaucratic institutions while the European settlers played a distinctly inferior role. Initially, the interests of the settlers and the army dovetailed, but soon the army replaced the

Algerians as the chief barrier standing in the way of the settlers extending their power. Military antipathy drove the settlers to embrace Republicanism.

The settler stage of colonialism began in 1870 when the Third Republic replaced the Second Empire in France, and civilians replaced the military in Algeria. Whereas the illiberal Second Empire had kept a relatively tight institutional rein on the settlers, the liberal Third Republic inadvertently allowed them to create local pockets of power in the interstices of the "looser" civilian administration. In Bône and elsewhere in colonial Algeria the official bureaucracy was controlled by representatives of metropolitan France while the unofficial patronage network was dominated by the European settlers. Thus, control of the bureaucratic system and the patronage network corresponded by and large to two of the three main forces contending for hegemony in Algerian affairs. No one actualized more the potential of this distinctive political culture—a combination of patronage, bossism, and corruption in a settler colonial situation—than Jérome Bertagna.[3]

Still reeling from the violent imposition of French colonial rule, the Algerians were kept politically quiescent during the formative decades of settler society. Only during the period of decolonization did the Algerians emerge powerful enough to rival the settlers and metropolitan French, and to win independence as a result. This third stage of colonialism can be dated from the 1945 Sétif riots, and culminated in the Algerian Revolution of 1954–62. But that gets ahead of our story.

Jérome Bertagna's father was an Italian naturalized French; born in Nice, he ran a bakery in Bône. Jérome himself was born in Algiers and educated in Marseille. He joined the *Ponts et Chaussées*, the French corps of civil engineers, but quit to work for the Maison Lavie as a commercial agent specializing in flour milling and selling wheat.

François-Marc Lavie arrived in Bône in 1834. General Monk d'Uzer, commander of the Bône region at the time, wrote that having "arrived in Bône with . . . several letters from the Minister [of War], I thought it was my strict duty to support and favor M. Lavie" (quoted in Maitrot 1934: 319). By 1840 Lavie had estab-

lished the first flour mill in the city of Constantine. In 1848 he
moved to Héliopolis, located between Bône and Guelma, where he
obtained a large amount of property. After Lavie's death in 1863,
his son Pierre took over the family's operations in Constantine,
and his son Louis took over the family business in Guelma. One
of his grandsons became a leader of the Opportunist Republican
party in Constantine; another married the daughter of one of Bône's
twentieth-century mayors. In short, the Lavies became one of the
four or five richest families in eastern Algeria (data from Montoy
1982: 50–51, 173, 210, 319, 382, 489, 724).

Some of Lavie's success must have rubbed off on Jérôme Bertagna,
because when he quit he founded the Maison Bertagna and made his
fortune before the age of forty when he won the government contract to supply the French army during the takeover of Tunisia in 1881
(APCA, Opérations Electorales, Conseil Municipal; AOM, F 80 1836,
1837; AN, BB 18 2006; Ageron 1968: 501–6). His economic position
secure, Bertagna proceeded to boost his social status by plowing his
business profits into land purchases and became one of the biggest
colons in the Bône region. His 7,500-acre estate in Mondovi included
1,500 acres of vineyards; he employed five hundred workers including
one hundred convicts.

Guébar-Bou-Aoun
When, from Mondovi, you notice, above the lofty tops of euca-
lyptus, which form a moving emerald belt around it . . . the slate
dome of Guébar flanked by its two cupolas, you think you see rising
in the midst of the verdant banks of the Seybouse [River] one of
those Muscovite temples, with a hieratic profile, and the enigmatic
attitude of an Oriental *koubba* [*qubba*] on the Russian horizon. . . .
It is the largest domain under exploitation which the Bône
region can rightfully pride itself on. . . .
In its present state, the domain is subdivided into several small
farms and groups of dwellings, of which the most important are:
Saint-Charles, Nathalie, Sidi Den-Den, Bou-Farah, Berkani, Dar-
Zitoun, etc. (Blanc 1887: 66–67)

Already it was clear how Bertagna combined his practical
background—civil engineering, construction, grain—with an élan
brought to bear on business. He had a knack for being the right person

in the right place at the right time, and he knew it. Bertagna parlayed his economic wealth into not only social prestige but political power as well. He was only 27 when as deputy to the mayor of Bône he was revoked in 1870 by Marshal MacMahon, then presiding over the violent birth of the French Third Republic. Demonstrating his talent for political survival, Bertagna soon regained his seat on the Bône city council, worked his way up again to deputy mayor, and crowned his comeback by becoming mayor in 1888, a post he held continuously for fifteen years until his death.

It was while mayor that Bertagna enjoyed his greatest successes and experienced his biggest scandals. He had false invoices drawn up for municipal money spent on public works. He lent a local building contractor 100,000 francs in exchange for a cut of the profits. He taxed brothel keepers for each prostitute—a flagrantly illegal municipal law. He colluded with government engineers to deceive the French state by deliberately and grossly underestimating costs for the construction of the port of Bône. And when port construction halted after nine years due to lack of funds because the money had run out, the government was interpellated in the *Assemblée Nationale* in Paris over Bertagna's role.

But the biggest scandal Bertagna was ever involved in was the so-called Tébessa phosphates affair. Getting wind of a vast deposit of phosphates south of Bône, Bertagna peddled his influence to obtain the necessary prefectoral authorization to insure that the concession would be sold to an English businessman in Bône named Jacobsen.

> On 14 September 1893 Jacobsen wrote to an intermediary: "I hope M. Bertagna will not complain if I don't walk at a rapid enough pace. To which you will probably offer your favorite motto: 'You cannot dance faster than the music.' I say to you: But there are ways to make the musicians play faster. Find them! Once the ground is broken, we will deploy the same activity and with the precious aid of the Messieurs Bertagna, I hope that we will outdistance our rivals." (AN, BB 18 2006: 16 March 1896, 19 June 1896)[4]

When word reached Paris that the phosphates of Tébessa—termed a "national treasure" by one French engineer—were to be sold to a foreigner, the government was interpellated again, the prefect's authorization rescinded, the prefect revoked, and a judicial investigation launched against Bertagna and his coconspirators.

> Five days later on 19 September 1893, Bertagna telegraphed the following from Tébessa to the intermediary: "You will probably be able to announce to your principals [*à vos mandants*] solution day after tomorrow." Finally, on 22 September Jacobsen telegraphed, "Very good. Sincere compliments Messieurs Bertagna. Now forward!"
> (AN, BB 18 2006: 16 March 1896, 19 June 1896)

This list of Bertagna's corrupt practices could be extended *ad nauseum*, since no fewer than twenty-eight separate *instructions judici-aires* (analogous to grand jury investigations) were launched against him during his career. Yet the significant point here is that Bertagna was never indicted let alone convicted of any wrongdoing. Why? Because Bertagna successfully played off his position as a settler-leader against metropolitan France. As long as settler interests coincided with those of metropolitan France, the colonial French bureaucracy cracked down only on the most egregious excesses of local patronage politics. This situation continued from 1870, when the settlers were given virtually a free hand in determining Algerian policy in exchange for their staunch support of the Third Republic, to the early 1890s. This period coincides precisely with the era when Bertagna was becoming the boss of Bône. What Bertagna did was to capitalize—literally—on opportunities opened up after 1870 for all settlers, profiting ultimately at the expense of the Algerians. Beginning in the 1890s, however, the situation began to change. It was then that a series of reports issued in quick succession alerted Parliament in Paris to settler abuses in Algeria: the Rapport Burdeau (1891), Rapport Jules Ferry (1892), Rapport Jonnart (1892), and Rapport Isaac (1895) (see Ageron 1968: 447–77). For a while, it looked as though things were about to change. No less convinced a colonialist than Jules Ferry, for example, demanded that France arbitrate between the settlers and Algerians rather than side with the settlers against the Algerians.

> Ferry criticized "*l'état d'esprit* of the *colon* vis-à-vis the vanquished Algerians: it is difficult to make the European *colon* understand that there exists other rights besides his in an Arab land," and that "the

indigenous people are not at his beck and call." Ferry concluded that France should act as an arbiter in Algeria, in this land which was "necessarily given over to the conflict between two rival races," and mediate between the European settlers on the one hand and the Algerians on the other. (quoted in Ageron 1974: 48)

The 1890s debate in Paris over reform in Algeria was conducted primarily in terms of those who were either for or against the colonial policy of assimilation. By and large, the terms of this debate are carried over in the historiography. In the name of assimilation to the Republic, the settlers pushed to establish the full panoply of political institutions in Algeria. But the practice of assimilation in Algeria differed markedly from the theory of assimilation as adumbrated in Paris. Rooted in Jacobin universalism and the revolutionary tradition of 1789, assimilation may have been a progressive, liberal policy when applied in France, but it was clearly a retrogressive, illiberal policy when applied selectively in Algeria. For in the name of assimilation the settlers carved out their own power base within the civil regime which they used to gain hegemony over the Algerians. "Algeria 'assimilated to France' was in reality in the hands of colonization," that is, the settlers (Ageron 1974: 49).

At the level of theory, association replaced assimilation as official French policy after 1900 (Ageron 1968: 989–1002). In fact, it made little, if any, practical difference to Bertagna and other settlers in Algeria whether Paris adopted assimilation or association as official colonial policy. What was crucial for the settlers was not the particular colonial policy determined in Paris, but its implementation in Algeria; what mattered was not theory but practice. On the one hand, assimilation had clearly proven advantageous to the settlers. On the other hand, Bertagna could argue apropos the debate on assimilation versus association, "We are destined to live with the Arabs, to utilize their special capacities for the development of this land, and our first duty is to respect their customs by banishing any idea of assimilation" (quoted in Ageron 1968: 575, translation mine).

Key was the manner in which Bône politicians formed patronage chains with politicians elsewhere, the most important of which connected Bertagna in Bône to deputy Gaston Thomson in Paris, the longest-sitting deputy of the Third Republic. In fact, local settler power throughout Algeria was linked to and cemented by an influential settler lobby in Paris, comprised largely of the so-called *élus algériens*, the French representatives of Algeria who sat in the *Assemblée Nationale*. In turn, these *élus algériens* played a major role in the *parti colonial*, the foremost interest group lobbying for colonial expansion during the Third Republic.

Recent work on the *parti colonial* and its parliamentary component, the *groupe colonial*, bears out this line of interpretation (Andrew and Kanya-Forstner 1971, 1974, 1976, 1981; Kanya-Forstner and Grupp 1975; Andrew 1976; Ageron 1978; Abrams and Miller 1976; Persell 1983; Binoche 1971). The *parti colonial* emerges as a highly successful pressure group, largely responsible for late nineteenth- and early twentieth-century French expansion rather than any widespread, mass-based enthusiasm emanating from ordinary Frenchmen. It is worth stressing that European settlers from Algeria and their representatives comprised the major faction within the *parti colonial*. Eugène Etienne, deputy from Oran, was the unquestioned titular head; he was seconded by Thomson, representative of Bône. So far the *parti colonial* has been studied mostly from "above" rather than "below," from Paris rather than Algeria. Yet interest groups such as the *parti colonial* could not have functioned, indeed, would have had no *raison d'être*, had it not been for precisely the sort of grassroots support provided by settlers in local Algerian cities like Bône.

When the showdown came between France and the settlers, the *métropole* learned to its dismay how powerful the settlers had become with their patronage-based political network extending from the local municipalities of Algeria to the settler lobby in Paris. The city of Bône and Mayor Bertagna played a key role in this settler political network and were at the center of the ensuing conflict.

Amidst calls for reform, Jules Cambon was named Governor General in 1891. To clean up local Algerian politics, Cambon began a wide-ranging purge of European mayors. From the end of 1895 to the end of 1896 he suspended or revoked no fewer than nine mayors. Within the context of his purge, Bertagna was clearly Cambon's biggest and most important prey.[5] At this very moment in 1895 the scandal over the phosphates of Tébessa surfaced. Pending the outcome of the judicial inquiry of Bertagna and his cronies, Cambon first suspended then revoked Bertagna as mayor. When the French jurist Broussard investigating the case concluded that Bertagna had indeed peddled his political influence and recommended that Bertagna be tried, it looked for a minute as though Bertagna was through.

> MM. Jérome and Dominique Bertagna have sold to M. Jacobsen, who wanted to obtain a favor or a profit resulting from an agreement concluded with the public authorities, the influence which their electoral mandates gave them.
> —Procureur-Général Broussard (AN, BB 18 2006:
> 16 March 1896, 19 June 1896)

But in fact it was already too late. Despite his suspension and revocation as mayor, Bertagna had already been triumphantly reelected by loyal Bône voters in 1896. At the time of his investiture, he went on the offensive lambasting the state administration in general and the judicial system in particular.

> The judiciary, unable to prove my guilt after six months of tortures which it has inflicted on me, has invented for me a penalty unknown in our legal codes: "perpetual investigation" [*l'instruction perpétuelle*]. This justice system has prostituted itself and has submitted to political demands. I await proudly all the persecutions which can still afflict me strengthened by my past of rectitude and honesty, for without blemish and without fear I have the legitimate conviction of being invincible. (quoted in *Le Réveil Bônois*, 18 May 1896)

And so he was, for the Bône *juge* who conducted the phosphates investigation concluded—as did every other judge who ever investigated him—that there was insufficient evidence to bring Bertagna to trial (AN, BB 18 2006: 19 June 1896).

In the end it was not Bertagna but Cambon who was removed from office. With his failure to unseat Bertagna, Cambon's mayoral purge sputtered out; the *coup de grâce* came in 1897 when the settlers connived to have Cambon ousted as Governor General. A contemporary politician from nearby Constantine, Emile Morinaud, wrote in his memoirs that Cambon was removed as a result of "the repeated intervention of [Gaston] Thomson and [Eugène] Etienne." Charles-Robert Ageron, the leading historian of colonial Algeria, claims that Thomson was Cambon's "most decided adversary," and that Morinaud's contention that Thomson and Etienne were involved in Cambon's removal "is impossible to verify . . . but more than likely" (Ageron 1968: 479, 531).

> I am Governor, and I do not govern. I command, and I am not obeyed. I want to do right, and I am powerless to prevent wrong. I have received the mission to have the administration of France liked and respected: I do not have the power to wrest it from the jaws of sharks [aux griffes des aigrefins].
>
> —Jules Cambon in a speech to Parliament
> (quoted in Le Réveil Bônois, 3 January 1896)

The confrontation in Bône in 1896 which pitted the settlers against the government, and the bureaucracy against the patronage system had clearly been won by the settlers and their representatives. Elsewhere in Algeria, the settlers also beat back the metropolitan French challenge, but somewhat differently.

The attempt by metropolitan France to reform Algeria, to act again as an intermediary between Europeans and Algerians, spawned a settler reaction which is usually discussed in terms of an anti-Semitic crisis between 1898 and 1901, but which amounted in reality to a revolution manquée. Regarding anti-Semitism, Algeria experienced an outbreak at the very moment the Dreyfus affair peaked in France. Scholars concur that Algerian anti-Semitism was primarily an electoral phenomenon born as a result of the 1870 Crémieux decree which enfranchised en masse the Jews of Algeria. Yet it became more than simply an electoral phenomenon in fin-de-siècle Algeria. "Racial anti-Semitism can be considered one of the givens of colonial Algerian psychology" (Ageron 1968: 588). It functioned as a lightning rod which collected and deflected, as much as it focused, a whole range of collective resentments.

Anti-Semitism constituted in turn one aspect of a larger Algerian crisis which also included colon insecurity vis-à-vis the Algerians, French settler fears of non-French settlers ("foreign peril"), an economic crisis over colonization, plus a movement for autonomy. Crisis in Algeria fueled the *crise de conscience* felt in France over the course the settlers were steering, and led to a political confrontation, the opening round of which cast Cambon against Bertagna in 1896. But if Cambon's defeat at the hands of Bertagna resolved in large measure the Bône situation, Cambon's removal failed to still emotions elsewhere in Algeria. "With Cambon gone," Ageron writes, "the political crisis only worsened until the revolutionary attempt of the years 1898–1901, misunderstood as the anti-Jewish crisis, and by which the Algeria of the Europeans meant to obtain its autonomy" (Ageron 1979: 39–40).[6]

Cambon's departure in 1897 failed to resolve the Algerian crisis, therefore, because it was more than a crisis over anti-Semitism.[7] To anti-Semitism were added calls for autonomy, and even outright separation from France. As Ageron explains, the ties between France and Algeria consisted in "a sort of contract" whereby the task of France was to defend the settlers and to maintain their social supremacy over the Muslims; should it fail to do so, the settlers had the right to claim their independence. By 1898 large numbers of settlers felt France had broken this contract (Ageron 1979: 133).

At the height of the Dreyfus affair, therefore, a besieged Republic needed all the support it could get, and in the end caved in to the settlers' more moderate demands in exchange for their support against the anti-Dreyfusards. In a series of decrees issued in August 1898 and completed by a 1900 law, the settlers failed to obtain outright political autonomy, but they did gain financial autonomy, the creation of a colonial assembly (*Délégations Finançières*), and perhaps most important, the "unwritten promise that metropolitan interference would cease" (Ageron 1979: 39–40). These concessions satisfied all but the hard-core anti-Semites, tensions attenuated from the end of 1898, and by the parliamentary elections of 1902 Algeria returned to the Opportunist fold.

But at what a cost. Algerian reform had been shelved. And measures for autonomy only strengthened the hand of the settlers at the expense of the *métropole*. Just as Bertagna had bested Cambon in 1896, therefore, so did the European settlers emerge victorious in their confrontation with metropolitan France at the turn of the century. By capitalizing on among other things the possibilities of patronage politics in a settler colonial situation, they had taken a giant stride forward in securing their de facto control over colonial Algeria.

Yet it is not the big men alone, the bosses of the cities, that made Algeria a settler colony. Bertagna was extraordinary in the sense that he realized the possibilities more than most; he actualized the potential of the colonial situation in Algeria after 1870. But what was extraordinary about colonial Algeria was that it offered similar opportunities to the mass of ordinary European settlers. They, too, seized their opportunity and in so doing created a new society, part French, part Italian, part Spanish, part Maltese, part Jewish, part Algerian; in short, a settler colonial society. "A new race" is precisely how André Gide, who was in the Maghreb at the time, described what he saw (quoted in Baroli 1967: 214). Already by 1900 more than sixty percent of the settlers lived in cities as opposed to the countryside. Algerians outnumbered Europeans six to one in Algeria as a whole, but in the main cities along the Mediterranean coast, Europeans preponderated over Algerians two to one. Thus, the port cities of Algiers, Oran, and Bône constituted the loci of colonial Algerian society, and played thereby a disproportionately large role in assuring settler predominance throughout Algeria (Lespès 1925: 89; Lespès 1938, graphique v; APCA, Listes nominatives, 1848–1926; Prochaska 1990: 135–37). In Bône (see table), Europeans outnumbered Algerians two to one between 1848 and 1926. And in making Bône a European city in the nineteenth century, the French blocked social evolution, attempted to contain history, and precluded thereby any genuine rapprochement with the Algerians in the twentieth century.

To take the argument a step further, the single most striking feature of this colonial society is that it not only existed in objective terms, but that it became subjectively aware of its own existence. Not simply formed around the turn of the twentieth century, it formed itself, it became conscious of itself. It is no coincidence, therefore, that at the very time Cambon was tangling with Bertagna, the settlers in Bône and elsewhere in Algeria were beginning to refer to themselves as the "Algerians," the "Algerian people." When the enormously popular literary character, Cagayous of Algiers, is asked, "Are you

Bône Population, 1907

Category	Percent	No.
Native French	22	(8845)
Jews	4	(1588)
Europeans naturalized French	29	(12041)
Other Europeans (primarily Maltese and Italians)	18	(7455)
Algerians	27	(11227)
Total	100	(41156)

SOURCE: Gouvernement Général de l'Algérie (1908: 132–33).

French?" he answers, "We are Algerians!" (quoted in Ageron 1979: 128). As for the Muslim Algerians, they were called the "*indigènes*." Thus, at one blow the settlers proclaimed their hegemony in Algeria and at the same time obliterated the Algerians in the very words they used to describe themselves.

Nowhere is this settler colonial society, this settler consciousness more evident than in the culture they created, in the language they spoke, and the literature they wrote. Consider language first. The language the European settlers of Algeria spoke consisted of an amalgam of the various languages they brought along with them as part of their cultural baggage, namely, French, Spanish, Italian, Maltese, plus Arabic. This language, or more precisely, dialect of French was termed *pataouète*.

> Alors Coco y s'avance et y lui dit: "Arrête un peu, arrête." L'autre y dit: "Qu'est-ce qu'y a?" Alors Coco y lui dit: "Je vas te donner des coups.—A moi tu vas donner des coups?" Alors y met la main derrière [à la poche-revolver] mais c'était scousa. Alors Coco y lui dit: "Mets pas la main darrière, parce qu'après j'te choppe le 6–35 et t'y mangeras des coups quand même."
>
> —Albert Camus (1950: 66)[8]

Pataouète was a language of the cities more than the countryside, especially of the large port cities where the largest number of settlers concentrated. Moreover, accents and usage varied from city to city. In Oran, Spanish predominated; in Bône, Italian. In the Bône case, the variant of *pataouète* was called, naturally, *patois bônois*. Italian loan words were known as *bônoises*, that is, related to Bône; parodies of classical literature sprinkled with Italian phrases were termed *hipponismes*, that is, related to Hippo, the city of St. Augustine, situated on the same site as Bône (Lanly 1962; Bacri 1983; Gautier 1920; Audisio 1931; Brunot 1948: 209–10).

ACTE I

Scène III

Dodièze: "Avec gloire et honneur je me port' la cravate,
             Pourquoi moi et Fernand nous s'avons fréquentés
             Du temps que manque encore il était député."

Gongormatz: "Tout député qu'il est, c'est pas pluss que les autes!
             Laisse aujord'hui qu'y passe et le monde qu'y vote,
             Tu oiras comment qu'c'est qu'y prend le saucisson,
             Çuilà-là qu'y s'oblie aux amis à de bon!"

—Edmund Brua 1941 (quoted in Bacri 1983: 208)[9]

Although it is more difficult to track the rise and diffusion of spoken discourse than it is to read the literary survivals which remain, there are a number of clues in the case of the *patois bônois*. For one, there is the local character, Luc, a housepainter by vocation, a bard and balladeer by avocation. Luc gained a certain local fame for his poems and songs, all expressed in *patois bônois*.

The Opportunist candidate
Lies night and day with skill. . . .
He says, 'I am a Republican,'
But he is only a vile opportunist. . . .

Algeria is a land of gold
And Bône would be flourishing
If its treasury were not squandered [*gaspillait*].

So who is to blame for our turmoil and our ruin? . . .
It is *messieurs* the Opportunists.

—Luc (quoted in Le Réveil Bônois, 27 July 1895)

We also know that Bône's two opposing political factions congregated in two cafes on opposite sides of Bône's main street, named the Cours Bertagna after Bertagna's death.

> The "Crown" [*Couronne*] cafe had always been the place where all the groups (they were numerous and diverse) gathered which combatted the Municipality whether that of Prosper Dubourg or Jérome Bertagna.
> On the other side of the Cours [Bertagna] was the cafe St. Martin [today: cafe de Paris], headquarters of the friends of the Municipality.
> On those days when the election campaign reached fever pitch, the regulars of these two cafes worked themselves up against each other.
> From each one of the terraces, which faced each other diagonally across the street, could be heard howls or cheers, insults, cries, gibes, guffaws and those guttural and farting-like onomatopoetic words, which are, it is said, a veritable Bône specialty. (Arnaud 1960: 92) [10]

These strange sounds are, of course, those of the *patois bônois*. Bône political culture, exemplified in Bertagna's political corruption, employed as its favored mode of discourse, the *patois bônois*.

Turning next to the literature of colonial Bône, the first texts written in the *patois bônois* consist of a series of columns which appeared under the pseudonym of Pepino. Eighteen of his "Croquis Naturalistes" were published in *Les Clochettes Bônoises* between 4 May 1895 and 6 November 1897. Another five "Croquis Naturalistes" appeared in *Les Gaités Bônoises* between 21 February and 21 March 1897.

> Ils [André, Jean-Jean, Petites-Moustache, Courtes-Jambes, Grand Victor and Guigui] se précipitent l'un vers l'autre et se battent. Passe un Monsieur ganté, portant gibus.
>
> Le Monsieur
> Ganté: "Voulez-vous bien, jeunes galopins, cesser ce pugilat qui n'a aucune raison d'être?"

Patatrac:	"Arga-moi ce long, dio patanae, avec son décalitre; va compter les fèves chez Xiberras. . . ."
Le Monsieur Ganté:	"Veux-tu bien te taire, galopin sans vergogne."
Petites-Jambes:	"Entends-le qué parisien gros bec, pas mieux y va travailler aux phosphates. . . ."
Grand-Victor:	"Te veux cinq sous pour la barbe. . . ."
Guigui:	"Y me ressemble tout à Jacob. Aille mà la lampa! . . . C'est un juif, je crois. . . . Attention les coups de revolver. . . ."
Patatrac (chantant):	"Igna-ce! Igna-ce! . . ."
Le Monsieur (furieux):	"N'y a-t-il pas ici d'agents de police?"
Jean-Jean:	"La police? Nous s' l'affoguons pas moi et Grand-Victor? O va vendre le fromage pour le broumège, dans la rue du Quatre-Septembre! . . ."

Un agent de police point à l'horizon. La bande se disperse avec la rapidité d'un train du Bône-Guelma.

—Pepino ("Croquis Naturalistes," *Les Clochettes Bônoises*, 4 May 1895) [11]

In 1898 an entire newspaper in *patois bônois* was published, *Le Diocane Bônois*. Satirical in intent, shocking in effect, *Le Diocane Bônois* caused a furor because it featured on its masthead the Italian blasphemy, *Diocane!*, the Italian version of *nom d'un chien!* (Goddammit!). Due to the scandal, only one issue appeared, dated 31 December 1898. Then the name was changed to *Le Scandale Bônois*, and two additional issues appeared on 7 and 14 January 1899.[12]

Notre Nouveau Titre

Avant-hier on s'a fait une grande réunion à la buvette aarab' de Moham . . . ed ben Kouider Abderahman ou Taraz Faraz.

Ordre du jour: *Qué nouveau* nom pour le journal!

P'tit Malade:	"*Le Diobone. Le Diobone Bônois*, oh! sauve!"
Sale Fatty:	"*Le Zacounas.* Zacounas toi-même!"

Marie-la-Longue:	"*Le Bourmetche*. A qui te veux empoisonner?"
Mikal F:	"*La Troumba*. Mala nous devons donner des lave-ments . . . pour rien?"
O. Z'Yeux:	"*La Grappe poileuse*. Qué dio-sfax de toqué de la jetée!"
Goualio:	"*Le Coutelatche*. Oh! va pecher les oursins baveux!"
Moi:	"*Le P'tit bon sang à la mihiel*. Mà ce titre y se rem-plissait les quat' pages. Alors oui!"

Enfin tant de discussion, qu'à trois heures du matin pas un il était d'accord. Juste y passe le gérant, ô vilain!

Quel nom? *Le Scandale*.

Oui, oui, *Le Scandale*. Je vous jure pas même un il avait compris. Enfin marche pour *Le Scandale*. Ca veut dire: *La Chaussette Puante*.

—La Rascade d'ses morts [pseud.] (*Le Scandale Bônois*, 7 January 1899)[13]

Not only newspapers but also books in *patois bônois* were published. Although the books generally came later, they usually returned to an earlier period, to the local legends and personalities of the age of Bertagna. There is, for example, *Harmonies Bônoises* by Louis Lafour-cade (n.d.).[14] Jérome Bertagna himself appears, as well as Thaddo, guardian of the European cemetery, and Carloutche, humble Italian fisherman and devoted Bertagna follower. Carloutche served as the model for the fisherman sitting at the base of the statue of Bertagna, which was the largest and most important statue in Bône before it was torn down by the Algerians in 1962. But this local literary genre culminates in Edmund Brua's *Fables Bônoises* ([1938] 1972), "one of the summits of *pied noir* literature" (Lentin 1982).

A MONSEIGNEUR LE DAUPHIN

Vous à qui nous devons & nos coeurs & nos têtes
Et nos voix, si du moins nous savions qui vous êtes!
J'aimerois, pour ma part, vous avoir révélé
Le langage barbare en ces Fables parlé.
Vous connoissez sa mort, apprenez sa naissance.
Votre aïeul Charles Dix en jeta la semence

Et le rameau grandit sur la souche du franc.
Plus d'un siècle passa. Charles Onze le Grand
Vint, ouït Salvator, Sfatchime, Badiguelle,
Bagur, auxquels Ahmed avoit cherché querelle,
Et les deux bras levés pour apaiser leurs cris,
Philologue imprudent, dit: "Je vous ai compris."
Hélas! il lui manquoit le secours d'un lexique,
Au rebours d'un Soustelle instruit par le Mexique.
Six mois plus tard, Bagur, Sfatchime, Salvator,
Badiguelle ahuris oyoient: "Vous avez tort."
Je chante ces héros, mais non pas dans la guerre,
Dans la paix de jadis (d'autres pensent: naguère).

—Edmund Brua ([1938] 1972: 10) [15]

The language of the *Fables Bônoises* is *pataouète*, the literary model the tales of La Fontaine, and the tone ironic, satirical. In these tales transplanted from La Fontaine's France to Brua's Bône, we meet Malakoff the milkman and also the Maltese *curé*, plus Bagur, Salvator, and Sauveur. And when the *Fables* were collected together and first published in 1938, they were reviewed by that other writer from the Bône region, Albert Camus, who wrote that "the singular flavor of these ironic moral tales belongs only to Brua, and through him to those robust people, the Bagurs, the Sauveurs, and the Salvators, who make love and go swimming, who cheat and jeer and bluster in the very places where St. Augustine meditated on the tragedy of the human soul" (*Alger-Républicain* 1938, reprinted in Brua [1938] 1972: 7).

It is time to draw up a preliminary balance sheet. The political culture of Bône, typified by the political corruption of Jérome Bertagna, and the linguistic and literary culture, exemplified by Pepino and Luc, Lafourcade and Brua, together demonstrate the formation in Bône of a distinctive settler society and culture around the turn of the twentieth century. Settler colonialism in Algeria was the necessary but not sufficient prerequisite for the creation of settler colonial culture. In turn, colonial culture contributed to the formation of settler society.

As such, the creation of settler society and culture in Bône constitutes one chapter in making Algeria French in the decades prior to the First World War.

Perhaps the most striking feature about the formation of settler colonial society and culture is the way the Algerians tend to drop out of the picture. Bertagna achieves preeminence in Bône not by taking the Algerians into account but by leaving them out—and getting away with it. Likewise, Bône's *pied noir* literature was written by, for and about the Europeans, not the Algerians. It records like a seismograph European preoccupations, but rather than dealing with, let alone coming to terms with the colonial situation in Algeria, the relationship between European colonizers and Algerian colonized, the Algerians are curiously absent. Yet they were there, if one only bothered to look.

Even the Bônois could not fail to see the Algerians in 1909 when they staged a mass meeting, twelve hundred strong according to European estimates, three thousand according to Algerian sources—that is, somewhere between ten and twenty-five percent of Bône's nearly 11,000 Algerians (Gouvernement Général de l'Algérie 1908: 132–33). Ostensibly, they gathered to support a recent French law which required French military service of all Algerians, but in actuality they used the occasion to call for reforms. The meeting was organized by none other than Sadek Denden and Khélil Kaid Layoun, who delivered two of the three speeches the crowd heard. Denden urged that Algerians who served in the French military be given the option of becoming French citizens. Kaid Layoun argued that special punitive laws applicable only to Algerians, the *Code de l'Indigénat*, "constitute an insurmountable obstacle to the assimilation dreamed by French and Arabs" (*L'Islam*, 30 December 1909). The next day accounts of the gathering appeared under banner headlines in the local Algerian newspaper edited by Denden, *L'Islam*.[16]

Ageron points out that this was very likely the first mass meeting of Algerians, and that it followed soon after the 1908 Young Turk revolution in Turkey plus a 1908 visit of *Jeunes Algériens* who met with

Georges Clemenceau in Paris (Ageron 1968: 1037–38; 1979: 235). At
the same time, this meeting in Bône constitutes one of the first and
most important gatherings anywhere in Algeria of the *Jeune Algérien*
movement, that movement of Frenchified Algerians who sought the
assimilation of Algeria to France. As we have seen, assimilation was
official French policy in theory; in practice, however, it was stymied
by settler intransigence. The *Jeunes Algériens* appealed over the heads
of the settlers in Algeria to French reformers in France to implement
assimilation. In seeking closer ties to France at the beginning of the
century, the *Jeunes Algériens* pursued a course of action which ironically
the *Front de Libération Nationale* (FLN) was later to term "collabora-
tionist."

In 1909 Sadek Denden was thirty-eight years old; it was an eventful year for him. He had joined the colonial administration after studying in a French *lycée*. In 1909 he quit the administration, cofounded
L'Islam, and organized the mass meeting at the end of the year. He
edited *L'Islam* in Bône until 1912 when he moved to Algiers and took
L'Islam with him, where it appeared until the First World War. In
Algiers Denden became friends with Dr. Benthami, one of the most
influential *Jeune Algérien* leaders in the capital, and the Emir Khaled,
grandson of Abd al-Qadir, the leader of Algerian resistance to the
French in the 1830s and 1840s. In 1919 Denden, a candidate for the
Algiers city council on a ticket headed by Benthami, was defeated
by a ticket led by Khaled. A talented journalist, a scathing editorial-
ist, a skillful political organizer, Sadek Denden made *L'Islam*, first in
Bône, then in Algiers, the single most important *Jeune Algérien* newspaper. He himself became one of the acknowledged leaders of the
Jeune Algérien movement.[17]

> This jovial, potbellied patriot [Si Saddek Dendene], this marvel-
> ously reddish, erudite countenance under a *chechia kalabouche* [a kind
> of hat], always alert in spite of his weight and his enormous billow-
> ing pantaloons . . . came from one of the oldest families [of Bône],
> Dar Ed-Dendène. . . . (Derdour 1982–83: II, 463)

While Denden moved to Algiers, Khélil Kaid Layoun remained
in Bône (Montoy 1982: 468, 1347). A year older than Denden, Khélil

came from a lower middle-class Bône family; he worked as a clerk in a French law office. At the time of the French reform effort back in the 1890s which culminated in Bône with Governor General Cambon's attempted ouster of Mayor Bertagna, Khélil helped publish an Algerian newspaper in Bône called *El Hack*, Arabic for "the truth." Sliman Bengui directed the paper, and Omar Samar served as editor (Montoy 1982: 468). Scrupulously apolitical, legalistic, and assimilationist, *El Hack* called on French reformers to prevent settler abuses. It objected to holding Algerians responsible collectively for crimes committed by individuals, and it waxed indignant when all Algerians were lumped together and termed "bandits."

> Aujourd'hui, dimanche, les français et les étrangers naturalisés déposent dans l'urne le nom du candidat de leur choix. . . .
>
> Pendant ce temps, l'Arabe reste muet, il voudrait bien donner son opinion, mais il se tait, il n'en a pas droit, pourtant il a intérêt autant que les colons et plus que les étrangers naturalisés. . . .
>
> Pour le moment reste dans ton gourbi, fellah, patiente, résigne-toi, car la France est trop généreuse pour t'abandonner à tes malheurs, et le jour ne tardera pas, où revenant de l'erreur où l'ont induite tes ennemis, elle te délivrera et te donnera autant de droits que tes frères les colons,—les véritables colons, non pas les gros propriétaires qui te mangent, mais les autres ceux qui partagent tes déboires et ta misère.
>
> —Zeid ben Dieb [Omar Samar]
> ("Les Elections," *El Hack*, 20 August 1893) [18]

El Hack was printed in French, not Arabic; French sympathizers known as *indigènophiles*, as well as Algerians, contributed articles. *El Hack* criticized the practice of French colonialism, but it did not question the theoretical foundations of the colonial regime; it did not seek separation from France, but pushed for French reforms in Algeria. What is striking about the reforms advocated by *El Hack* is not how conservative they strike us today, but how radical they seemed to the settlers then. Nearly the entire European press in Bône plus papers in Algiers and Oran fulminated against *El Hack*'s alleged "anti-French" and "anti-Algerian" tendencies, claiming it was guilty of urging the Algerians to revolt.

> Monsieur le Gouverneur Général and Monsieur le Procureur de
> la République in Bône ought to read this press [*El Hack*] and then
> tell us whether it is the French who have suddenly become the sub-
> jects of the Arabs or if the latter still remain under our domination.
> ("Chronique locale: Appel à la révolte," *Le Bônois*, 26 Septem-
> ber 1893)
>
> This dumping ground [i.e., *Le Réveil Bônois*, which defended
> *El Hack*] finds it quite natural and entirely legitimate that the more
> or less educated *indigènes* have the audacity to abuse the liberty of
> the press. . . . ("Chronique locale: Appel à la révolte," *Le Bônois*,
> 20 February 1894)

Freedom of the press notwithstanding, the settlers demanded *El Hack*
be suspended, the colonial administration banned its sale in rural areas,
and in 1894 it folded after publishing twenty-six weekly issues between 30 July 1893 and 25 March 1894 (Montoy 1982: 468–75, 1347–50;
Ageron 1979: 233).

> For what reason would anyone ban us? In all the countries
> where the *indigènes* are subject to a dominant race, they have news-
> papers, including the United States, and unless entirely in thrall to
> the Jews, the French would not want to appear less liberal than the
> Yankees, those exterminators of so-called inferior races.
> —El Rachid [X. Gaultier de Claubry]
> ("Mise au point," *El Hack*, 15 October 1893)

The same editorial staff consisting of Khélil Kaid Layoun, Sliman Bengui, and Samar Omar launched *L'Eclair* the following year,
which soon changed its name to *La Bataille Algérienne*. However, these
latter papers appeared only between 24 March and 30 June 1895 before
they, too, folded (Montoy 1982: 475–76, 1353–55; Ageron 1968: 1036;
Ageron 1979: 234.)

> We request that metropolitan France cast a glance of pity on
> the innumerable French and Arab proletarians who are starving
> due to lack of work while the foreigners [i.e., Europeans] who
> flock to Algeria fatten themselves at their expense. . . . (*L'Eclair*,
> 25 March 1895)

Khélil Kaid Layoun surfaced again in 1900. As part of the metropolitan French reform effort of the 1890s now winding down, a group

of senators on a fact-finding tour passed through Bône. Khélil addressed them on behalf of a group of "young Bône Muslims." He described the situation of Francophone young Algerian males such as himself, who favored Algerian assimilation to France but could not convert their French education into a job, who were less and less Algerian but prevented from becoming more and more French, who were in short "floundering in civilization."

> Educated Muslim youths are floundering in civilization . . . No jobs to hope for, not even a way to let their voice be heard, in order to state their opinion in some effective way, even on exclusively indigenous matters, even when it comes to local affairs. It is the right to vote that these youths are calling for. . . .
>
> —Laioun ([Layoun] 1901: 661)

What Kaid Layoun wanted was the vote extended to young Algerians with a French education and to Algerian businessmen licensed by the French. His deposition was the most far-reaching the senators heard.

Earlier in 1900 Khélil had attempted to form the *Djemâ'a El Kheiria El Arabia*, or Muslim Benevolent Society. Organized by Kaid Layoun and Mahmoud Hassam, a young tobacco merchant, the society consisted of older, honorary members and younger, active members. The honorary members included many of Bône's Algerian elite; mostly they were landowners and businessmen, white collar employees, and professionals. The active members were neither as well-established nor as well-off; they ranged from artisans and businessmen to clerks, journalists, and commercial employees. Two occupations in particular were overrepresented, white collar clerks such as Khélil and those who worked with tobacco—either cutting it, selling it, or making cigarettes from it—such as Khélil's cofounder Mahmoud Hassam.

Benyacoub Ali
   age: 45
   profession: propriétaire-agriculteur
   membre honoraire

Benyacoub Mihoub
   age: 25

profession: propriétaire-cultivateur

Benyacoub Abderrrahman
    age: 21
    profession: clerc chez M.———

Caid Laioun Khélil
    age: 30
    profession: clerc chez M. Boivin, notaire

Denden Ahmed
    age: 35
    profession: employé chez M. Charmardy, avocat

Hassam Mahmoud
    age: 36
    profession: propriétaire, fabricant de tabacs

Samar Omar
    age: 28
    profession: secrétaire-interprète chez M. de Peretti, avocat.

(APCA, Affaires Indigènes, folder on *Société Djemâ'a El Kheiria El Arabia*, February 1900)

These occupations corresponded to the same two groups of Algerian businessmen and French-educated Algerians which Khélil had singled out in his deposition. At an initial meeting of the Muslim Benevolent Society, eighty-four Algerians attended and Khélil was named provisional president. All that needed to be done was to obtain authorization from Mayor Bertagna (APCA, Affaires Indigènes, folder on *Société Djemâ'a El Kheiria El Arabia*, 1900).

Khélil Kaid Layoun's activities in 1900 are noteworthy for two reasons. First, Ageron argues that Khélil's deposition can be compared both in form and content to a later and more widely known *Jeune Algérien* manifesto published in 1912 (1968: 1031). Thus, Khélil formulated early what became later *Jeune Algérien* principles. Moreover, "the young Bône Muslims" of 1900 soon became Bône's *Jeune Algériens*, which demonstrates Bône's precocity within this Algeria-wide movement—that is, it demonstrates why Bône and Algiers were "the two *Jeunes Algériens* capitals" (Ageron 1979: 232).

Second, and perhaps even more important, Khélil's statement together with the formation of the Muslim Benevolent Society reflect significant changes occurring in Algerian society at the turn of the twentieth century. It has been argued before that after the Algerians resisted the French actively from 1830 until roughly 1870, they resisted the French passively, largely by retreating into the Islamic religion and holding onto the Arabic language (Desparmet 1931, 1932a, 1932b, 1933). In fact, during the decades after 1870 the French confidently predicted that the Algerians, like the "aborigines" of Australia and America, soon would die out. But around the turn of the century a sea change occurred in Muslim society and manifested itself in the *Jeune Algérien* movement. Although the mass of Algerians continued to live in the countryside and were poverty-stricken, a small number of Algerians in the cities were carving out niches within the French colonial economy. Some, like Sadek Denden and Khélil Kaid Layoun, attended French schools, learned French, and worked in the tertiary or service sector of the urban economy as clerks in French law offices or the colonial administration. Others either grew tobacco on their land and sold it to the French government tobacco monopoly each year when it bought in Bône, or sold it to merchants who cut, dried, and rolled it into cigars and cigarettes which were sold in Bône and beyond.

Clerking in law offices and raising tobacco may not appear at first glance as particularly promising avenues to economic wealth and social prestige, but in *fin-de-siècle* Algeria they were. And it is precisely these same Algerians making their way in French Algeria who were now clamoring for a political role concomitant with their economic role, and who were now joining the *Jeune Algérien* movement. One example is Hadj Omar Bengui, the primary financial backer of *El Hack* in the mid–1890s, and whose son Sliman was director of the paper. Bengui was the only Algerian businessman on Bône's main street, the Cours Bertagna, where he sold tobacco from a kiosk (APCA, *Situation Industrielle*: 1883; Montoy 1982: 468, 1349). Another example is the Benyacoubs, one of Bône's two leading Algerian families, who had been in eclipse since 1830, and who slowly reconsolidated their wealth and family position due in part to tobacco profits. Cofounders of a tobacco cooperative, the *Tabacoop*, with other Europeans after the First World War, and today one of the leading families of Annaba, the Benyacoubs before the First World War were making money from tobacco, investing in Denden's *L'Islam*, and participating in Kaid Layoun's Muslim Benevolent Society.

> Benyacoub Hamidou (1858–1899)
> > Fought against the French after 1830.
> > Born enemy of the Boumaiza family.
> > Produced tobacco in plain of Bône.
> > 1898: elected to *Délégations Financières*, created as result of French reform effort to woo Algeria away from anti-Semitism.
>
> Benyacoub Mihoub (1875–1948)
> > 1900: Member, *Djemâ'a El Kheiria El Arabia*.
> > 1919: Represents tobacco planters at *Union agricole de l'Est* (Bône).
> > Post-World War I: One of three founders, *Tabacoop*, Bône tobacco cooperative.
> > Married Frenchwoman.
>
> Benyacoub Ali (1855–1927)
> > 1900: Administrator, *Djemâ'a El Kheiria El Arabia*.
> > 1910: Involved in *L'Islam*.
>
> Benyacoub Amar (1874–1928)
> > 1917: Vice-President, Syndicat de Planteurs de Tabac.

(Sources: APCA, *Liste nominative*, 1911: 1180, 1182–83, 1188; APCA, *Listes électorales*, 1908, 191; APCA, Opérations électorales, Conseil Municipal 1900; AOM, 6 H 33, 16 H 31)

Not surprisingly, Mayor Bertagna viewed the *Djemâ'a El Kheiria El Arabia* differently than Khélil Kaid Layoun. He agreed with his close Algerian collaborator and head of Bône's other leading Algerian family, Mohammed Tahar Boumaiza . . .

> The Boumaizas claim descent from one of the companions of the Prophet Muhammad. When the French invaded in 1830, the head of the family was Si el Hadj Ali Boumaiza. He soon "rallied," as the French say, to the French cause; in 1842 his support led to the "pacification" of Algerians in the Edough mountains outside Bône. Ali had three sons, Mohammed Tahar, Brahim, and Nafa. The most impor-

tant, Mohammed Tahar Boumaiza (1832–1919 or 1920) looked after the family's 15,000 acres in the Edough mountains, the Algerians in Bône as *adjoint indigène*, and opposed himself to the Benyacoub family (APCA, *Liste nominative*, 1911: 246; *Listes électorales*, 1908, 1912; AOM, 6 H 33, 16 H 31; Montoy 1982: 231, 733, 905).

. . . that Khélil Kaid Layoun and his coorganizer Mahmoud Hassam were "as everyone knows two militant politicians," that the Muslim Benevolent Society had been created with an exclusively political aim, and that the society's slogan ought to have been "political society and not charitable society" (APCA, Affaires indigènes, folder on *Société Djemâ'a El Kheiria El Arabia*, February 1900). As a consequence, Bertagna banned it. Earlier, Khélil Kaid Layoun's *El Hack* had been hounded out of existence by the settler press in the mid–1890s only to return stronger, more independant, and more militant with Sadek Denden's *L'Islam* in 1909. Khélil's 1900 deposition had no immediate consequences, and his Muslim Benevolent Society was aborted by Bertagna before it got off the ground, but a decade later a number of similar but longer-lasting Algerian societies appeared in Bône and elsewhere, and in 1909 Khélil organized with Sadek Denden their mass meeting attended by many more of Bône's Algerians than the 1900 society had ever dreamed of attracting. Algerian voluntary associations formed in Bône included *la Sadikiya*, *Société islamique constantinoise*, *le Croissant*, and *le Cercle du Progrès*; again, Bône was precocious in this regard (Ageron 1968: 1034; 1979: 234).

What can we conclude from these tales about Denden, Kaid Layoun, and their *Jeune Algérien* activities? First of all, the *Jeunes Algériens* were a movement not of the majority of Algerians but of a tiny minority. A new Algerian society was germinating around the turn of the twentieth century, it took root among a number of *évolués*, (literally, Algerians who had "evolved" linguistically, culturally, and politically towards France), it sprouted with *El Hack* and the *Djemâ'a El Kheiria El Arabia*, and it blossomed in the *Jeune Algérien* movement. Second, the *Jeunes Algériens* were pro-French, not anti-French. It could not be otherwise considering the historical soil in which they arose. Initially, they emerged as one of the intellectual and political manifestations of the social and economic transformations occurring in Algerian society. Thus, the *Jeunes Algériens* were pressing for a more active role; they were reacting against the constraints posed by the rules of the colonial game in Algeria, rules determined primarily but not entirely by the European settlers.

The long-term historical significance of the Bône *Jeunes Algériens* lies in the fact that along with their confrères elsewhere they constituted one of the three main strands of what became Algerian nationalism.[19] To foreshorten a lengthy historical process, we can say that from the beginning of the twentieth century the *Jeunes Algériens* pushed for a larger Algerian role in an essentially French Algeria. Their biggest hope and first major disappointment was the so-called Jonnart reforms of 1919, which were aimed at enfranchising those Algerians who were most French, that is, the *Jeunes Algériens* themselves. But in exchange for French citizenship, the Algerians were required to renounce their Muslim personal status, and in the end only a miniscule number accepted such terms (Ageron 1968: 1211–27). In 1919 municipal elections were held in their two leading centers of Algiers and Bône, and the *Jeunes Algériens* split over this very issue. In Bône on a slate headed by Ali and Mihoub Benyacoub, Mahmoud Hassam—Kaid Layoun's co-organizer of the *Djemâ'a El Kheiria El Arabia*—was the top vote-getter (Kaddache 1970; APCA, Opérations électorales, Conseil Municipal, 1919; and Ageron 1979: 282). Thus, 1919 marked their first major disillusionment: the *Jeunes Algériens* had tried to become more like the French, but the French had failed to overcome settler opposition and enact meaningful reform.

The initiative passed next to the *Salafiyya*, or Islamic Reform movement, associated in Algeria with Abd al-Hamid Ben Badis.

> This town of Annaba is crushed under the weight of two outrageous forces, one implanted by force and which possesses nearly all the material wealth [e.g., the French], and a more reactionary one from

Sicily and Malta which occupies our neighborhoods and imposes on us its flotsam and jetsam.
—Ben Badis (quoted in Derdour 1982–83: II, 462)

Where the *Jeunes Algériens* had attempted to embrace French society and culture, the Reformists turned away to rediscover the fundamentals of Islam. As such, they waged a battle on two fronts: first, against the secular *Jeunes Algériens*, and second, against the *tariqa*-s, Sufi brotherhoods, and *mrabtin*, holy men, both of which had strayed from the teachings of Muhammad. Pan-Arab in orientation but advocates of Algerian nationalism, religious at base but implicitly political, the Reformist movement began in the mid–1920s but made significant headway only in the 1930s. Nonetheless, it was already clear by 1939 that Ben Badis and his followers could not transform alone a primarily religious movement of the traditional bourgeoisie into a mass-based nationalist political party (Merad 1967; Colonna 1974: 233–54; Gellner 1981).

> Had I discovered the Algerian nation, I would be a nationalist and I would not blush as if I had committed a crime . . . However, I will not die for the Algerian nation, because it does not exist. I have not found it. I have examined History, I questioned the living and the dead, I visited cemeteries; nobody spoke to me about it.
> —Ferhat Abbas, 23 February 1936 (quoted in Nouschi 1962: 89)

> History shows that the Muslim Algerian nation [*le peuple musulman d'Algérie*] has been created like all the others . . . [I]t has its culture, its traditions and its characteristics, good and bad. This Muslim population is not France, cannot be France, and does not wish to be France.
> —Ben Badis, April–June 1936 (quoted in Nouschi 1962: 89)

The impetus passed then to Messali Hadj and his successive political organizations, namely, the *Etoile nord africaine* (ENA), the *Parti populaire algérien* (PPA), and the *Mouvement pour le triomphe des libertés démographiques* (MTLD). To the Islamic nationalism of the Reformists, Messali Hadj opposed his own secular nationalism.

At the same time as the Reformists arose to challenge the *Jeunes*

Algériens, and the Messalistes challenged in turn the Reformists, the earlier groupings were displaced but not discarded. Thus, the Reformists succeeded in institutionalizing and legitimizing their program only after independence in 1962 (Colonna 1974). And the same process is clear also in the case of the *Jeunes Algériens*, who continued to play a significant role at least through the 1930s. The *Fédération des Elus indigènes*, the chief organization of elected Algerian officials in the interwar period, was *Jeune Algérien* in outlook. Ferhat Abbas, the single best known Algerian leader between the wars, answered to the name *"Jeune Algérien"* (Salah el Din el Zein el Tayeb 1986). The Blum-Violette reforms proposed in 1936 were aimed again primarily at those Algerian *évolués* who still called themselves *Jeunes Algériens*. In opposition to the Blum-Violette proposals, the European mayors of Algeria resigned *en masse*; the last best chance to enact meaningful reform had failed egregiously (Ageron 1979: 449–66). And even later during the Algerian Revolution 1954–62, the *interlocuteurs valables* the French sought but could not find were the *Jeunes Algériens'* putative successors, that is, intermediaries with whom they could deal.

After riots at Sétif in 1945 had occasioned massive European repression . . .

> My sense of humanity was affronted for the first time by the most atrocious sights [at Sétif]. I was sixteen years old. The shock which I felt at the pitiless butchery that caused the deaths of thousands of Muslims, I have never forgotten. From that moment my nationalism took definite form.
>
> —Kateb Yacine (quoted in Horne 1978: 27)

. . . schisms occurred as nationalist groups disagreed on ways to breach the stone wall of *pied noir* intransigence. One such split led to the formation of the *Organisation Secrète* (os), the secret army of the *Parti Communist Algérien* (pca). Compared to the earlier *Jeunes Algériens*, the social composition of the os, like the ppa, was decidedly plebeian. In Bône, employees, workers, storekeepers, and artisans predominated; one leader was a chauffeur, another a gas station attendant (Alleg, et al. 1981: I, 350, III, 496). The French dismantled the os, but several militants incarcerated in Bône escaped, including four of the *"neufs historiques,"* the nine leaders of the *Comité Révolutionnaire d'Unité et d'Action* (CRUA), which now formed. On 1 November 1954 CRUA launched the Algerian Revolution.

Only during the Algerian Revolution did the Algerians succeed in driving a wedge between the *pieds noirs* and metropolitan France. At Constantine, Ferhat Abbas's nephew was killed in 1955 for criticizing FLN excesses. In December of the same year an alarmed Camus arrived from France to float a joint European-Algerian "civil truce" initiative. But at a public meeting which he addressed jointly with Ferhat Abbas—in one of his last appearances as a moderate nationalist—Camus was booed by the *pieds noirs*, and only later learned that the two Muslim leaders he had selected had both secretly become FLN members. Overtaken by spiraling communal violence, Camus retreated back to France, never to write about Algeria again, save once. At the beginning of 1960 Camus died instantly when the car he was riding in from Aix-en-Provence to Paris careened wildly and went out of control on a straight stretch of empty road.

Finally, a cease-fire was agreed to in March 1962. In Bône between 20 and 22 June 1962 the *Organisation Armée Secrète* (OAS), abetted by the *colons*, destroyed what they could. Jérome Bertagna's statue on the Cours was dismantled and shipped to France where today it sits in the garden of a Bertagna family member somewhere in the Rhône region (Amato 1979: 174–76).[20] The Bônois then left en masse 3 to 5 July. In a strange premonition dating from 1939 Camus had written, "The whole coast is ready for departure; a shiver of adventure ripples through it. Tomorrow, perhaps, we shall leave together" (quoted in Horne 1978: 531). On 5 July 1962 the Annabis took over Annaba. They tore down what remained of Bertagna's statue. They changed the name of the city from Bône to Annaba. And they changed the Cours Bertagna to the Cours de la Révolution.

> Providence had willed it that the two cities of my passion should have ruins nearby, in the same summer twilight, so near Carthage; nowhere are there two such cities, sisters in splendor and desolation, that saw Carthage sacked and my Salammbô disappear, between Constantine, the June night, the collar of jasmine blackened under my shirt, and Bône where I lost my sleep for sacrificing the abyss

of the Rhummel to another city and another river, on the track of
the strayed gazelle who alone could tear me from the shade of the
cedars, of the father killed the eve of my birth, in the cave that I
alone could see from this balcony, beyond the fragrant peaks, and
with the unknown woman's father I left the ruins of Cirta for the
ruins of Hippo. What does it matter that Hippo is disgraced, Carthage buried, Cirta ruined and Nedjma deflowered. . . . The city
flourishes, the blood dissolves, appeased, only at the moment of the
fall: Carthage vanished, Hippo resuscitated, Cirta between heaven
and earth, the triple wreck restored to the setting sun, the land of the
Maghreb.

—Kateb Yacine (1961: 243–44)[21]

APPENDIX

It was one of those days. At the entrance to the Annaba *mairie* [city
hall], the only foreigner in a mass of Algerians clamoring to be waited on,
the guard waved me by. Upstairs I was passed from office to office until I
saw M. le secrétaire-général himself. Everyone scrutinized my authorization to the archives, everyone balked—this American, he cannot just walk
in here—and everyone dared not do as the letter of authorization from
the *Conseil de la Révolution* in Algiers ordered. I was passed back down the
hierarchy, alternately stalled and entertained as a key was searched for. A
young Algerian "gofer" finally appeared, and I was conducted upstairs to
the low-ceilinged third floor, where the door opened on the richest local
archives extant in Algeria.

No inventory exists that I was ever able to discover, but a cursory
survey of archival series organized by the wooden cabinets in which they
are stored would include:

Cabinet 1: Politique générale. Conseil général.
Cabinet 2: Administration municipale. Services municipaux. Maires et
Adjoints. Impôts arabes.
Cabinet 3: Sociétés de secours mutuels et autres. Consulats. Banques.
Cabinet 4: Budgets. Comptabilité générale.
Cabinet 5: Contentieux. Actions judiciaires. Avocats de la commune.
Cabinets 6–7: Instruction publique.

Cabinet 8: Port de Bône. Pêche.
Cabinet 9: Affaires militaires et indigènes. Constitution de la propriété
   individuelle. Sociétés secrètes des indigènes. Demandes de secours.
Cabinet 11: Culte. Catholique. Protestant. Hebraique. Musulman.
Cabinet 12: Conseil Municipal. Procès-verbaux des séances.
Cabinet 18: Milices.
Cabinet 19: Taxes municipales.
Cabinet 20: Affaires indigènes. Secours aux indigènes. Renseignements
   et affaires indigènes divers, 1868–1900.
Cabinet 22: Police générale, 1836–1949.
Cabinet 29: Personnel.
Cabinet 38: Coup d'état, 1851.
Cabinets 40–41: Conseil Municipal. Déliberations (1849 on).
Cabinet 41: Etats Récapitulatifs, 1840–1948. Statistique agricole. Statis-
   tique industrielle. Dénombrements.
Cabinet 46: Recrutement registres, 1884–1912, 1914–1917. Naturalisa-
   tion (1849 on).

On open shelves were located:

Maitrices cadastres des propriétés baties.
Listes nominatives, 1848, 1861, 1866, 1872, 1876, 1881, 1886, 1891, 1896,
   1901, 1906, 1911, 1926, 1931, 1936, 1948.
Mouvement de la population, 1853–1854.
Actes de naissance (1830s on). Actes de mariages (1833 on). Migration
   (1874–1912).

The first of three rooms which housed the archives was lined on two
walls with wooden cupboards; in the middle stood a metal cabinet. Inside the cabinet hung the former French archivist's white coat and feather
duster, which I and the young Algerian "gofer," with whom I was to
spend many hours, examined together. Out came a bronze statuette of
Bertagna, a miniature replica of the one previously located downstairs on
the Cours. We placed it ceremoniously on the table and laughed at the
incongruity of it all.

Notes

This essay is based primarily on the Bône/Annaba municipal archives; I thank R. Ainad Tabet, former director of the Archives Nationales de l'Algérie, for granting me authorization to use these archives. I also thank Jatni Brahim, secrétaire-général of the Assemblée Populaire et Communale de Annaba, for facilitating my research in Annaba; Jean-Claude Vatin, Edmund Burke III, and Paul Rabinow for their support and solidarity. The French government; the University of California, Berkeley; and the University of Illinois provided extensive research support. Lynn Dumenil, Irving Elichirigoity, Harry Liebersohn, Sally Prunty, Dan Segal, Margarida de Souza Neves, and Ron Toby provided useful comments and encouragement. Huguette Cohen provided valuable help with the translations.

1. The name is the same, and the leading contemporary local historian of Annaba, H'sen Derdour, told me Sadek Denden was Sidi Denden's descendant, but I have no conclusive evidence linking the two. See Derdour (1982–83).

2. Italicized passages without other attribution are by David Prochaska.

3. That the settlers constitute a blind spot in the historiography, a datum literally too large to be seen, raises a related issue. The scholars of the so-called *Ecole d'Alger*, based at the Université d'Alger, played a disproportionately large role in the French academic tradition of Orientalism, and at the same time were closely tied to the settler milieu of Algeria when not settlers themselves. This suggests that an analysis of their scholarly production from the perspective of their social backgrounds and political involvements, that is, from the angle of colonial discourse, would be highly illuminating. See Colonna (1976); Valensi (1984); Burke (1977, 1980 in progress).

4. Jérome's brother, Dominique Bertagna (1856–1916), was also involved. At the time, he sat on the city council and *Conseil Général* of Morris, located in the plain of Bône.

5. Ageron (1968: 478–543) details Cambon's attempts at reform, but the history of Algerian reforms in general and Cambon's reforms in particular is the history of the failure of those reforms. In nearly every case, reform attempts failed due to unrelenting settler opposition.

6. The terms *antijuif/antijudaisme* and anti-Semite/anti-Semitism are often used interchangeably in the Algerian case. *Antijudaisme* is technically more accurate, but anti-Semitism has the advantage of explicitly linking anti-Semitism in Algeria to anti-Semitism elsewhere.

7. Ageron (1979: 489, 491, 511–12, 527) recognizes Cambon failed to

achieve anything, but argues he prefigured the reforms enacted in 1919. But just as settlers stymied Cambon in the 1890s, so they prevented France from enacting meaningful reforms in 1919 and again in 1936. Rather than a series of missed opportunities, as Ageron argues, I contend that the history of colonial Algeria constitutes a classic case of settler colonialism where the *colons* enjoyed a virtually unbroken string of successes.

8. Certain passages have been left in French in the text, and English translations provided in the notes, where it was important to convey the flavor of the original. In English, Camus' text reads: "Then Coco steps forward and says to him: 'Wait a minute, wait.' The other one says: 'What is it?' Then Coco says to him: 'I'm gonna slug you.'—'Me? You're gonna slug me?' Then he reaches in his hip pocket, but it was just for laughs. Then Coco says to him: 'Don't reach in your back, because, after that, I'm gonna grab your 6–35, and what a hammering you're gonna get anyway.' "

9. Brua uses pastiche, or imitation, to at once evoke Corneille's *Le Cid* (1659) and parody it. Thus, Dodièze (C sharp) is Brua's pastiche for Don Diègue, father of Rodrigue, the leading man in Corneille's play, while Gongormatz is Don Gomès, Comte de Gormas, father of Chimène, the leading lady. In English, the text reads:

ACT I

Scene III

Dodièze (C sharp): "With glory and honor I wear the ribbon [of the Legion of Honor]
I and Fernand, we used to see each other
At the time when he was not a deputy."

Gongormatz: "He can be a deputy all he wants, he is still no better than the rest of us!
Let him come today and let the world vote,
You will hear how it is that he takes a beating at the polls,
The guy who really forgets his buddies!"

10. The "friends of the Municipality" refers to the Opportunist Republicans, while the Radical Republicans "combatted the Municipality." Prosper Dubourg was Opportunist mayor of Bône 1878–88, immediately prior to Bertagna.

11. They [André, Jean-Jean, Short-Whiskers, Short-Legs, Big Victor and Guigui] throw themselves against each other and start fighting. Comes a gloved gentleman, wearing an opera hat.

The Gloved
Gentleman: "Please, little rascals, will you stop this fistfight which there is no point to?"

Patatrac: "For God's sake, look at this long-legged one, with his décalitre [hat]; go cool your heels at Xiberras. . . ."

The Gloved
Gentleman: "Will you please keep your mouth shut, impudent rascal."

Short-Legs: "Listen to this big mouth Parisian; sounds like he is getting a job at the phosphates. . . ."

Big Victor: "Gimme five sous to shave your beard. . . ."

Guigui: "He is an exact copy of Jacob. Hey, it's a curse! . . . I think it's a Jew. . . . Beware the gunshots. . . ."

Patatrac
(singing):   "Igna-ce! Igna-ce!"

The Gentleman
(furious):   "Are there no policemen around?"

John-John: "The police? Don't we scare them away, me and Big Victor? We're gonna sell the stinking cheese to make *broumège* in September 4th Street [located one block from the Cours Bertagna, and named after the day the French Third Republic was declared in 1870]. . . ."

A policeman's figure appears on the horizon. The gang breaks up with the swiftness of a train of the Bône-Guelma [the railroad company, headquartered in Bône, which ran in eastern Algeria, i.e., very slowly].

12. *Diobone!*, *Diocane!*, *Diocane à Madone!*, *Diosaxaphone!* were all blasphemies current in Bône.

13.   Our New Title

The day before yesterday we had a big meeting at Mohammed ben Kouider Abderahman's or Taraz Faraz's Arab cafe.

Agenda: A *new* name for the newspaper!

Little Sick one: "*Le Diobone. Le Diobone Bônois*, oh! God!"

Dirty Fatty: "*Le Zacounas.* Zacounas yourself!"

Twiggy Marie: "*Le Bourmetche.* Who do you want to stink out?"

Mikal F: "*La Troumba.* Better we give enemas for nothing?"

O. Eyes: *La Grappe poileuse (The Hairy Grape).* That goddam crazy one at the pier!"

Goualio: "*Le Courtelatche*. Hey! Go fish for dribbling sea urchins!"

Me: "*Le P'tit bon sang à la mihiel* [a pun on Mont Saint-Michel]. But this title will fill up the whole four pages. Really!"

There was so much debate that at three AM nobody agreed. Then the manager passes by, that wicked one!

What name? *Le Scandale*.

Yes, yes, *Le Scandale*. I swear to you that not one of them got the message.

Then OK for *Le Scandale*. In other words: *The Stinking Sock!*

14. Another work in *patois bônois*, which I have been unable to locate, is *Moi et Augu. Histoires bônoises* (Bône: Imprimerie Centrale, n.d.).

15.   TO HIS LORDSHIP THE DAUPHIN

You to whom we owe our hearts and our heads
And our voices, if only we knew who you are!
I, for one, would have liked to teach you
The barbaric language spoken in these Fables [i.e., *pataouète*].
You are aware of its demise, now learn about its birth.
Your ancestor Charles the Tenth scattered the seeds
And out of them a branch grew on the stump of the French idiom.
More than a century came to pass. Big Charles the Eleventh
Came along, listened to Salvator, Sfatchime, Badiguelle
Bagur, with whom Ahmed had picked a quarrel,
And raising both arms to calm down their shouting,
Reckless philogist, he said: "I understand you."
Alas! He missed the help of a lexicon,
Contrary to someone like Soustelle, trained in Mexico.
Six months later, Bagur, Sfatchime, Salvator,
Badiguelle were amazed to hear: "You are wrong."
I sing of these heroes, but not at war,
At peace like long ago (others think not so long ago).

This passage is part of the preface Brua added to the 1972 edition. It was during Charles X's reign that France invaded Algeria in 1830. "Big Charles the Eleventh" refers to Charles de Gaulle, who was six feet four inches tall. The quarrel between Salvator, Sfatchime, Badiguelle, and Bagur, on the one side, and Ahmed—the generic denomination of the French for a male Algerian—on the other, refers to the Algerian Revolution. Jacques Soustelle, anthropologist of Mexico, was Algerian governor general during 1955–56. He became a die-hard supporter of *Algérie française*. In a 1958 speech to the *pieds noirs* in Algiers, Charles de Gaulle uttered the words, "Je vous ai compris," which were widely taken to mean he supported them and *Algérie française*. No sooner had he done so, however, than he began slowly but nimbly to distance himself from the *pieds noirs* and to extricate France from Algeria, which he succeeded in doing by 1962.

16. The first director of *L'Islam*, 'Abd al Aziz Tebibel, founded a second *Jeune Algérien* paper in Bône, *L'Etendard Algérien*, which appeared from 22 November 1910 to 29 January 1911 (Montoy 1982: 663–64, 1529–30). I thank Prof. Louis P. Montoy for kindly providing unpublished biographical data regarding 'Abd al Aziz Tebibel and a host of other Bône residents gathered in the course of research for his massive doctorat d'état, "La Presse."

17. On Denden, see APCA, *Liste nominative* (1876: 285); Montoy (1982: 639, 662, 670, 759, 1515). He died penniless in 1938, despite modest financial support from H'Sen Derdour's father, among others (interview with H'Sen Derdour, July 1983). See Ageron (1968: 1040, 1049, 1050–52); Ageron (1979: 234); Kaddache (1970: 42); Derdour (1982–83: II, 463–64).

18. "Today, Sunday, the French and Europeans naturalized French cast their ballots for the candidate of their choice . . . During this time the Arab remains silent, he would certainly like to give his opinion, but he keeps his mouth shut, he doesn't have the right, although he has as much at stake as the settlers and more than the Europeans naturalized French . . . For the time being, stay in your hut, peasant, be patient, resign yourself, because France is too generous to abandon you to your misfortunes, and realizing how it has been misled by your enemies, it won't be long before it will set you free and will give you as many rights as your brothers the settlers enjoy—the genuine settlers, not the big landowners who gobble you up, but the others, those who share your hardships and your misery."

19. On nationalism and colonialism in Islamic societies, see Lapidus (1987, 1988). On the cultural logic of nationalist discourse, see Handler (1988) and Segal (1988).

20. In a note Amato adds, "At the request of M. Claude Bertagna I have not mentioned the exact location of the statue."

21. Gustave Flaubert's historical novel *Salammbô* (1862) is set in Carthage. Carthage is located just outside present-day Tunis, one hundred fifty miles east of Annaba. Cirta is the Phoenician name of present-day Constantine, which lies one hundred miles south of Annaba. Constantine is built on either side of the Rhummel gorge. "Maghreb" means "land of the west" in Arabic.

REFERENCES

Abrams, Larry, and D. J. Miller. 1976. "Who Were the French Colonialists? A Reassessment of the *Parti Colonial, 1890–1914.*" *Historical Journal* 19:685–725.

Ageron, Charles-Robert. 1968. *Les Algériens musulmans et la France 1870–1919.* 2 vols. Paris: Presses Universitaires de France.

———. 1974. *Histoire de l'Algérie contemporaine 1830–1973.* Paris: Presses Universitaires de France.

———. 1978. *France coloniale où parti colonial?* Paris: Presses Universitaires de France.

———. 1979. *Histoire de l'Algérie contemporaine 1871–1954.* Paris: Presses Universitaires de France.

Alleg, Henri, et al. 1981. *La Guerre d'Algérie.* 3 vols. Paris: Temps Actuel.

Amato, Alain. 1979. *Monuments en exil.* Paris: Editions de l'Atlanthrope.

AN. See under Archival Sources.

Andrew, C. M. 1976. "The French Colonialist Movement during the Third Republic: The Unofficial Mind of Imperialism." *Transactions of the Royal Historical Society.* 5th ser., 26:143–66.

Andrew, C. M., and A. S. Kanya-Forstner. 1971. "The French 'Colonial Party': Its Composition, Aims and Influence, 1885–1914." *Historical Journal* 14:99–128.

———. 1974. "The *Groupe Colonial* in the French Chamber of Deputies, 1892–1932." *Historical Journal* 17:837–66.

———. 1976. "French Business and The French Colonialists." *Historical Journal* 19:981–1000.

———. 1981. *The Climax of French Imperial Expansion, 1914–1924.* Stanford: Stanford University Press.

AOM. See under Archival Sources.

APCA. See under Archival Sources.

Arnaud, Louis. 1960. *Bône. Son histoire, ses histoires.* Constantine, Algeria: Damrémont.

Audisio, Gabriel [Auguste Robinet]. 1931. Introduction and lexicon in Musette. *Cagayous. Ses meilleures histoires.* Paris: Librairie Gallimard.

AWC. See under Archival Sources.

Bacri, Roland. 1983. *Trésors des racines pataouètes.* Paris: Belin.

Baroli, Marc. 1967. *La vie quotidienne des français en Algérie, 1830–1914*. Paris: Hachette.

Binoche, Jacques. 1971. "Les élus d'outre-mer au Parlement de 1871 à 1914." *Revue française d'histoire d'outre-mer* 58:82–115.

Blanc, A. 1887. *Tableautins sur l'Extrême-Ouest algérien*. Bône: Puccini.

BNV. See under Archival Sources.

Brua, Edmond. 1941. *La Parodie du Cid*. Algiers: Collections du Cactus. Excerpted in Roland Bacri, *Trésors des racines pataouètes*.

———. [1938] 1972. *Fables Bônoises*. 3d ed. Paris: Balland.

Brunot, Louis. 1948. "Sabirs." *Journal des Instituteurs d'Afrique du Nord*. April: 209–10.

Burke, Edmund, III. 1977. "Fez, the Setting Sun of Islam: A Study of the Politics of Colonial Ethnography." *Maghreb Review* 2:1–7.

———. 1980. "The Sociology of Islam: The French Tradition." In *Islamic Studies: A Tradition and Its Problems*, ed. Malcolm Kerr. Malibu, CA: Undena Publications.

———. Forthcoming. "Orientalism Observed: France, Islam, and the Colonial Encounter."

Camus, Albert. 1950. *Noces*. Paris: Gallimard.

Colonna, Fanny. 1974. "Cultural Resistance and Religious Legitimacy in Colonial Algeria." *Economy and Society* 3:233–54.

———. 1976. "Production scientifique et position dans le champ intellectuel et politique." In *Le mal de voir*. Paris: Collection 10/18.

Denoon, Donald. 1983. *Settler Capitalism: The Dynamics of Dependent Development in the Southern Hemisphere*. New York: Oxford University Press.

Derdour, H'sen. 1982–83. *Annaba. 25 siècles de vie quotidienne et de luttes*. 2 vols. Algiers: Société nationale d'édition et de diffusion.

Desparmet, Joseph. 1931. "La réaction linguistique en Algérie." *Bulletin de la société géographique d'Alger* 36:1–33.

———. 1932a. "Les réactions nationalitaires en Algérie." *Bulletin de la société géographique d'Alger* 37:173–84.

———. 1932b. "La conquête racontée par les indigènes." *Bulletin de la société géographique d'Alger* 37:437–546.

———. 1933. "Elégies et satires politiques de 1830 à 1914." *Bulletin de la société géographique d'Alger* 38:35–64.

Eisenstadt, S. N., ed. 1987. *Patterns of Modernity: Beyond the West*. Vol. 2. London: Frances Pinter.

Gautier, Emile-Félix. 1920. "Les émeutes antijuives en Algérie," in *L'Algérie et la métropole*. Paris: Payot.

Gellner, Ernest. 1981. *Muslim Society*. Cambridge: Cambridge University Press.

Gouvernement Général de l'Algérie. 1908. *Tableau général des communes de l'Algérie*. Algiers: Imprimerie Algérienne.

Guerin, Jenyves, ed. 1986. *Camus et la politique*. Paris: L'Harmattan.

Handler, Richard. 1988. *Nationalism and the Politics of Culture in Quebec*. Madison: University of Wisconsin Press.

Horne, Alistair. 1978. *A Savage War of Peace: Algeria 1954–1962*. New York: Viking Penguin.

Kaddache, Mahfoud. 1970. *La vie politique à Alger de 1919 à 1939*. Algiers: Société nationale d'édition et de diffusion.

Kanya-Forstner, A. S., and P. Grupp. 1975. "Le Mouvement colonial français et ses principales personnalités 1890–1914." *Revue française d'histoire d'outre-mer* 62:640–73.

Kerr, Malcolm, ed. 1980. *Islamic Studies: A Tradition and Its Problems*. Malibu, Ca: Undena Publications.

Lafourcade, Louis. n.d. *Harmonies Bônoises*. Algiers: Baconnier.

Laioun, Khélil Caid. 1901. "Mémoire présenté par Khélil Caid Laioun." *Procès-verbaux de la sous-commission d'étude et de la législation civile en Algérie*. pp. 661–63. Annexe no. 1840 au procès-verbal de la 2e séance du 9 juillet 1900. Tome XXXI. Paris: Imprimerie de la Chambre des Députés.

Lanly, Albert. 1962. *Le Français d'Afrique du Nord. Etude linguistique*. Paris: Bordas.

Lapidus, Ira. 1987. "Islam and Modernity." In *Beyond the West*, ed. S. N. Eisenstadt. Vol 2, *Patterns of Modernity*. London: Frances Pinter.

———. 1988. *A History of Islamic Societies*. New York: Cambridge University Press.

Lentin, Albert-Paul. 1982. "El Cid: Portrait d'Edmond Brua." In *Les Pieds-Noirs* ed. Emmanuel Robles. Paris: Philippe Lebaud.

Lespès, René. 1925. *Alger. Esquisse de géographie urbaine*. Algiers: Carbonel.

———. 1938. *Oran*. Paris: Alcan.

Lottman, Herbert. 1980. *Albert Camus*. New York: Braziller.

Maitrot, Albert-Charles. 1934. *Bône militaire*. Bône: Mariani.

McCarthy, Patrick. 1982. *Camus*. New York: Random House.

McMichael, Philip. 1984. *Settlers and the Agrarian Question: Foundations of Capitalism in Colonial Australia*. Cambridge: Cambridge University Press.

Merad, Ali. 1967. *Le reformisme musulman en Algérie de 1925 à 1940. Essai d'histoire religieuse et sociale*. Paris-La Haye: Mouton.

Montoy, Louis P. 1982. "La presse dans le département de Constantine (1870–1918)." 4 vols. Thèse de doctorat. Aix-en-Provence: Université de Provence.

Mosley, Paul. 1983. *The Settler Economies: Studies in the Economic History of Kenya and Southern Rhodesia, 1900–1963*. Cambridge: Cambridge University Press.

Musette [Auguste Robinet]. 1931. *Cagayous. Ses meilleures histoires*. Paris: Librairie Gallimard.

Nora, Pierre. 1961. *Les français d'Algérie*. Paris: Julliard.

Nouschi, André. 1962. *La naissance du nationalisme algérien (1914–1954)*. Paris: Les éditions de Minuit.

O'Brien, Conor Cruise. 1970. *Camus*. London: Collins.

Persell, Stuart Michael. 1983. *The French Colonial Lobby, 1889–1938*. Stanford: Hoover Institution Press.

Prochaska, David. 1990. *Making Algeria French: Colonialism in Bône, 1870–1920*. New York: Cambridge University Press.

Robles, Emmanuel, ed. 1982. *Les Pieds-Noirs*. Paris: Philippe Lebaud.

Salah el Din el Zein el Tayeb. 1986. "The Europeanized Algerians and the Emancipation of Algeria." *Middle Eastern Studies* 22:206–35.

Segal, Daniel. 1988. "Nationalism, Comparatively Speaking." *Journal of Historical Sociology* 13:300–321.

Valensi, Lucette. 1984. "Le Maghreb vu du Centre: Sa place dans l'école sociologique française." In *Connaissances du Maghreb*, eds. Jean-Claude Vatin, et al. Paris: Editions du CNRS.

Vatin, Jean-Claude, et al. 1984. *Connaissances du Maghreb*. Paris: Editions du CNRS.

Yacine, Kateb. 1961. *Nedjma*. New York: Braziller.

ARCHIVAL SOURCES

AN Archives Nationales de France.

AOM Archives Nationales Dépôt des Archives d'Outre-Mer.

APCA Archives de l'Assemblée Populaire et Communale de Annaba (specific series of APCA are cited in the text).

AWC Archives de la Wilaya de Constantine.

BNV Bibliothèque Nationale Annexe de Versailles

Of the newspapers cited in the text, *El Hack*, *L'Eclair*, *L'Islam*, and *La Bataille Algérienne* may be found in AWC; *Le Diocane Bônois*, *Le Scandale Bônois*, *Le Bônois*, and *Le Réveil Bônois* in BNV; *Les Clochettes Bônoises* and *Les Gaités Bônoises* in both AWC and BNV; and *L'Etendard Algérien* in Hoover Institution, Stanford University.

6
Cosmopolitan Moments
Echoey Confessions of an Ethnographer-Tourist

James Boon

This essay executes an intertextual, first-person account attuned to coincidence. After narrating—through a pastiche of self-promoting styles of travel-telling—a true encounter with a Javanese mystic who construed the narrator coincidentally, my essay multiplies fragments that multiply this motive. Over the long history of the so-called West's inscriptions of so-called Others—one stretching back at least to A.D. 400 (Campbell 1988) or indeed longer still (Boon 1982)—magical-coincidence (in Indonesian, *kecokcokan*) keeps being given back from the margins that ethnography values and in whose nature it shares.

First Attempt at Preliminaries

My previous works (e.g., Boon 1977) treated texts and contexts since the sixteenth century marked by complex encounters between European and East Indies societies. The difficulty-laden discourse produced at intersections of Indonesian, Dutch, British, and Indicized cultures has been saturated with ambiguities and reversals in the play of power, gender, language, and other constructions. As a general rule, older ethnologies and newer ethnographies alike (including my own) contain multiple contradictions, even when they appear to support straightforward political or apolitical interests (Boon 1990). Cultures are never crossed, nor their crossing represented, *simply*, regardless of the period and circumstances in question—whether early modern mercantilism (or before), subsequent "high colonialism's" labor-intensive plantations for export crops, late nineteenth-century ethical policies accompanied by intensified philological enterprises, or developing nationalist movements, postwar nationalism, and now commercial "internationalism" (with their distinctive varieties of tourism). Although the present study is conspicuously situated in the post-1968 (u.s.) and post-1965 (Indonesia) "internationalist" context, its ironies form part of the *longue-durée* of languages and cultures in tragicomic collision. But to insist on this fact may be to place too much weight on a jocose essay.

My principal scene is Bali, a cornucopian "chronotope" or place-in-time. Bali harbors a minority Hindu polity amidst an Islamic (although hardly orthodox Koranic) majority in a nation (Indonesia) that was constructed out of the remains of the Dutch East Indies (controlled by the British only during Napoleon's occupation of the Netherlands), after the brief and traumatic Japanese occupation during World War II. Bali also features a diverse society inclined to hierarchy that has assumed flexible identities over a mottled, multilingual and long-literate history in the margins of several so-called world systems, including missionizing (or its decided absence) and, of course, tourism.

Consider a few characteristic twists in events from colonial Bali (the north subjugated by the Dutch in the 1840s, the south only after 1906–8, with the complicity of certain royal houses). Hindu-Bali, declared off limits to Dutch missionary efforts in the late nineteenth century, became a kind of religious preserve said to illustrate the value of new ethical policies for fostering "self-rule." The 1880s and after found Bali an ideal haven for Dutch steamship tourism for the same reasons it had been of strategic interest to Britain during the heyday of eighteenth- and nineteenth-century Anglo-Dutch rivalry: it lay just off, and insulated from, Java. Between the World Wars, Bali's international renown was cultivated by the cosmopolitan artist Walter Spies, hired away from a Javanese sultan by a Balinese raja who hoped to enhance Balinese arts and courtlife by attracting foreign devotees and to preserve Hindu-Balinese identity from "Javanization" (Boon 1986). I mention those convolutions in colonial encounters, including pragmatics of packaging Bali for tourist markets still accelerating today, to suggest historical continuities with the present essay lest it be mistaken as postmodernist (Boon 1990).

In an oral/aural delivery the prose "moments" that follow were made to do-si-do with canned musical examples to which they refer. My patently outlandish tactic struck some listeners more precisely as outrageous, not to mention unscholarly; others found its devices perfectly pertinent to neglected aspects of culture-crossing, or so they confessed. That difference of opinion is likely to remain among readers. These transgressions are as true as I can possibly make them; they attempt to take seriously both commercialized culture and one anthropologist's comic beginnings; they strive to bother comfortable old-fashioned certitudes that something like ethnography is altogether distinct from something like travel of the most touristic sort; yet they are equally wary of newfangled certitudes that everything is a phantasmagoria of Baudrillardian *simulacra*. By professional standards I commit a regression, moving backwards in memory from increased ethnographic expertise to recapture first impressions, wondering whether the process of marginalizing or repressing them does not belie how cultures really get crossed.

Scholars and nonscholars from diverse disciplines recurrently challenge pat claims "authentically to know" the Other (or for that matter the Self) and question possibilities of authoritative descriptions. Goals of penetrating anyone else's "essence" have been contested by anthropologists of different persuasions and their observers; I might just mention Lévi-Strauss ([1955] 1973; see Boon 1972, 1982), Geertz (1983, 1988), and Clifford (1988). Now, the discourse that questions either the epistemological possibility or the political advisability of "going native" (or deluding oneself into thinking one can) has a longer history than many contemporary critics, often working in the wake of Edward Said's *Orientalism* (1978), like to acknowledge (Boon 1972: 141; 1977: 66; 1982; 1990). It is not, however, that issue but the other side of the coin pursued here. I do not engage that zenith of imagined anthropological authenticity: an ethnography that achieves perfect congruence with a different language or culture or "other," however demarcated. Rather, I engage its flip side, that nadir of imagined anthropological inauthenticity: superficial touristic experience. To challenge anthropology's zenith (or what some take it to have been) is necessarily to reopen the issue of its nadir; the two critical tasks, such that they are, are inseparable. I wish to explore ludic possibilities of inauthentic cross-cultural encounters taking on fuller authority, while remaining within the ranks and traditions of prolonged ethnographic documentation that I continue to prize.[1]

This, then, is my point of departure: if would-be authentic ethnography is only a disguised brand of self-involved description (a proposition too comfortably avant-garde to buy, and one to which I do not subscribe), must not manifestly inauthentic touristic-mystic coincidence be seen as a disguised brand of profounder comparative knowledge? To agitate that provocative prospect, I peer into the abyss of cross-cultural subjectivity-written, hoping to push it so far as to explode it and renew efforts for some kind of ethnography deflective of patent ideology in this imperfect and imperfectible political world.

My paragraphs parody recourses to first-person accounts that conventionally claim to be more genuine by earnestly advocating a liberation politics, or a self-therapeutic ideal regardless of partisan slant (Boon 1982: 263; 1989b). But even to parody first-person accounts runs the risk of sounding self-indulgent, and unserious to boot.[2] Readers are therefore respectfully referred here to Stendhal's *De l'amour*, written of and through his displacement to Italy and Germany for fifteen years after 1815 and the break up of the Napoleonic empire—just one of the texts with which this essay is in intimate contact. (From Stendhal's gradually recognized classic in philosophical travel-telling I have borrowed the "first attempt/second attempt" formulation of these overlong preliminaries:)

> I may be charged with egotism for the form I have adopted. But a traveller is allowed to say: "*I* embarked at New York for South America. *I* went up to Santa Fe de Bogota. Midges and mosquitoes bothered *me* on the journey, and for three days *I* could not open *my* right eye."

The traveller is not accused of being too fond of the first person singular; all these *I*'s and *me*'s are forgiven him because to use them is the clearest and most interesting way of relating what he has seen.

It is to be clear and graphic, if he can, that the author of this journey into the little-known regions of the human heart says: "I went with Mme Gherardi to the salt mines of Hallein. . . ." All these little things have really happened to the author. . . . (Stendhal 1975: 25)

Second Attempt at Preliminaries

Professional anthropologists engage in a specialist activity that is ideally interlingual and other-encountering. "Fieldwork" ushers intensely observed elsewheres into ethnography, a kind of writing-to-be-read. Even fieldworkers of domestic situations—the late Erving Goffman, to take a renowned example—may frame evidence as if it were witnessed cross-culturally. These are familiar facts, indeed nowadays increasingly familiar and routinely self-conscious facts (Clifford and Marcus 1986, and everything since).

Less familiar, perhaps, is the fact that the strategic isolation designed into fieldwork occasionally folds over on itself, to yield sudden distance from distance. Whether this flush of double alienation returns full circle to the too-ordinary or spirals to higher planes of remove is exquisitely difficult to decide. To sustain, prolongingly, such difficulty is to cultivate what I shall be calling the cosmopolitan moment. To inscribe, paradoxically, such difficulty is to engage some inescapable ironies of representation.

The pages that follow (and, by now, precede) gather many motives from the history of travel tales, including fragments of Vladimir Nabokov's *Lolita*, like this one, where Humbert Humbert is writing (Alfred Appel, mercifully, has annotated; the passage should be read in a Russo-Cambridge-Berliner-Parisian-upstate New York accent, but not necessarily in that order):

I remember as a child in Europe gloating over a map of North America that had "Appalachian Mountains" boldly running from Alabama up to New Brunswick, so that the whole region they spanned—Tennessee, the Virginias, Pennsylvania, New York, Vermont, New Hampshire and Maine, appeared to my imagination as a gigantic Switzerland or even Tibet, all mountain, glorious diamond peak upon peak, giant conifers, *le montagnard émigré* in his bear skin glory, and *Felis tigris goldsmithi*, and Red Indians under the catalpas. That it all boiled down to a measly suburban lawn and a smoking garbage incinerator, was appalling. Farewell, Appalachia! Leaving it, we crossed Ohio, the three states beginning with "I," and Nebraska . . . (Nabokov 1970: 211–12)

The present account of post-1968 crossings of cultures will commemorate equivalent, venerable ambiguities: Appalachia, Switzerland, Bali, or Tibet? As Humbert Humbert writes, not even Dolores ("Dolly"), alias Lolita, knows.[3]

My exercises in "Nabokovian" coincidence—which, as we shall see, could just as well be called "Javanese"—also claim affinities with the Marxist-mystic snapshots and illuminated aphorisms of Walter Benjamin and, if that isn't cosmopolitan enough, with the less profane contradictions dotting the novels and essays of Walker Percy. First, Benjamin (to be read with a universal accent, one tragically so):

We penetrate the mystery only to the degree that we recognize it in the everyday world, by virtue of a dialectical optic that perceives the everyday as impenetrable, the impenetrable as everyday. . . . The reader, the thinker, the loiterer, the *flaneur* are types of illuminati just as much as the opium eater, the dreamer, the ecstatic. And more profane. (1978: 190)

And now, Percy (to be read carefully, with any comically regional accent):

After a lifetime of avoiding the beaten track and guided tours, a man may deliberately seek out the most beaten track of all . . . (Such dialectical savorings of the familiar as the familiar are, of course, a favorite stratagem of the *New Yorker Magazine*.) The thing is recovered from familiarity by means of an exercise in familiarity. . . . Such a man is far more advanced in the dialectic than the sightseer who is trying to get off the beaten track. . . . this stratagem is in fact, for our complex man, the weariest, most beaten track of all. (1975: 48–49)

The cosmopolitan moments inscribed below from Indonesia and elsewhere oscillate among motives of Nabokov's redoublings, Benjamin's Baudelairian loitering, and Percy's profound moviegoing plus passionate post-sightseeing—not to mention Proust.

When glimmers of second-order alienation interrupt the course of crossing cultures, ethnographers may neglect to document them, so enchanted are we with having gained, ostensibly, the first-order alienation of fieldwork proper. My as-if confessions—proceeding from self-satire to other-parody and (I hope) beyond—are offered to fill this regrettable gap in the cross-cultural record. These notes of an ethnographer-rebecoming-a-tourist (a mystic?) invite fellow readers-travellers to heed Percy's advice, regress, and go further than simply leaving the beaten track. Now then, *allons-y*; or in other words, *marilah kita*. (N.B.: All Indonesian terms in this interlingual essay are pronounced approximately as in operatic Italian.)

Part the First: Exotic Moments

We interrupt these preliminary intertextualities to narrate a dramatic entry into Indonesia's most storied isle:

> My wife, daughter, and I arrived, malaised and different, in Bali, which, being Bali . . . .

Not bad, I guess, but better try again.

Oh, I had struggled all right during those dark and stormy days. Drilling Indonesian and Dutch; beginning Balinese; mastering kinship theory; conquering comparative social structure; advancing through Viet Nam protests and grant competitions; doubting throughout 1968–71, along with everyone else, anthropology's and everything else's relevance. When suddenly, through the kind offices of several professors, a well-intentioned foundation, and an eminent Indonesianist, I found myself assigned to help survey local social science researches, such that they were, in Java and Bali (ostensibly to help; I was far too green to matter). Nothing, however, in my struggles, training, or doubts prepared me for those initial encounters.

First Specimen: Native to Native, or Me-me-me

Foretastes of first meetings in Bali began in central Java while interviewing a range of participants from all social classes, peasant to general, active in "mystical" *kebatinan*—a vigorous movement with important implications for Indonesia's political and religious future, especially since the collapse of communism (and Sukarno) in 1965. One affable charismatic I well remember greeted me by proclaiming precognition of my face and name. The latter recognition was familiar enough even from nonmystics during those "007" days of 1971 when all languages—or so it seemed—shared a universal feature: "James Boon" reminded the world's ears (not, alas, its eyes) of "James Bond." His foreviews of my visage, however, were more mysterious. The explanatory spiel he ingratiatingly spun was such that even my fledgling Indonesian could comprehend: We had met during his sleep last night in a dreamscape (*"Tadi malam saya bermimpi tentang Tuan* James Boon") that included, among other compatriots, Doris Day (in Indonesian, "Doris Day").[4] I failed, again alas, to record the specific extracts of fifties film fodder interlacing this magnetic seer's celluloid-informed insights. I only knew that I had seen them all. In Java, my quaint standards of authenticity precluded then absorbing lessons from what I later realized was a not-untypical mode of accessing exotica. An essay such as this one, perhaps unregrettably, couldn't be written then; but nowadays, during "high postcolonialism," do we have any choice?

The brief flight Baliward from Surabaya sustained that welcome's portent. Boarding a prop-job small during politics nervous, our passenger list was triple-checked, each of us summoned individually to his seat. The Third World loudspeaker blared "James Boon"; there followed the Indonesian equivalent of a crowd in uncontrollable titter, then a show of real disappointment when it was I who humbly filed on. A breathtaking pirouette round East Java's foremost volcano executed, we landed in equally theatrical Bali. In long-gone 1971, first year of the Pacific jumbo jets, airport taxis still wound through bustling lanes, past ricelands, shrines, and masses toiling on the nonstop labors and rites marking life 'neath the swaying palms of this oddly Hindu land.

Given political conditions that make research less than "free," upon arrival an ethnographer must quickly assure that he or she can exit too. Exit/reentry permits were particularly iffy in Indonesia during the first general elections since the 1965 massacres that preceded Sukarno's fall. These circumstances, plus a planned rendezvous with my wife and infant elsewhere in Asia before resuming work in Bali, led me straight to the then-only place to book flights and confirm requisite papers, or try to: the infamous, the international, the inauthentic Hotel Bali Beach. Tickets approved, exit/reentry argued into order, those other ubiquitous palms greased, I resolved at once to disassociate my anthropological self from this ultramediated zone offensive to all ideals of fieldwork "experience," not to mention travel. (It has since been outdone.) Object: a "real" Balinese (or bust), i.e., one behind neither a ticket counter nor a steering wheel. Relevant entries of my journal, labeled "First in-formant," read something like this:

> Exhausted, overstimulated, I slouch past sea-taxis hawking passage to Turtle Island, toward a barricade dividing me off from Bali's uncapitalized "beach" and, I assumed, from Bali. And it came to pass: at the border's edge, up popped a native, mine to befriend.

Our conversation began—as they do in Indonesia—with customary conventions of itinerary-checking: Where are you going? (*Mau ke mana?*) Where have you been? Where were you a little while ago? Where are you from (*Dari mana?*) We eventually arrived at the next plateau of interaction: "How many children do you have?"

He was pleasant enough, eventually successful, I suppose, although I never saw him again. I seasoned our Indonesian exchanges with Balinese terms and titles, to show I was by no means just a tourist; he seasoned our Indonesian exchanges with a stab at English ("daughter, er, ah, sister") to show, possibly, that he was by no means just an informant. I learned some things about Dewa Made Rai (I still think of him as "Dari Mana"): he had approached, actually, to peddle a younger brother's ("*kakak*, er, ah, *adik*") "genuine" Balinese paintings—a steal at seven hundred rupiah. I "promised to buy one next week when I returned from Hong Kong." He said I could find him in Gianyar or Den Pasar between which he motorbiked nineteen kilometers through-heat-to-school; he had been writing his *skripsi* for three years while earning extra cash. I still have the calling card he proffered: its first line gives his high-caste title (*Dewa*); its fourth his university; its third his "faculty" (in the continental sense); and its second his graduate division major: *Antropologi.*

I bypass the too painful and obvious ironies of this climax in a distant voyage round half the world to discover t'other. I sidestep implications pursued since: that Balinese anthropologists are "native" too, like British, French, Dutch, and American ones, etc. That in a seemingly shrinking world of folk less "indigenous" than "anthropologist," one does well to inquire how cultures became perceived as "native"—not to mention "cultures"—in the first place. Instead, I here celebrate that moment whereupon—oh, miracle of translation— Indonesian *antropologi* was transfigured into American "anthropology" during an incipient fieldwork encounter that strikes me now—more than fifteen years later, forgetfulness having accomplished its task— as momentously cosmopolitan and appropriately coincidental.[5]

Second Specimen: Our Song

Mysteries more embarrassing still link three separate fieldwork stints and, I begin to suspect, all future stints as well. The self-contrived connection is T.V.'s ultimate classic—need I name it?—"Perry Mason," the original, of course. In eventful 1968, the wife, who calls me "the husband," and I—first year graduate students, newlywed and dirt poor—economized by cultivating a therapeutic connoisseurship in late-night reruns, cheaper by far than psychiatrists, particularly in Chicago. Some are born predisposed to overtures and what were once happily (before Derrida) called "prefaces": devices that allusively and/or flamboyantly establish powerful, pervasive, and short-lasting moods and mediations, thus modulating passage between business as usual (life) and the world of the book, the screen, the performance. The immortality of "Perry Mason" had been assured by its opening titles, rivaling many a cultural system. Initial shots for each morality play—revised just twice (wasn't it?) during the series' nine-year history—disassembled the courtroom into a composition sweeping from balcony past judge's bench, prosecution table, and defender's amanuensis (friends call her Della), round the pivotal, inward gaze of ever-present Perry. This miniaturized music drama was paced by that un-forgettable fifties themesong, the only thing preservable in remakes. I can't describe it; you have to know it; and ASCAP rules prohibit playing it now. A little like "Hubcaps and Taillights" and then mer-cifully free of the droning beat of deconstructive disco, its sliding syncopations captured much that was worthy in the rhythms of this world. In solemn '68, "the wife and the husband" would end each day of historical defeat in mock-upbeat enthusiasm, converting the show's final strains of recapitulation to a private choreography we called the "Perry shuffle." (You see, children, those years were pre-VCR; we had to watch what was on when it was, and trudged fifteen blocks through-snow-to-school.)

Our silliness persisted as long as local programming allowed. That bit of home therapy must have been important: for, in 1971, when asked abruptly by a distinguished scholar, mentor, and patron what kind of study I hoped to write about Indonesia, I could only think to respond, without (believe it or not) elaboration, "Something like the 'Perry Mason' credits." That he kindly disregarded the slip and took me half-seriously anyway has sealed my eternal, blushing gratitude. What, then, could be more beside any point whatsoever than this: ever since, for this fieldworker, Bali and Perry have remained inextricably intertwined. And yet . . . and yet. . . . Itemized evidence of selective affinities follows. Sure, it's circumstantial; but don't forget, I've got Perry on *my* side.

DEFENSE EXHIBIT A   Still sheepish over my amateurishly dropped guard and "off-the-wall-ism" before a thoroughgoing professional, I put it out-of-mind en route to Indonesia in May, 1971. Whereupon, entering my initial *toko buku* in steaming Jakarta, the first thing I spied was *Simanis dan Harta Warisan* (loosely: "sweetie-pie's inherited wealth") translated from the American original, *The Case of the Sulky Girl*. Out of all the books, the billions and billions of books, in earth's uncounted bookstores, Erle Stanley, it had to be you. I bought just one copy and commenced memorization. (Language drill wasn't par-ticular, as long as it was Indonesian.)

DEFENSE EXHIBIT B   Back again in 1972, my project in bilingual Bali altered through the year. Most projects do, and all fieldworkers have their explanations and rationalizations, their "Because, whys." Because of unforeseen developments in the dynamics of Balinese status, I focused increasingly on ancestor group activities. Because of a debilitating disease, my wife, daughter, and I remained in one location rather than sampling three. Because my wife taught deaf Balinese children nearby, we minded less. Because our illness periodically sapped most energy and all strength, I worked more in Indonesian and less in Balinese. Because our hospitable hosts were opponents of the local leadership, I traced interregional networks and marriages, including ties with Javanese, Buginese (markedly Islamic) and Chinese, plus ancestor group endogamous unions (weddings between patriparallel cousins: i.e., children of brothers or children of children of brothers) favored under certain conditions. Because a Socialist party past of many friends and subjects alienated them from the Nationalist party powers that be, including segments of the academic establishment, I felt obliged to offer requisite scholarly reciprocities not to social scientists in Bali's university but to its law school. Here is the drift of this expandable list: While my fieldwork ordeals, local Balinese politics, and some deep concerns of informants (e.g., ancestral legacies) and of intelligentsia (e.g., property law) seemed disparate indeed, in a funny way they converged. I had hundreds of books with me in Bali: in Balinese, Indonesian, Dutch, and so forth. But one and only one of them turned out to be a concentrated word-list of research opportunities at hand: good old, translatable Erle.

DEFENSE EXHIBIT C   I wrote a dense dissertation and then a complicated book about contradictory values in contemporary Balinese hierarchies and the corrosive history of "evidencing" them. Gardner's *Simanis* was playfully acknowledged in a dedication to my co-victim who alone knew that, somehow, just as Perry had gotten us through epochal 1968, he helped us survive near fatal 1972. Then in 1981, coincidence (Indonesian *cokcok*), and even, as it were, description, thickened; things got serious.

I had set up ethnographic shop in a tourist area that facilitated quick access to parts of Bali where commercial pressures were altering cremation ceremonies and, to a lesser extent, marriage rites. Bearing gifts, I wished to visit but not to disrupt our hosts from before. Revised fieldnotes from 10 June 1981 convey a (to me) poignant and information-laden return:

A.M. Feel good; still drilling Indonesian and reviewing a bit of Balinese. Toast, jam, and coffee. Unruly bladder, perhaps because of crab asparagus soup last night (*sup asperg kepeting tadi malam*) . . .
7:00. *Naik bemo* (board a jitney) to Den Pasar. Slightly fatigued, I slip into a "café" to order unsweetened coffee, request access to a urinoir (*boleh ke belakang?*), and pick up clove cigarettes before the long busride. All three tiny goals achieved (rare in fieldwork, comprised almost exclusively of little defeats); thus, elation . . . . I learn, alas, that the antique vehicles once plying the route to Tabanan have been replaced with streamlined models: faster, dangerous, diminishing the views over housewalls provided by highslung busrides of yore. I successfully jockey for a window seat on the landscape side; could be worse; *relative* elation . . .
News on view: The roadside is littered with portable Bali-Hindu shrines for sale as garden decorations to motorists (many of them Muslim) en route to Java. The school called Saraswati (Hindu goddess of learning) has been expanded. Untouristic Tabanan sports a new arts pavilion named for its celebrated interwar dancer (Mario), complete with gigantic, post-social realism statue of a peasant woman bearing burdens on her head (*memikul*). Other political rumblings are evident in the new district office, now headed by a Javanese, handpicked by Jakarta over Balinese rivals, including one from that once Socialist faction mentioned above. And so forth, darkeningly.
Felt emotions: I de-bus on a crossroads next to the shop owned by a fond father (*Bapak*) from before. During our unBalinese bearhug he informs me, chokingly, that *his* father had indeed been exhumed and cremated (*diaben*, i.e., the corpse has received the ritual respects required of dutiful descendants). His greeting reacknowledged me as a friend and admirer of that extraordinary elder who had spent his final months wanting to recollect his own life and Bali's recent history with a devoted outsider, and doing so (he died several days after our departure at the end of 1972). That was then. Now his son and I talk family affairs and *plus ça change*. He managed his many chil-

dren's schooling with profits from the shop's photocopy machine—
long the only one in the district. The old neighborhood has really
developed: fulltime electricity, piped water, phones, and just recently
T.V. broadcast from ever-watchful Jakarta. Worries include his wife's
ongoing complaints, an unseemly dearth of grandchildren, and a son
who had married out to Australia, now back temporarily. That son,
intricate in his own right, I later discover had learned to apply words
like "workaholic" to his father: not disrespectful, perhaps, but different from the lapsing honorifics indigenous to Bali. Whether this son
will permanently return home is a pressing concern.

My original notes continue, halting and goosefleshed.[6] The present
narrative's climax, however, is not the jottings themselves (no post-
structuralist, I), but their backdrop. Returned to my wee bungalow that evening, sworn forever off asparagus soup, I settled on the
veranda to record *minutiae* of observation and conversation. (Never
turn in before completing your day's fieldnotes, that mentor once
wisely advised, as he himself had been counseled and I counsel today;
some things continue.)

I checked a few key references in my own book on Bali, per-
chance brushing past its aforementioned dedication and, pen poised,
readied to write the account extracted above. I must now confess that
I had not failed earlier to notice a peculiar foursome in the adjoining
cabin: two California lads plus "consorts" ("pick-ups"?—their native
term I overheard was less delicate) from downunder. Suddenly those
old sweet sounds, or nearly so, wafted through the frangipani. God's
truth: Unbelieve-able. Granted, this version *was* disco. (What would
you expect from the ghetto blaster, or should I say boombox—1981
was pre-Walkman, remember—of two surfing studs and their Aussi
chicks [birds?] cruising-carousing through what they wished were
Tijuana?). But heard at that precise moment on that day of days, "our
song," even degraded, might as well have been Perry himself shuffling
to a Balinese *gamelan*. *This* was authentic. I'll never get over it. And
yet . . . and yet. . . .

Ordinarily, what should we, Nabokov's children, make of ultra-
outlandish coincidence? Ordinarily, not much, I profess; and please,
nothing at all, if it deflects one from fieldwork proper. Coincidences

confessed are no substitute for ethnography. Yet they do happen. And
every now and again, just to set the record straight (or crooked), one
feels inclined to commend coincidence much as Della Street in *Simanis*,
echoing the jury, commends Perry:

Anda menang.
You win.

Karma, or showbiz? Not even Della, delightful Della, knows.

Commentary: Qu'est-ce que c'est qu'un Cosmopolitan Moment?

Weary of mythemes, gustemes, épistémès, and the like, I propose to
designate my topic not the high analytic "cosmomeme" but the low
comic "Cosmome": rhymes not with "phoneme" but with "tome,"
"foam," "Om," "Rome," and in my native dialect "poem." The Cosmome (alternate spelling Kozmōm): irreverent rejoinder to brand-
name methodologies—a comedically concrete, sheepishly particular
spurt of intersensory (mystical?) fluttering.[7]

Difficult to define, impossible to predict, the beast is unmistakable
when it strikes. Ingredients of a vintage Cosmome are multilingual,
ambiguous, cross-temporal, a little learned (a dangerous thing), super-
cilious and winking, with so many elbows poking out in convergence
that its foreordainedness seems Karmic, or is it Calvinist? (Compare
Gita Mehta's *Karma Cola*: "That's either Karma. Or it's showbiz"
[p. 146].) Either way Cosmomes bring factors distant into propin-
quity teasing. The fleet leaps effected are less than Kierkegaardian, but
no less exhilarating for being so. Simultaneously self-dissolving and
self-indulgent, Cosmomes achieve both perspectives through incongruity (per Kenneth Burke) and incongruities through perspective,
or contradictory perspectives, yet ones less comfortable, cozy, and
clichéd than your average Escher etching.

Circumstances conducive to Cosmomes include: (1) when random broadcasts are within overhearing distance; (2) when music,
text, conversations, scene, and temporal flux half-mockingly corre-
spond; (3) when disparate channels of sight, sound, taste, and touch

stretch across languages; and (4) when the grand and the frivolous do a do-si-do. There would, in dialectical brief, be no Cosmomes were languages not diverse; cultures not plural; time not ongoing; the present not displaced; intentions not subvertible; the senses not transposable; form not fragmentary; media not multi, the arts not, *de temps en temps, gesamt*; disciplines not many; understandings not partial; interpretations not . . . inter-; experience not ironic; messages not clumsily communicated; life not written; the universe not, conceivably, a closed book; and subjunctive conditions not liable negatively to be itemized. Because all these nots *are*, the Cosmome *is*!

During a cosmopolitan moment, the trivia maddeningly, perversely, and involuntarily retained in everyday life effect unspeakable synapses between the ordinary and far-flung, producing an echo of concerted performance or, failing that, a concoction of pseudo-punchlines. "Cosmopolitan" in this case implies no pat universal order achieved by some citizen of a postrevolutionary world, although this possibility, too, remains in play. Rather Cosmomes enact collisions of provincialisms, tribal enthusiasms, narrow views, and "local knowledge" so intense and multiply allusive that they cancel each other out, empty one into the other, launch equivalent stereotypes, as if all parties in history's carnival of cultures might be ready mutually to celebrate the outlandishness of each in quasi-apocalyptic parodies of redoubled dialectics, of too radical remove. *Voilà: c'est ce que c'est qu'un* Cosmome.

Even at home the crazy currents of a Cosmome strike only an aficionado or two amidst others who do not get it. ("Others who do not get it" are guaranteed during fieldwork.) Your ideal-type Cosmome is thus both social (involving others) and nonsocial (unshared to the hilt). *Un*promising contexts for Cosmomes include pushy happenings that jab captive audiences to the brink of outrage: P. T. Barnum, Monty Python, the stridently experimental, the contentedly Pop (although these shows also have their appeal). Likewise ill-suited are in-the-know groups relishing innuendos at the expense of a hypothetically insensitive outgroup, as in campy filmbuff audiences, angry protests, and movements countercultural (although these demonstrations, too, have their importance). Cosmomes, in contrast, incline the one in-the-know to feel not so much superior as kind of silly in "getting it," yet gradually to give in.

Additional attributes of a Cosmomer caught in the act: (1) You don't know whether to laugh or cry, and do. Reading, for example, "Mahasiswa Antropologi" on my first Balinese interlocutor's calling card, I knew not whether to laugh or cry and did. Or did I giggle, tearingly? I can't remember, I can't remember (check the notes). (2) Intersensory rhythms become duple and then some; the pace is multiply quick, very quick. It may feel like Wagner's conclusion to Act I of *Siegfried*, like some of Strauss (Richard), and maybe all of Mahler, his Symphony No. 1, at least. Here ostensible ditties recur, becoming leitmotivic to wind up archetypal. Indeed, the final thunder reveals that they (the ditties) are all there is, and all there need be. This essay's confessions are accordingly offered in the paradoxical hope of promoting Cosmome-musicality even among the Cosmome-deaf.

Lower-brow analogies derive from filmdom, or rather movie-land. Cosmomes evoke mobile cameras, booms and zooms, revolving stages, invisible treadmills, with overlaid narrative and undercurrent score. Their coordination is nearer Busby Berkeley than his pale revival in video. (Between MGM and MTV there is, I churlishly declare, a loss, dammit, a loss.) Devoid of the total technological control and nonstop exhilaration now standard in slick *Star Wars*–style spectaculars, Cosmomes remain reminiscent of musicals gone by, ragged extravaganzas and rather intimate: mine, all mine; to each his own. I once met a mystic and movie buff who seemed to share this view, and I dedicate these notes to that empathetic cross-cultural encounter between Doris Day familiars: one Javanese, the other not.

Parenthetically, friend Freud called certain Cosmome-potential the uncanny plus, perhaps, a dash of oceanic; he seems to have neglected the zany, or did he? Freud's aftermathers trap matters between, on the one hand, the whole, the true, and the proper, and, on the other hand (the left one), the damaged, the false, and the deviant. I question such crisp distinction. Cosmomes prove corrosive of models of "other" today prevailing: Heideggerian, structuralist, deconstructionist, dialogicist, Marxo-feminist, hermeneutico-phenomenological, lit-crit Lacanian, whatnot. Cosmomes offer time-outs, brief respites —or the illusion thereof—from such threadbare dilemmas as "Je est un autre," or "L'autre est un je (un jeu?).," or "L'autre est un autre autre, *oder noch ein anderer*." Any such othering is itself othered when a Cosmome effects bursts of *ostrenanie* in overdrive or *verfremdung* all over again. You make contact with the *données immediates de la connaissance* of distanced distance, thus raveling too-determinant polarities of unremitting consciousness-raising frequent among solemn theorists of Otherdom. Altogether to ignore the occasional ultralocal Cosmome is to diminish the human relevance of our high-critical manifestoes. End of prolegomenon.

Cosmomes twinklingly imbue the detritus of living, reading, thinking, traveling, viewing, listening, and remembering with, if not purpose or form, at least point, edge, lilt, contour, effervescence, fizz. Sounds like pop Proust, *nicht wahr*: Americanized, consumerized, minus that ultimate heightening onto the stilts of cumulative retrospect wherefrom Proust salutes ART in capital letters as redemptive, albeit ironically so. Although Proust's *madeleine* moments of synesthesia that recapture times lapsed are not cosmopolitan moments, the two may sometimes start to taste the same. Moreover, writing Cosmomes, like Marcel writing madeleines or Martinvilles, may actually induce concrete circumstances to allemand with words. Proust, moreover, recommended that we write as we read (especially Ruskin): *in situ*, between the page and the landscape, eyes/fingertips tacking between page and topography: sentences read or written interpenetrated by ones overheard.

The Proustian thrill's spectrum of senses sustains an encyclopedic "fictioning" of the whole *belle époque* and its wartime postlude. Less epiphanal than Proust's *ex post facto* advance into as-if coherence, Cosmomes rather retract into overlapping disconnectedness. Still, without Proust (a personal favorite), just as without fieldwork, this travelreader could never have recognized a Cosmome and certainly would never have tried writing one. And it took a Javanese mystic moviegoer—content in his counterorthodoxy—to bring it all home.

Part the Last: At Home with Cosmomes

My final confessions illustrate a not-Bali-but-New-York–New-York
state of mind—or is it Switzerland, Nabokov's Nebraska, or Tibet?
Regardless, the Big Apple remains a locus classicus of Walker Percy's
"dialectical savorings of the familiar as the familiar," or contacting the
alien known.[8]

Third Specimen: Rockefeller Plaza, NYC, USA, New World, Earth, Universe, Cos . . .

Rockefeller Plaza, off-season, is a virtual Automat of Cosmomes, a
precast scene from which "A Friend Writes." Those pages, and the
plaza they taste like, package alternative zones of high urbanity, confident enough in its privilege to sympathize with the off-beat, down-
to-earth, and everyday. While both pages and plaza sometimes seem
smug, their sage councils and arch devices include quick-witted de-
bunkings of their own pretentiousness as well. And neither, readers
may have noticed, eschews ads, provided the salespitch is upscale. A
final parallel is happily conspicuous: Rockefeller's bronzes and *The
New Yorker's* cartoons.

> September 10, 1983. "A Friend of Ours writes from Rockefeller
> Plaza." Awash in bromeliades and epigrams. Like Bali's riceland, the
> promenade's pavement slopes; the fountain's water can't. Slope-sided,
> flat-watered fountains sport flexible floral borders and would-be
> permanent sculptures, vandal-thwarted. "Wisdom and Knowledge
> shall be the stability of thy times." Similar-but-different denizens of
> the deep astride variant sea-creatures, poise opposite cute critters,
> also marine. My on-the-scene ethnographic catalogue of these oozie
> metamorphoses:
>
> 1. Crab; *en face*: merman, prick-finned on a buck-lipped carp.
> 2. Turtle; *en face*: mermaid on a dolphin, sidesaddle.
> 3. Starfish; *en face*: mermaid again, this mount long-snouted.
> 4. Starfish again; *en face*: finless female astride a shark.
> 5. (Missing [vandals?]); *en face*: mermaid unsidesaddling less baroque
>   carp.
> 6. (Missing [intake valve?]); *en face*: horned trumpeter on carp.

The garden surrounds are foursquare, punctuated by palmettos:
hence Palmsquare, so near and yet so far from Times Square.

Although "there is nothing more wonderful than a list, instrument of
wondrous hypotyposis" (Eco 1983: 73), that last bit strikes even *me*
as too contrived; familiarly familiar estrangement may be hardest to
enlist at home, particularly in the first person. May I, then, offer fragmentary ingredients for some other "friend to write": Soaring Gothic
mullions and integrated pigeon-stops; promenade's slopes; Prometheus's pit. The sound of water's reflection in Singer shop windows
(since then, there's been a change in brand). Multilingual bookstores.
Polyglot guests. Travel bureaus. The gilt; the banners, the *grande place*
Brussels-likeness of it all.

Another visit, less inviting but profounder, found Prometheus's
restaurant a rink whose music is concentrated and canned: Canned
concentrate. In Manhattan's March, 1984, doubly off-seasoned because February and it had do-si-doed, a narrow ray of sun glinted
off Prometheus *et moi*, we alone spotlighted, loitering. Fountains
frozen, Christmas lights retained, intermission declared, the ice machine cometh to smooth the ice. Avoiding cheap coincidence (e.g., on
this trip my funding was also by Rockefeller), I only recall the piped-
in music, not quite Muzak: "Fly me to the Moon," and "My kind
of town, Chicago is . . ." Oh, fond dislocation. "Crossing Cultures:
Essays in the Displacement of . . ." Skaters, resume.

During Rockefeller's less untropical, friendlier-for-writing off-
season, background songs remain dispersed, along with background
speech and signs.

> September 10, 1983, again. Winds polydirectional. Diverse *flaneurs*
> converge on Prometheus's pit, less abyss than eddy. Aeschylus's
> words—toward which bromeliads slope, o'er which Radio City
> towers—in truth divert through multiple currents and many wave-
> lengths a plural flow. The inscription: "Prometheus teacher in every
> art brought the fire that hath proved to metals a means to mighty
> ends." The separate-but-equal other words: "Nikon Takes New
> York," "Newsweek 11:07," "Chase Manhattan Bank." The passers-
> by (I level languages): "Gorgeous. . . . Look at the turtle. . . . Well,

I like that. . . ." The wooden benches. *My* friends, the bromeliads.
Foodstands. A woman dabs/ a tissue in/ the shark pool/ wipes/ the
edges of/ her lips. John D.'s creed: ". . . Only in the purifying fire of
sacrifice is the dross of selfishness consumed and the greatness of the
human soul set free." What a friendly place for friends to write! Yet
flaws in the multinational flagstaffs are strengthened by makeshift
braces that conceal from view meant-to-be-seen snatches of what
Prometheus bears—his message—whose circle is the zodiac, names
written *inside the ring*.

Some spaces are, as space, as eccentric as those *Eccentric Spaces* that
Robert Harbison has revealed in prose, guidebooks, catalogues, and
subway maps. All Cosmomes are. Rockefeller Plaza is one of them.[9]
This place, I now realize, is no barrier (cabbies to the contrary notwithstanding) to the never-sleeping city's gridded streetscape. It is
more a ha-ha, a sunken separator—*not* a fence. Yes, *I*, illuminated
loiterer, find echoes of ha-has here (and in Cosmomes else- and everywhere), much as Gary Schmidgall's *Literature as Opera* finds ha-has
prefigured in Handel:

> The position of the English garden in the history of landscaping
> bears some interesting parallels to the place Handel occupies along
> the continuum between the older Italian Baroque opera and the
> Classical opera of Mozart. . . . The new emphasis in landscaping
> was upon the picturesque. Walpole praised the invention of the ha-
> ha (a sunken, concealed fence) [one blocking cows from the lawn,
> thus letting vistas of pasture appear continuous] for making the
> walk through a fine garden like the experience of a "succession of
> pictures" . . . .
>   The "sunk fence" brought the art of man and the art of nature
> closer together, made the distinguished line more subtle. . . . In
> opera, Handel was having the same effect. In his operas we see the
> struggle between traditional formulas and the urgency of natural,
> truly dramatic expression—in other words, the struggle between
> artificial "neatness" and incisive, direct "rudeness." We see the re-
> linquishment of the da capo aria where it would be painfully re-
> dundant, the development of differing emotions in duets and trios,
> a new simplicity of utterance (which looked forward to the artis-
> tic Rococo). . . . We frequently see Handel abandon what Walpole
> called the "prim regularity" of tradition. (Schmidgall 1977: 45)

Rockefeller Plaza: Manhattan's ha-ha; Cosmomes: life's (cultural anthropology: disciplines'). Thank you, John D. R.: The money may be dirty, but the Cosmomes are pure. Ha-ha. Sunk fence. Which brings us to the punchline.[10]

Fourth and Final Specimen: An Afternoon at the Opera Shop

Fieldworkers to Manhattan (perhaps many a native as well) often seek spots to escape the sensory assault, to render it background, to displace the place. "Crossing Cultures: Essays in the Displacement of . . . ." In inclement weather, Rockefeller Plaza precluded, my outs include the Grand Central balcony bar and the nearby waters of the equally Grand Hyatt: post-ostentatious lobbydom, plus free jazz ensemble. To this list of briar patches, I add one place called "metropolitan," including its Opera Shop. Cynical query: Is the shop here for the opera or the opera for the shop? Which "motivates" which? Parallel question: Do products promote movies or movies products? Such unanswerably circular needs/desires drive the history of hybrid arts, commercial reproduction, and the culture industry (Horkheimer and Adorno 1970; see Boon 1983: 119).

So reflecting, innocently, I entered in 1984 (wasn't it?) the Metropolitan Popera Shop. I exited guilty, a fully aware consumer: VCR-victorious, desiring to Xerox life itself in reprints now moving, already Technicolor, soon Cinemascope (registered trademark). Indeed it was this field experience—along with Doris in Java, Perry in Bali, and reading Proust and Nabokov, among others—that fixed for all time Cosmomes in my once unrisen consciousness. Here are my notes:

> *I* have capitulated, purchasing Puccini placemats, *Ring Cycle* glossies, a cut-rate *Rosenkavalier*, and other high culture gift suggestions. Appropriately, a Pioneer Laser Video Disc Player punctuates this Lincoln Center scene with strains of—guess who?—"Hello, Dolly!" (exclamation point theirs). "Hello, Dolly: the Movie!," that is, not the authentic original. A strikingly *artistique* duo of Asian mien wanders up; one nudges his friend, gestures screenward, uttering "Herro Dorry, Calor Channing." I barely stifled a blurted correction: "No, no; Balbla Stleisand!"

(Forgive my notes; twice forgive me. How superior is his near-expertise in u.s. stardom to all my gaffes in Balinese cosmology. Would that my manglings of Indonesian pronunciations were as subtle as his lilting Japanese reversals of liquid consonants. I not only prefer his charming English to my ghastly Balinese; I favor his accent in American over my own.)

> As Louis Armstrong trumpets onto center screen for his famed cameo, the twosome approvingly approaches an *Aïda* poster, deep in discussion of their favorite *corolatula lore*: "Rucia de Ramamool."
>
> Meanwhile, sixteen folk or so (I'm jotting quickly) gather gazing at the celebrated production number. An errant flash, the screen goes blank. Hushed pause. Stylish cashier abandons post to fumble with the apparatus, to flip (switch?) the disc. Between the title song's conclusion and its recap (da capo?) that makes literal that incomparably final "Aaaggaaaainn!"—she must switch (flip?) the disk. Can you follow me, readers? Altogether now, repeat: Between the Metropolitan Opera Shop's Lazer "Hello, Dolly's" climax and renowned reprise, the disck gets flitched. (Oh, for an instant replay/reprise of prose!).

Enough. I apologize to non–Opera-Shop-goers for the eccentricity of this example. I apologize to all Occidentals and Orientals for alluding to (y)our accents (this letter-play marks the poignant point of this paper). I, an eastern Westerner displaced, apologize to universal readers for attempting a representation that may require being read repeatedly and in intertextual relation even to itself, where ironies abound. I apologize for everything, which is purely coincidental. "I may be charged with egotism for the form I have adopted."

Is enough. Amidst these cross-cultural, multimedia comminglings: pop/serious, Orient/Occident, stage/screen, screen/screen, absent/present, viewing/writing, hearing/reading, Opera/shop; during this *gesamt*-like instant of anti*gesamt*, I seek beseechingly among the assembled eyes awaiting the blank screen's "Aaaggaaaainn" again for mutual recognition. Nothing. *I* soar into disparity; they stay. I prance; *they* price the Pioneer. The inescapable pathos: I alone get/got it. I only am escaped alone to tell thee, to commemorate the Cosmome! Call me Satchmo.

Last Confessional Note: I, an opera-going Appalachian anthropologist, once a *Mahasiswa*, in the field wherever, am sporadically drowning, drowning in the variations, the coincidence, the mad, mad, mad, movie-mad rush of inauthentic magical affinities, whose concoctions may yield, winkingly, intersensory pleasure, not bliss . . . or *is* it? Am *I*: *Where* am I? In the field? Not? Where *am* I? Bali? Busby? Baudelaire? Benjamin? Broadway? Hello? Hollywood? Herro? Anybody there? *Dari mana*? Rockeferra Praza? Perry? Percy? Della? Dolly? Dorry? Doris . . . Day? Dolores? Lolita? Dolly? Dolly, Doris will never go away *again* . . . Wonderful woman.

NOTES

Dan Segal and Harry Liebersohn made extremely helpful suggestions for extending the paper, and Polly Strong and other participants in the Claremont conference offered sympathetic responses. Julie Ellison, Susan Stewart, and Judith Becker expressed different varieties of tolerance of an earlier version presented at the University of Michigan; Tom Sebeok and Svetlana Alpers reacted in kindly fashion to another version at the University of Rochester. Thanks to all.

    1. Put it another way. Abundant polemicists alert to power-knowledge have now deemed "expropriating" any claims of fieldworking authority, not to mention authenticity. Filmmakers, too, including one superb one, have rushed in, sometimes unfortunately confusing that style of high-handed ethnographic documentary that they despise with dimensions of ethnographic texts that they show little evidence of having seriously scrutinized or "really read" (e.g., Minh-ha et al. 1989). Now, even the best of critics (e.g., Clifford 1987) cannot avoid reinscribing the pretension of expertise—indeed superiority, yea mastery—at least over those works they deem critically naïve or passé. Similarly, even fresh efforts to embed critical insights in renewed forms of travel-writing (e.g., Greenblatt 1983) still cannot but imply they have managed to draw nearer, say, China—despite their manifest lack of language or any other variety of "expertise"—than have those less critically alert *voyageurs* they would supersede. One work I know that avoids this inconsistency, or rather incorporates it as an irony, is a fiction of travel-scholarship remarkably versed in the ambiguities of authoritative reading and describing alike: *Flaubert's Parrot* (Barnes 1984).

2. I can only hope against hope that readers will remain mindful of the medley of Balinese, Indonesian, European, and Indo-European views that I elsewhere address and of the fuller range of comparative discourse (both "theirs" and "ours") with its many angles, voices, rhetorics, dilemmas, promises, setbacks, gifts, and victimages.

3. For phonetic and etymological resonances among "Lolita, Dolores, Dolly," and similar names coinciding in sounds and meanings that help orchestrate the hyperorchestrated *Lolita*, see Appel's commentary in Nabokov (1970: 334), along with all Appel's and others' notes (including Nabokov's) on Nabokov's play of nomenclatures. The present paper's inching toward a burlesque of ethnographic confession—i.e., towards both a parody of confessions and a confession—is prompted, but only in part, by Nabokov's "number" (called *Lolita*) on literary-psychotherapeutic confessions. I accordingly proceed by offering "winks" toward any "works" mentioned, including books, cultures, and filmstars. For example, any resemblance between certain formulations that follow these "preliminaries" and Geertz's (1973) celebrated study of Balinese cockfights or his influential definition of religion as a cultural system is purely coincidental. Coincidence-writing, by the way, like the magics it echoes, is necessarily very intricate, layered, and both explicit and allusive.

4. On Doris Day, see (seriously) Updike (1983: 791–801); this courageous essay by the most arrived of litterateurs and most prominent of *New Yorker* writers, entitled "Suzie Creamcheese Speaks," confesses past and present involvement, even complicity, with pop-plastic productions from history's most hegemonic culture industry. Updike's moving insights into Doris Day's autobiography coincide in his collected essays with "Pinter's Unproduced Proust Printed" (reviewing *The Proust Screenplay*), which piece in turn happens to fall in juxtaposition with his ongoing salute to Borges (see also Boon 1982: 204–5): "Whereas the polylingual erudition of Eliot and Pound was part of a worldwide search for an authenticity that would help make the native language and tradition new, Borges's erudition, with its quizzical touchstones of quotation and its recondite medieval and Oriental references, is a parody of erudition wherein the researched and the fabricated lie side by side ironically—a vast but claustrophobically closed system that implies there is no newness under the sun. The must of alchemists' libraries pervades his learning; his chaos of texts . . ." (Updike 1983: 780).

5. At this juncture in the performance version of this paper, a few moments of the song discussed in the following section was broadcast as a prelude; a still scratchier version was repeated at the end of the section as a postlude.

6. These notes move so quickly that some listeners missed the fact that my confessions include considerable evidence of post-1965 Balinese unrest and dilemmas. Perhaps it is worth noting here that this kind of paper, with its parodic writing (and indeed the kind of multifarious fieldwork it reports) questions standards of political seriousness (and economic power) that dismiss popular culture—and often as well ritual and carnival—as superficial (I address this issue at length in Boon 1990). It is, after all, commoditized popular culture that already supersaturates the "First World," and increasingly the "Third World," and may sooner than we thought, it now seems, engulf the "Second World." This is as profound a development as any other and one not so easy to "rise above" as proponents pining for human relationships unmediated by commodities would have us believe. For the fact is that human relationships, including cross-cultural ones, are mediated even by such hypercommodities as Doris Day movies and "*Antropologi*" calling cards; how possibly to make something of this fact is the subject of this essay, attuned to mysticisms, tourisms, literary coincidence, and related magics.

7. Lévi-Strauss's *Tristes Tropiques* remains more inviting, or at least more accessible, than his *Mythologiques* for eschewing "mythemes" when pursuing his distanced gaze, his compassionate *regard éloigné* (see Boon 1972, 1982, 1986, 1990).

8. I apologize, of course, to Californians, Balinese, and other Pacific-rimmers for the provincialism of the following example. Any resemblance between this representation—styled to suggest that Cosmomes can be quiescent even when they happen in New York—and the *New Yorker*'s format is purely coincidental.

9. So too may ethnography be deemed the space (place, *topos*) of cross-cultural inscription (Boon 1982, 1990).

10. At this juncture in the performance version of this paper, moments were played from the title song of the musical comedy discussed in the concluding example. (Uncoincidentally, a derivative of this same number, with other lyrics, became Ferdinand Marcos's last campaign song). The original piece ends with a female solo backed by a male chorus; the lyrics go "Dolly will never go away again"; the last word is sustained, and the chorus is repeated, as is customary in popular finales, even when not written by Jerry Herman.

REFERENCES

Barnes, Julian. 1984. *Flaubert's Parrot*. New York: McGraw-Hill.

Benjamin, Walter. 1978. *Reflections*. Ed. P. Demetz. Trans. E. Jephcott. New York: Harcourt, Brace, Jovanovich.

Boon, James A. 1972. *From Symbolism to Structuralism: Levi-Strauss in a Literary Tradition*. New York: Harper & Row.

———. 1977. *The Anthropological Romance of Bali, 1597–1972: Dynamic Perspectives in Marriage and Caste, Politics and Religion*. New York: Cambridge University Press.

———. 1982. *Other Tribes, Other Scribes: Symbolic Anthropology in the Comparative Study of Cultures, Histories, Religions and Texts*. Cambridge: Cambridge University Press.

———. 1983. "America: Fringe Benefits." *Raritan* (Spring): 97–121.

———. 1986. "Between the Wars Bali: Rereading the Relics." In *History of Anthropology*, ed. George Stocking. Vol. 4. Madison: University of Wisconsin Press.

———. 1989a. "Lévi-Strauss, Wagner, Romanticism: A Reading Back." In *History of Anthropology*, ed. George Stocking. Vol. 4. Madison: University of Wisconsin Press.

———. 1989b. "Against Coping Across Cultures: Some Semiotics of Self-Help Rebuffed." In *Semiotics, Self and Society*, ed. Benjamin Lee and Greg Urban. Hawthorne, N.Y.: de Gruyter.

———. 1990. *Affinities and Extremes: Crisscrossing the Bittersweet Ethnology of East Indies History, Hindu-Balinese Culture and Indo-European Allure*. Chicago: University of Chicago Press.

———. Forthcoming. "Why Museums Make Me Sad." In *Exhibiting Cultures*, ed. Ivan Karp and Steve Levine. Washington, D.C.: Smithsonian Institution.

Campbell, Mary. 1988. *The Witness and the Other World: Exotic European Travel Writing, 400–1600*. Ithaca: Cornell University Press.

Clifford, James. 1988. *The Predicament of Culture: Twentieth-Century Ethnography, Literature and Art*. Cambridge and London: Harvard University Press.

Clifford, James, and George F. Marcus, eds. 1986. *Writing Culture: The Poetics and Politics of Ethnography*. Berkeley: University of California Press.

Eco, Umberto. 1983. *The Name of the Rose*. Trans. W. Weaver. New York: Harcourt, Brace, Jovanovich.

Geertz, Clifford. 1973. *The Interpretation of Cultures*. New York: Basic Books.

———. 1983. *Local Knowledge*. New York: Basic Books.

———. 1988. *Works and Lives*. Stanford: Stanford University Press.

Greenblatt, Stephen. 1983. "China: Visiting Rites." *Raritan* (Spring 1983).

Harbison, Robert. 1977. *Eccentric Spaces*. London: Andrew Deutsch.

Horkheimer, Max, and T. Adorno. 1970. *The Dialectics of Enlightenment*. Trans. J. Cumming. New York: Seabury.

Lévi-Strauss, Claude. [1955] 1973. *Tristes Tropiques*. Trans. J. and D. Weightman. New York: Atheneum.

Mehta, Gita. 1979. *Karma Cola*. New York: Schocken Books.

Minh-ha, Trinh T., ed. 1989. "Introduction" to "(Un)naming Cultures." Special issue of *Discourse*. 11 [2]: 5–17.

Nabokov, Vladimir. 1970. *The Annotated Lolita*. Ed. Alfred Appel, Jr. New York: McGraw-Hill.

Percy, Walker. 1975. *The Message in the Bottle*. New York: Farrar, Straus and Giroux.

Said, Edward W. 1978. *Orientalism*. New York: Random House.

Schmidgall, Gary. 1977. *Literature as Opera*. New York: Oxford University Press.

Stendhal [Beyle, Marie-Henri]. 1975. *Love*. Trans. G. and S. Sale. New York: Penguin Books.

Updike, John. 1983. *Hugging the Shore*. New York: Knopf.

CONTRIBUTORS

JAMES BOON teaches anthropology at Princeton University and is the author of *From Symbolism to Structuralism* (1972), *The Anthropological Romance of Bali, 1592–1972* (1977), *Other Tribes, Other Scribes* (1982), and *Affinities and Extremes* (1990).

MARY CAMPBELL teaches English at Brandeis University. She is the author of *The Witness and the Other World* (1988) and a book of poetry, *The World, The Flesh, and Angels* (1989). She is also coeditor (with Mark Rollins) of *Begetting Images: Studies in The Art and Science of Symbol Production* (1989).

HARRY LIEBERSOHN teaches history at the University of Illinois, Urbana–Champaign. He is the author of *Fate and Utopia in German Sociology* (1987).

PETER LINEBAUGH teaches history and literature at Harvard College. He is an editor of and contributor to *Albion's Fatal Tree: Crime and Society in Eighteenth-Century England* (1975), and the author of *The London Hanged: Crime and Civil Society in the Eighteenth Century; Or, History by the Neck* (1991). He is also the editor of *Midnight Notes.*

DAVID PROCHASKA   teaches history at the University of Illinois, Urbana-Champaign. He is the author of *Making Algeria French: Colonialism in Bône, 1870–1920* (1990). He has also published on the Algerian resistance and French colonial photography.

MARCUS REDIKER   teaches history at Georgetown University. He is author of *Between the Devil and the Deep Blue Sea: Merchant Seaman, Pirates, and the Anglo-American Maritime World, 1700–1750* (1987), and a contributing editor of volume I of *Who Built America? Working People and the Nation's Economy, Politics, Culture, and Society* (1989).

DEREK SAYER   was born in London, England, in 1950. Educated at the Universities of Essex and Durham, he has taught in Britain, Tanzania, and Canada. Currently he is Professor of Sociology at the University of Alberta, Canada. His most recent books are *The Great Arch: English State Formation as Cultural Revolution* (with Philip Corrigan, 1985), *Society* (with David Frisby, 1986), *The Violence of Abstraction* (1987), *Readings from Karl Marx* (1989), and *Capitalism and Modernity: an Excursus of Marx and Weber* (1991).

DANIEL SEGAL   teaches anthropology and world history at Pitzer College in Claremont, California. He is the author (with Richard Handler) of *Jane Austen and the Fiction of Culture: An Essay on the Narration of Social Realities* (University of Arizona Press, 1990). He received his Ph.D. from the University of Chicago in 1989 for a study of nationalism and state formation in Trinidad and Tobago. He has published on the medical profession in the United States and is currently writing a multicultural, world history text to serve as an alternative to existing 'Western Civilization' texts.

PAULINE TURNER STRONG   is Assistant Professor of Anthropology at the University of Missouri-St. Louis. Educated in philosophy at Colorado College and cultural anthropology at the University of Chicago, she takes an interdisciplinary approach to the study of intercultural encounters, historical representation, and the cultural construction of identity and difference. In addition to the work on North America represented in this volume, she has undertaken comparative research on Jamaica and Australia. She is currently studying representations of Native Americans during the Columbian Quincentenary.

Index

tic working class, 105, 110,
114, 115, 117, 118, 129; Native
Americans as, 46, 51, 60, 86
n. 20, 87–88 n. 27
Slave uprisings, 113, 129
Smith, John, 33, 42, 49, 56, 80
Sociocultural evolutionary theory,
xi–xii
*The Sovereignty and Goodness of
God* (Mary Rowlandson), 44,
61–66, 72–76
Spenser, Edmund, 4, 8, 26
Spies, Walter, 227–28
Squanto. *See* Tisquantum
Standish, Captain Miles, 51
Stanley, John Mix, 39, 41, 79
Statesman (Calcutta), 149
Stendahl, 229
Stockwell, Quentin, 64
Strauss, Richard, 242
Strikes, historical origins of, 124
Sumner, Lord, 171
Surtees, Brigadier General, 164
Swarton, Hannah, 44, 68, 69, 70,
73, 74
Sydenham, George, 165
Syphilis. *See* Disease

Tarring and feathering, 115
Tate, Nahum, 17, 24
Taverns, 105. *See also* Cafes; Hotels
Taylor, A.J.P., 144
Tébessa phosphates affair. *See*
Bertagna, Jérome, scandals of
Thanksgiving, 33, 81 n. 1
Thomson, Gaston, 189, 190, 192
Thoreau, Henry David, 89 n. 34
Times (London), 161, 163, 166, 167
Timothy, Peter, 117

Tisquantum, 33, 44, 46, 49, 50, 51,
55, 63
Todorov, Tzvetan, 5, 7, 8
Torture, 53–55, 59, 60, 63, 68, 78, 88
n. 29
Tourism, xvi, 227–29, 234, 237
"Tradition": British, 161, 162
Translation, 235, 236, 237
Travel writing, 11, 58, 226, 229–30
Triangular relations of settlers,
metropole and Algerians, xvi,
184, 188–93, 195, 201
Typification, 40, 42, 66, 72–74, 76,
79, 83–84 n. 9; of gender in
representations of captivity,
35–39, 41–42, 66, 68, 74; of
races in representations of captivity, 39, 42, 70–71, 73, 74,
76

Vanderlyn, John, 37, 39, 79
Vaughn, Robert, 57
Vespucci, Amerigo, 9
Viet Nam protests, 232
Vincent, Sir William, 156
Virgil, 15, 19, 20, 21

Wagner, Richard, 242
Waldseemüller, Martin, 9
Walpole, Horace, 124
Wampanoag legend of first contact
with Europeans, 45–46, 70–81
Wampum, 52, 53, 54, 55
Warfare, 42, 44, 52, 54, 55, 56;
condolence rituals, 52, 53;
mourning wars, 52, 53
Weber, Max, xv
Wedgewood, Colonel, 164–65
Weetamoo. *See* Wetamo
"The West," xi–xiii, xvi–xvii, 35

Wetamo, 60, 62, 69, 73, 74, 88 n. 30
White, John, 48
Whiteboy movement, 120–24
Wilberforce, William, 108
Wilkes, John, 123–24
Will (a slave), 113
Williamite confiscations, 119
Williams, Eunice, 72, 74
Williams, John, 44, 63, 68, 72, 74, 75, 78
Williams, Raymond, 40, 84 n. 11
Wilson, Sir Henry, 160, 161
Wolf, Eric, xiii

Wood, Peter, 114
Working class: contradictions within, 106, 130; Hydra as image of, 107–10, 118; interracial solidarity of, 105–6, 110, 114–15, 117–18, 125, 128, 162; from Ireland, 119–25; polyglot, community, 106, 110; slaves as component of Atlantic, 105, 110, 114, 115, 117–18, 129

Yacine, Kateb, 212
Young, Alfred, 115